BUSINESS CREATIVITY AND INNOVATION

PERSPECTIVES AND BEST PRACTICES

Bassim Hamadeh, CEO and Publisher

Mazin Hassan, Acquisitions Editor

Amy Smith, Project Editor

Christian Berk, Associate Production Editor

Jackie Bignotti, Production Artist

Sara Schennum, Licensing Associate

Natalie Piccotti, Director of Marketing

Kassie Graves, Vice President of Editorial

Jamie Giganti, Director of Academic Publishing

ISBN: 978-1-5165-4194-2 (pbk) / 978-1-5165-4195-9 (br)

FIRST EDITION

BUSINESS CREATIVITY AND INNOVATION

PERSPECTIVES AND BEST PRACTICES

LEN FERMAN

cognella® | ACADEMIC PUBLISHING

CONTENTS

ABOUT THE AUTHOR

Len Ferman is an adjunct professor of management at the University of North Florida where he developed the course he teaches on business creativity and innovation. Len is also a faculty member of the American Management Association where he teaches Creative Thinking in Business and Design Thinking.

In 2013, Len founded Ferman Innovation to help companies generate and evaluate breakthrough ideas to improve the customer experience. Previously, he spent 25 years managing innovation at AT&T and Bank of America where he introduced several new products, led the front end of innovation and served as head of ideation.

Len is a frequent speaker at major business conferences on innovation and holds two master's degrees from Duke University (MBA in Marketing and MA in Economics).

ACKNOWLEDGMENTS

I would like to acknowledge several people for their contributions to this project.

Many thanks to all of the staff at Cognella, including Mazin Hassan, Amy Smith, Abbey Hastings, Theresa Winchell, and Susana Christie, who provided expert guidance throughout the development of this book and whose continuously positive outlook and enthusiasm made them a delight to work with.

In addition, I enjoyed the opportunity to receive feedback and input from professors and business colleagues who reviewed portions of the draft material, including Greg McGiffney, Steve Reed, Jacob Goldenberg, Rom Schrift, Robert Tucker, and Debapratim Purkayastha.

Finally, and most important, I would like to extend my appreciation to my family, who serve as a constant source of inspiration, including my beautiful bride, Heather; my parents, Arlene and Stanley; and my three amazing children, Jeremy, David, and Shira.

INTRODUCTION

Innovation has been one of the most common buzzwords in twenty-first-century business. Corporate CEOs regularly cite innovation as being one of the most critical areas in which their organizations need to focus. And innovation is viewed as equally important for small companies and start-ups as well. I define innovation as successfully commercializing a new idea that solves for a customer problem. There is ample reason that all companies need to be innovating. Advances in technology and globalization have enabled new market entrants to spawn at a faster rate than at any time in history. This has created a business landscape in which innovation is essential for company survival.

In recent years, several great companies that failed to effectively innovate have gone bankrupt. A classic example is Blockbuster, which once dominated the video rental industry. Companies that have embraced innovation, like Netflix, have thrived. Netflix created not one, but two new revolutionary new business models for video rental distribution—internet mail order and streaming. It is no surprise that some of the world's most innovative companies such as Apple, Alphabet (the parent of Google), and Amazon are now also among the largest, most successful, and most admired companies in the world.

Yet, despite the recognizable need for innovation in today's business world and the extraordinary benefits that accrue to those that innovate successfully, many organizations still do not have a systematic process for managing innovation. In addition, most company employees have no innovation training. And even worse, few employees in large organizations are invited to have a role in the company's innovation efforts.

This book seeks to provide a selection of readings that enable students, business managers, and organization leaders to gain a broad perspective on the many facets of innovation and understand the innovation process. The book also strives to demystify various aspects of innovation, including how to identify needs for innovation and how to generate ideas to solve for those needs. Furthermore, the readings collectively deliver a sampling of the skill set and mind-set that employees, managers, and leaders need to innovate on a world-class level.

One of the great advantages of this type of anthology is that the reader benefits from multiple perspectives and writing styles. In selecting the readings, I have included some of the thought leaders in the field to ensure readers have direct access to some of the most brilliant thinkers about innovation. I have also included selections that were designed to stoke the curiosity of the reader, including pieces that contain short profiles of companies that are famous for their innovative practices. Finally, I have attempted to provide a variety of article lengths and styles to provide for a dynamic reading experience.

The book is divided into eight chapters. Within each chapter there are between two to five readings. At the beginning of each chapter and reading, I have provided a brief introduction. These introductions provide the context for each reading and preview key learnings. In addition, at the end of each reading I have provided questions for thought. These questions are an attempt to create an interactive experience for the reader. I encourage you to use these questions as a personal exploration exercise that will better enable you to reap the benefit of the readings and make the key points more memorable.

The following is a quick description of the contents of each chapter.

Chapter 1—Innovation Overview introduces a few general innovation topics that set the stage for the rest of the book.

Chapter 2—Creating a Culture of Innovation introduces the notion that great innovation must take place continuously and be embedded in the way a company operates to be most effective.

Chapter 3—Identifying Customer Needs for Innovation is the first of four chapters that describe specific phases of the innovation process. I regard this first phase as the most important in the spirit of placing the customer first.

Chapter 4—Generating Ideas to Solve for Customer Problems shares several perspectives on methods for tapping into your individual creative potential and the creativity of those in your organization to develop ideas.

Chapter 5—Evaluating Ideas provides specific methods for evaluating ideas and selecting the optimal ones to design and develop.

Chapter 6—Designing New Products & Services shares some approaches for how to take a big idea and design and cultivate it into a winning new product or service.

Chapter 7—Implementing an Overall Process for Innovation presents several viewpoints on how to put together a coherent process for innovation.

Chapter 8—Innovation Profiles delivers insightful overviews of how some of the most recognizable companies in the world actually innovate.

I hope you enjoy this first edition of the book. In the spirit of innovation and design thinking, I welcome all feedback from readers. Please contact me at Len.Ferman@unf.edu with any constructive comments you might have, as these will be helpful in making improvements to future editions.

Happy reading!

Len Ferman

1

INNOVATION OVERVIEW

Chapter 1 introduces a few topics that serve as a foundation to learn more about innovation. The first reading, packed with real world examples, introduces the fascinating theory of disruptive innovation and demonstrates the dangers that established companies face if they do not consider new business models. The second reading in this chapter reveals the important dichotomy between two ends of the innovation spectrum: incremental versus breakthrough innovations. The last reading in the chapter succinctly makes the case that innovation is the engine for company growth.

THE GREAT DISRUPTION

In 1997, Harvard University professor Clayton Christensen authored *The Innovator's Dilemma*. This landmark book introduced the theory of disruptive innovation. Disruption occurs when established companies with dominant market positions, making what seem to be at the margin all the right business decisions, nevertheless lose out to new entrants that are leveraging new business models. In many cases, the newcomer's disruptive innovation does not even appeal to the incumbent's best customers, thus blinding the incumbent to the disruptive force until it is too late to adequately respond.

It is interesting that Christensen's book appeared at the dawn of an age of disruption stemming from the advent of the internet. In recent years, we have seen several classic examples of disruption including Netflix overtaking Blockbuster, Uber and Lyft reimagining the ride hailing business, and, of course, Amazon becoming a force in many industries at the expense of long-established companies including many famous retail stalwarts.

The following journal article appeared in 2001 and was authored by Clayton Christensen in conjunction with Thomas Craig and Stuart Hart. Appearing in the *Journal of Foreign Affairs*, the article looks at how disruptive innovation played out on a macro scale from the 1960s to the 1990s during which time many Japanese companies initially disrupted American companies, only to then in turn be disrupted themselves. Disruption can happen to the initial disruptor when the company, having reached a high level of success and market share, retracts into a defensive mode. Many companies that reach the pinnacle of their industry act to protect current revenue and profitability without looking ahead and investing in experimentation around new business models, thus exposing themselves to the threat of disruption.

The article is valuable for its succinct overview of disruptive innovation and the innovator's dilemma. In addition, the many examples in the article help bring this theory to life and demonstrate why it is still a foundational concept for understanding innovation today. All students of innovation should have a grounding in the fascinating theory of disruptive innovation.

THE GREAT DISRUPTION

BY CLAYTON CHRISTENSEN, THOMAS CRAIG, AND STUART HART

REVERSAL OF FORTUNE

The booming Japanese economy from the 1960s through the mid-1980s was one of the most thoroughly studied and admired phenomena of modern times. From steel to automobiles, consumer electronics to watches, Japanese companies easily overran the fortifications of their American and European competitors. Western scholars praised Tokyo's careful economic planning and the focus of Japan's *keiretsu*—massive, interlocked networks of companies such as Mitsui, Mitsubishi, Matsushita, and Sumitomo—on building long-term competitive advantages. Other analysts attributed Japan's economic momentum to its workers' selfless dedication to improving productivity and to the extraordinarily high savings rates of its consumers. Scholars cited the absence of similar factors in Europe and North America, meanwhile, to explain the stagnation afflicting those countries. In the United Kingdom, for example, the huge share of GNP taken up by government spending was seen as crippling economic growth because it crowded out private investment capital.

The fortunes of these economies, of course, have now reversed. America has experienced the longest unbroken economic expansion in its history, and the United Kingdom has achieved levels of prosperity that few could have imagined 30 years ago. Japan, in contrast, has been mired for a decade in stagnation that appears to have no end. What happened? The answer lies primarily at the managerial and microeconomic levels and in particular with a phenomenon best termed "disruptive technology."

Disruptive technologies create major new growth in the industries they penetrate—even when they cause traditionally entrenched firms to fail—by allowing less-skilled and less-affluent people to do things previously done only by expensive specialists in centralized, inconvenient locations. In effect, they offer consumers products and services that are cheaper, better, and more convenient than ever before. Disruption, a core microeconomic driver of macroeconomic growth, has played a fundamental role as the American economy has become more efficient and productive. Once the micro-economic roots of disruptive technology are understood, policymakers can learn how to transform relatively stagnant economies such as Japan's, Germany's, and India's. Understanding disruptive technology can also help forecast the dangers lurking for strong economies such as South Korea's.

TOO MUCH OF A GOOD THING

Japan's macroeconomic puzzle has a microeconomic parallel. Why did so many companies that were once considered the best run in the world stumble so quickly? Many of these leading companies faltered not because they were ineptly managed but precisely because they were well managed. In fact, their leaders followed some of management's most sacred rules, such as staying close to their customers and focusing investments on the most profitable new products and services. But their innovations fell victim to disruptive technologies.

Every market features two types of "performance trajectory"—the rate at which the performance of a product or service improves over time. One trajectory measures the ability of customers to utilize the product improvements introduced by manufacturers. For example, even though carmakers keep developing new and better car engines every year, most drivers cannot take advantage of this improved performance because of outside constraints such as speed limits.

The second trajectory measures the actual pace of technological innovation. This pace of technological improvement almost always outstrips customers' abilities to utilize the improvements—so that companies with products and services centered on what customers need now nevertheless almost always overshoot what those same customers will be able to use tomorrow. A good illustration is Microsoft's popular Excel spreadsheet software. Microsoft can innovate at a much faster pace than its customers' needs, so most users are not even aware of 90 percent of this program's features. Well-managed producers overshoot the improvement rate that customers in any given tier of the market can absorb because they can improve their profit margins by selling more-sophisticated products to the most demanding customers. Companies that do not overshoot but instead keep their technology aimed at lower tiers of the market often find that competition drives profit margins sharply down. Hence good managers try to keep their profit margins healthy by moving their product lines out of the sluggish tiers of the market into those tiers where profitability is greater.

The tendency of good managers to overshoot, however, can allow disruptive technologies—cheaper, simpler, and more convenient products or services—to enter the tiers of the market where customers are already overserved by the existing (but more expensive) offerings. The leading companies in such industries are so focused on sustaining innovations and addressing the more sophisticated and profitable customers that they ignore the disruptive innovations piercing into the market from the low end. In this way, disruptive technologies have plunged many of history's best companies into crisis and, ultimately, failure.

There are four reasons why good managers become paralyzed when faced with disruptions. First, leading companies listen to their customers. Because disruptive technologies perform significantly worse than mainstream products in the beginning, the leading companies' most attractive customers typically will not use them. The more carefully companies listen to their best customers, therefore, the less they will recognize that the disruption is important. Second, such companies carefully measure the size of markets and their growth rates to understand their customers better. But disruptive technologies foster new products and services with a market impact that cannot be easily predicted. Third, good managers focus on investing where returns are the highest. Disruptive innovations, however, usually translate into cheaper products with lower profit margins. (It never made sense for IBM to market software in the 1970s—because the profits from making hardware were so much greater.) Finally, leading companies almost always pursue large markets. As companies become successful and grow, their managers are compelled to rake in more revenue each year to maintain their growth rates and boost stock prices. But the emerging markets for disruptive innovations are much smaller at first than mainstream markets and cannot provide the huge volumes of new business that keep a large company growing.

These four factors explain why most minicomputer companies could not position themselves well in the personal computer market when the PC emerged. At first, no customers of the large computer companies could use the new devices. They were like toys; indeed, firms like Apple often marketed them for children. Although PCs were developed as early as 1977, the ultimate size of the market and the computers' great potential for word processing and spreadsheet analysis did not become clear until about 1984. The evolution of this market—ultimately one of the world's largest bonanzas—defied the skills of the world's best corporate planners and market forecasters. Moreover, the gross profit margins in minicomputers for a firm such as Digital—the mid-range computer producer of the 1970s—averaged about 45 percent, and those margins were always under pressure from competition. The choice was between making higher-performance minicomputers, which promised margins of 60 percent and could be sold for more than $100,000 apiece, or personal computers, which yielded margins between 20 percent and 40 percent and were priced at $2,000 to $3,000 apiece. Hence personal computing represented a much smaller market than minicomputers did during the formative early years. Developing the PC, a classic disruptive technology, simply made no sense for minicomputer makers.

Of course, minicomputers themselves had once been a disruptive technology. In the 1960s, employees had to take punch cards to the corporate mainframe computer center and wait in line for the computer specialists to run the job. System crashes occurred almost daily. At the outset, minicomputers were not nearly as capable as mainframes, so the professionals who operated the sophisticated computers—and the companies that supplied them—discounted their value. But minicomputers eventually enabled engineers to solve the problems that historically only the centralized computing facility could handle. Later on, PCs enabled the less-skilled masses to compute in the convenience of their offices and homes. Even though desktop computers could address at first only the simplest of computing problems, they subsequently evolved into cheap, reliable, and convenient machines, which today do tasks far more complex than those that mainframes and minicomputers used to solve.

Photocopiers provide another example. Xerox once dominated the market with its complex, expensive machines. Employees needing photocopies had to wait at the corporate copy center until the operator could get around to the job. But then Ricoh and Canon brought their slow but inexpensive tabletop photocopiers to the market in the early 1980s. Xerox at first ignored these poorly performing machines; they were not good enough to address the needs of the customers who wanted better, faster machines for their high-volume, centralized copy centers. Yet as with minicomputers, the tabletop copiers allowed a larger population of unskilled people to make copies in closets and nearby supply rooms. From those disruptive beginnings, photocopying

Disruptive technologies have plunged great companies into crisis and, ultimately, failure.

has become so convenient that easy access to high-quality, feature-rich, and low-cost copying is now viewed as a constitutional right. High-speed photocopying facilities still exist, but they thrive by disrupting conventional printing businesses—enabling low-skilled operators to copy and bind printed matter on demand, which once required the time-consuming skill of professionals.

The examples abound. Alexander Graham Bell's telephone was initially rejected by Western Union, the leading telecommunications company of the 1800s, because it could carry a signal only three miles. The Bell telephone therefore took root as a local communications service that was simple enough to be used by everyday people. Little by little, the telephone's range improved until it supplanted Western Union and its telegraph operators altogether. Merrill Lynch brought equity ownership within the reach of middle-income Americans, and now firms such as E*Trade and Charles Schwab let college students and middle-class investors manage their own portfolios. Likewise, George Eastman's camera enabled amateur photography. In each of these examples, customers ultimately found products and services that were far more reliable, more convenient, and less expensive than what would have been available had these revolutions not occurred. Although they were simple and inadequate at the outset, the disruptive innovations that overturned their industries left people much better off and created huge new waves of economic growth—despite leaving the wrecks of the industry's prior leaders in their wake.

BIG IN JAPAN

Nearly all of the technologies that drove Japan's stunning economic growth through the 1960s and 1970s were disruptive relative to the dominant American and European manufacturers. For example, Japanese steel companies began exporting inexpensive steel targeted at the lowest-quality tiers of the American steel market in the early 1960s. As the Japanese captured these markets and drove the prices of their products down, Western steel makers simply exited those tiers of the market to focus instead where profit margins were higher. To improve their own margins, the Japanese steel makers then pursued the Americans into the higher tiers of the market. Today, Japanese companies such as Nippon Steel, Nippon Kokkan, and Kobe Steel are among the world's largest high-quality steel producers.

In similar fashion, Toyota attacked the lowest tiers of the North American automobile market in the 1960s with its Corona model. Over time, this strategy created new growth markets. The cars were so simple and ultimately so reliable that they became second cars in the garages of middle-income Americans. This track worked until Toyota encountered competition in this tier from other Japanese companies such as Datsun (Nissan), Honda, and Mazda. To maintain its profit margins, Toyota then introduced models targeted at more demanding consumers—first the Corolla and the Tercel, then the Camry, the 4Runner, and the Lexus, and finally the Avalon line. Honda and Nissan have followed Toyota in this upmarket march. From the small manufacturers of the cheap Japanese imports of the 1960s, these firms have grown into huge global corporations that make some of the highest-quality automobiles in the world.

Another good example is the Sony transistor radio. In the 1950s, Sony's battery-powered pocket radio was one of the world's first applications for the transistor, which was then a disruptive technology relative to the vacuum tube. The sound produced by these cheap radios was tinny and static-laced, but Sony's customers—teenagers who could listen to rock-and-roll out of the earshot of their parents for the first time—did not care. Within a few years, Sony and its Japanese competitors had driven American radio producers (who relied on vacuum tubes for their larger, higher-quality products) from the market. Sony disrupted the television market in the same way, starting with a cheap, portable black-and-white model and ending up with its Trinitron. Japan later followed the same tactic in the video-recording and home-sound-system markets. Far from the days when the "Made in Japan" label was considered an epithet, Sony, Matsushita, and Sharp are today among the largest makers of high-quality consumer electronics products in the world.

Over and over again, Japanese companies succeeded with this approach. But disruptive technologies also set their own trap. These very firms are now stuck at the high end of their own markets, paralyzed by the four practices of good management cited above. Their best customers are now the most sophisticated and demanding ones, with needs that cannot be served with just another round of disruptive products. The firms' skills at careful planning are legendary, enabling them to compete better in established markets, but they now work against aggressively creating new markets. Their profit margins now can be hurt only if they attempt to move back down-market. And the most successful of these companies—Toyota, Nippon Steel, Sony, Canon, and Matsushita—have grown to join the ranks of the world's largest corporations. They can no longer meet their needs for growth with the kind of modest revenues offered by the first transistor radios, portable televisions, tabletop copiers, and compact cars.

Japanese firms are now trapped at the high end of their own markets.

Again, Sony is a good example. Between 1950 and 1979, it introduced nine significant disruptive technologies, including pocket radios, portable televisions, consumer video cameras, and the Walkman. Because of their affordability and simplicity, these products allowed ordinary people to do things that previously had been limited to experts or the wealthy. But since 1979, Sony has not created a single new growth market of this genre. The company has adopted a strategy that is very different from the one that led to the dynamic growth of its first 30 years. Even though it now offers technologically innovative products such as its Playstation and the Vaio line of notebook computers, they are sustaining innovations, not market-creating disruptive ones.

Until the late 1970s, Sony's product-launch decisions were strongly guided by its chief executive officer, Akio Morita, who followed his intuition rather than conducting careful market research to unearth the potential for new products. But as the company became huge and successful in the 1980s, it had to hone its good management practices in market research, planning, budgeting, and resource allocation. These careful, rational processes, which are crucial to an established company's efficient operation, prevented one of history's most successful "serial disrupters" from succeeding at new market creation.

That said, Sony is exceptional in that it created new market after new market for 30 years before it succumbed to rational management. Most other companies, such as Toyota, Honda, and Canon, created markets only once. Once they secured their initial beachhead, they became fully engaged in exploiting the opportunity they had created and moved aggressively upmarket.

READING 1: QUESTIONS FOR THOUGHT

- Since the article was published in the year 2001, there have been many more companies and industries that have had their business models disrupted. Can you name a few?

- If a company has a successful business model and presently maintains a strong or even a dominant market share, why should they be concerned about innovation?

- What do you think established companies can do to avoid being disrupted?

- Imagine you are leading a company whose main business model for generating revenue has been successful for a long time. What types of activities would you institute to ensure that you can identify potential new business models for the future?

WHAT IS THE INNOVATION PARADOX?

As we learned in reading 1, successful companies can be disrupted if they overlook or discard the threat posed when new business models or new-to-the-world products and services are introduced by competitors. When new paradigms emerge from newly established businesses, as they often do with disruptive innovations, it is even easier for large established market leaders to ignore the threat.

A main reason this occurs is that the successful market leaders often focus solely on incremental innovations that improve profitability by making small improvements to their existing products and services. Start-ups or other market disruptors, on the other hand, focus on entirely new business models that could be characterized as breakthrough innovations.

The following reading is a chapter in the book *The Innovation Paradox: Why Good Businesses Kill Breakthroughs and How They Can Change*. Authors Marc Epstein and Tony Davila provide an excellent description of the dichotomy between incremental and breakthrough innovation. They also describe how these opposite ends of the innovation spectrum require a different set of innovation management routines. This concept of incremental versus breakthrough innovation is fundamental to understanding how to think about and oversee innovation efforts.

In most cases, companies need to be considering both incremental and breakthrough innovations. Much like an investor maintains a portfolio with some low-risk investments that provide a low but safe return while also holding other, higher-risk investments that offer a high potential return, companies should approach innovation the same way. After all, innovations are essentially investments that the company makes to support future growth. Thus, a focus on all incremental or all breakthrough innovations would be unwise. Focusing solely on incremental innovation could lead companies to miss large and possibly industry-changing opportunities, while focusing only on breakthrough innovations could lead to a gradual erosion of the company's current customer base as customer needs for small improvements are ignored.

This reading comes from two great thinkers on the subject. Marc Epstein is a frequent speaker on innovation. He was a long-time professor at Rice University and former visiting professor at both Harvard and Stanford. Tony Davila earned his PhD from Harvard Business School and is a former faculty member at Stanford University and a former visiting professor at Harvard.

WHAT IS THE INNOVATION PARADOX?

BY MARC J. EPSTEIN AND TONY DAVILA

Nokia was a fine-tuned machine when it came to grabbing the latest trends in mobile phone use and translating them into robust, profitable designs. Its scouters mixed up with young urban trendsetters, executives, and families, almost to the point where they understood their customers better than they understood themselves. Techniques ranging from in-depth ethnographies to early prototyping helped the company keep its healthy lead in mobile communication. For instance, the discovery that people in countries such as Morocco and Ghana would share phone conversations led Nokia to develop phones with more powerful speakers, making it easier for more people to participate in conversations.[1] Incremental innovations—gradual, regular improvements to existing products and services—allowed Nokia to maintain and extend their lead in the market as they knew it. What could possibly go wrong?

Nokia's market lead fell apart when the smart phone became the mobile device of choice. Since the company was so successful in the market for traditional mobile phones, when the market shifted away from their flagship products, Nokia was left with a nearly perfect organization innovating for a market whose relevance quickly eroded. Not only did Nokia lose its venerable market position, but it also lost any meaningful chance of making a dent in the smart phone market, allowing companies like Apple and Samsung to establish themselves.

Another example of creative destruction caused by breakthrough innovation—the kind of innovation that disrupts old markets and creates new ones—in the mobile communication industry is the ups and downs experienced by RIM (Research in Motion), the company behind the Blackberry. Blackberry was one of the early winners of the smart phone revolution, with a 22 percent market share in 2009. Executives praised its design and its security. *Businessweek* ranked it as the eighth most innovative company in the world. But by 2013, users were leaving Blackberry for new devices with more appealing features, and RIM's market share whittled down to 2.7 percent.[2] RIM kept executing on a strategy that had proven to be very successful, but one that had become obsolete in the fast-changing market.

The innovation paradox occurs when the aggressive pursuit of operational excellence and incremental innovation crowds out the possibility of creating breakthrough innovations. Its opposite is also often true—companies with a focus on developing breakthroughs can lose their starting-line position to companies that simply execute better. What happened to Nokia with the advent of the smart phone, and RIM with the growing popularity of touch screens and other smart phone features, are merely two of many examples of companies that have fallen victim to the innovation paradox.

Operational excellence and incremental innovation feed success within existing business models, but they can feed failure when it comes to creating new ones. The financial performance of incumbents frequently deteriorates quickly after an industry goes through a structural change. As Nokia and RIM discovered, by the time the structural change erodes the financial performance of incumbents, it is often too late for the leaders of the old market to catch up. Incremental innovation delivers results as long as the industry structure remains stable, yet it can fail miserably when breakthroughs redefine an industry.

Disruptive technologies and innovations cause drastic market changes.[3] The interesting thing is that incumbents often see them coming but then disregard them, to focus on incremental innovation. Nokia, for example, actually had a prototype of a smart phone. Yet their existing customers—the ones the company already knew and understood—were not asking for it. But if you simply ask people what they want, oftentimes the answer will be more of the same; consumers will often extrapolate from whatever is available today. Nokia was extremely successful with the phones they were selling, so why should they introduce a product their customers didn't even know they wanted? Hence, Nokia kept making improvements on models their customers liked. All the while a new market was about to form, taking with it many of those customers.[4]

Established companies can choose to disrupt markets through breakthrough innovation, or they can wait and hope: hope that their industries will not radically change, and that incremental innovation will keep on driving success. They can hope that the change will not be too abrupt and that they will be able to catch up; they can hope the change will only be a passing fad; they can lobby to stop the change; or they can be out in front and create the change.[5]

INCREMENTAL AND BREAKTHROUGH INNOVATION

Innovation is often mistakenly seen as a singular concept. Either your company is innovative, or it is not; either it's in your culture, or it's not. But innovation can best be understood as a range of types and intensities. At the ends of the spectrum are two markedly different phenomena—incremental innovation and breakthrough innovation (figure 2.1). Both have the goal of moving creativity to market, but similarities end soon after that.

Incremental innovation is about improvements, while breakthrough innovation is about discovery. Managers looking for the single best way to handle innovation are set to fail. As they search for the golden solution, they become frustrated when their innovation model fails to deliver the expected results. They conclude that their company does not have the culture and resources to achieve the feats they see in other organizations.

Operational excellence and incremental innovation succeed as long as an industry follows the predicted path. All industries experience breakthrough changes that make existing strategies obsolete. At these points, what made companies great can become their largest liability.

Innovation is not a single concept. Failing to capture the differences in types of innovation throughout the management process leads to problems and frustrations.

SPECTRUM OF INNOVATION

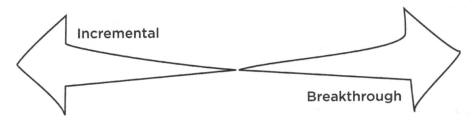

Figure 2.1. Types of innovation

Incremental and breakthrough innovation (and all the shades in between) can be visualized as coming from a range of technology and business models, some existing and others yet to be imagined (see figure 2.2).[7] Innovation works best when technological and business model dimensions are brought together. For example, the leadership of fashion firms often pair a creative mind—to come up with concepts that people had never considered—with a business mind—to bring those concepts to the market. Desigual, a fast-growing fashion firm, joined the creativity of Thomas Meyer with the business acumen of Manel Adell. Legendary design firms such as Christian Dior, Ralph Lauren, Prada, and Gucci also combine the separate talents of designers and businesspeople.[8]

Managing incremental innovation is about managing knowledge. Incremental innovation moves the current strategy forward. For instance, when Honda designs its new Odyssey, it isn't reinventing the automobile. Instead, a new version of an older model likely includes a nice set of novelties. Its safety features are better, its technology makes driving easier, and its entertainment capabilities are enhanced, but most of the parameters that define the car are unchanged.

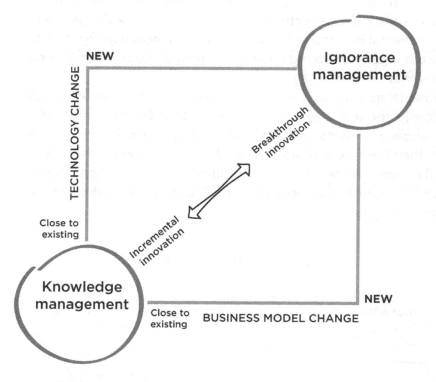

Figure 2.2. The innovation matrix[6]

In contrast, managing breakthrough innovation is about managing ignorance and uncertainties. For instance, consider the questions surrounding the driverless car: Which technology works best? How will people use it? How will it be commercialized? Will it coexist with or replace traditional cars? Will we need garages? How will traffic be regulated on driverless roads? As innovation efforts move away from existing products and services toward new technologies and new business models, uncertainty increases, risk goes up, and knowledge is sparser.

The two extremes of innovation are so different that they can't be managed the same way, and how you manage determines what you get.[9] If what begins as breakthrough innovation is managed as incremental, more likely than not it will become an incremental innovation. Sure, luck plays a substantial role, and a company may be lucky and get a breakthrough from an incremental innovation process. But putting more and more money into traditional incremental innovation processes will probably not significantly increase the already small odds of getting a breakthrough. Table 2.1 describes the main differences between incremental and breakthrough innovation.

INCREMENTAL INNOVATION

Most companies are good at developing innovations that build upon and advance the current strategy—innovations that fit within existing technologies and business models. Such developments help create operational excellence. A large percentage of investments go to feed this sort of innovation, the kind that keeps an organization in the game and gives it an edge over competitors. It is a hugely important type of innovation. Moreover, little steps, if they are taken faster than the pace of competitors, can put a company in the leadership position.

Winning in established markets requires executing faster through incremental innovation cycles. Even in maturing markets, the end-winner is the company able to better execute. Fast seconds—companies that come from behind to dominate markets—often end up at the top of the game.[10] Apple largely created the market for smart phones and tablets through the iPhone-iPad revolution, but Google and Samsung have been claiming territory with relentless efforts to bring incremental concepts to market. Pioneers such as Sixdegrees and MySpace

Breakthrough innovation deals with much higher levels of uncertainty and risk, and lower levels of knowledge. Thus, it needs to be managed differently from incremental innovation.

explored social media early on, only to see Facebook take the lion's share of the market, LinkedIn succeed in professional networks, and Twitter take the short communication space.

Table 2.1. Comparing incremental and breakthrough innovation

BREAKTHROUGH INNOVATION	INCREMENTAL INNOVATION
Talent combined for discovery and execution	Talent with strong weight on execution
Funding from separate budget	Funding from business units
Staged funding	Funding based on budgets
Low chance of success	Larger chance of success
Large returns on investment	Lower returns on investment
Discovery driven	Execution driven
Qualitative assessment	Financial metrics

Incremental innovation operates with relatively low amounts of uncertainty, large amounts of knowledge, and often large amounts of resources as well. It benefits from structured processes, because processes are good at managing knowledge and resources efficiently. For example, Logitech has dominated the computer peripheral market for more than a decade now. Every year, they come up with mice, keyboards, and web cams that are better than earlier versions. When Logitech goes into designing these new products, it already knows what the majority of these products will look like. It knows when the new products have to be on the market, the technologies that will go into them, their price points, their features, and a quite accurate development budget estimate. Of course, some uncertainties exist—like whether the new design will appeal to the consumer, or the new features will be better than those of competitors. But these uncertainties pale in comparison to the uncertainties of building industries around "not-yet" markets, like space tourism, nanorobots, or an ageless society.

Incremental innovation is extremely important for sustaining competitive advantage in current markets, and its inspiration benefits mostly from in-depth customer knowledge. Back in early 2000, Logitech, the leader in computer peripherals, had no presence in the keyboard market. One of its marketing department studies asked consumers to name the most important keyboard manufacturers, and even though Logitech had never made a keyboard, it came out as number three on the survey. A lot of companies would discard this information, or discount it as showing how ignorant consumers are—after all, Logitech knew that it had never sold a keyboard. Instead, the company interpreted it as a clear message to get into the market. In the minds of consumers, Logitech built and designed great mice, so they should also make great keyboards. Since keyboards use existing technology and were manufactured and distributed through the same channels as mice, Logitech's innovation was far from break-through. Yet it became a large and profitable business, and Logitech eventually ended up grabbing the number-one position.

Incremental innovation also benefits from going beyond customer needs into customer motivations. Design thinking and human-centered design effectively use careful observation and patient efforts to determine what people need and why people behave the way they do. They help understand that products not only fulfill a function but also have social and emotional meanings.

Overall, incremental innovation is a fundamental aspect of winning—it can result in rapid improvements for customers as well as for the organization, and it can keep company morale up by maintaining momentum. In fact, incremental innovation is central for staying competitive in current markets, and for defending new developments. While incremental innovation has barriers to achievement, the other end of the spectrum of intensity—breakthrough innovation—is a whole different beast altogether.

BREAKTHROUGH INNOVATION

In 1926, Henry Ford designed an airplane for the mass market—his idea being that everybody would fly an airplane much like they drove a car. The idea of personal planes is still appealing, and various research groups today are working to make this idea a reality. Should these groups successfully design the product and the business model to make it available to a large number of consumers, a lot of the infrastructure that we take for granted will be questioned, and additional infrastructure will need to be created. A world in which individuals pilot planes with the regularity that people now drive cars would certainly be a new paradigm, and would require a whole slew of support systems and structures.

Breakthrough innovation can shift existing paradigms. It is much riskier than incremental innovation, and the quest for it often fails, but it holds huge potential for growth. When breakthrough innovation succeeds, it creates new markets and redefines industries; incumbents often lose their dominant positions in favor of the mavericks who took the risk to change their industries and won. Its effects can be devastating to

Incremental innovation operates with relatively low levels of uncertainty, benefits from established processes, and is extremely important for sustaining competitive advantage in current markets.

Breakthrough innovations redefine paradigms and offer new ways to look at the world. Breakthroughs are often swift and spectacular, but they can also evolve over longer periods of time.

Incremental innovation is about employing creativity within existing strategies and industry structures. Breakthrough innovation is about employing creativity to come up with new strategies, new industries, and new societies.

companies that failed to gauge its implications on their customer base, and it can truly disrupt the status quo.

The most visible breakthrough innovations act quickly and revolutionize industries in very short periods of time. Often they create and leverage new technologies that rapidly make existing ones obsolete. For example, the iPod and the business model around it all but banished other portable music devices, while smart phones put companies focused on more traditional mobile devices in a difficult position. By the time the performance of disruptive technologies catches up with the incumbents' technologies, the incumbents are often hard pressed to develop a way to compete in the new market.

In other cases, breakthrough innovations are crafted over several years and take longer to fully transform industries. The international fashion company Zara is an example. In a market traditionally dependent on seasons and advertising in traditional media, trial and error in Zara's early years helped them shape a robust, disruptive, and winning business model. Whereas fashion was once an almost exclusively seasonal event, it is now a constant flow. Design cycles are measured in weeks rather than months; products that are sold out are not replenished; and print advertising is not needed to bring people into the shop. Zara has challenged deeply ingrained assumptions about how people shop for clothes, and how companies should serve them—and it has paid off. Breakthrough innovation is about questioning our values and beliefs, our mental models of how industries work, and our assumptions.

Breakthrough innovation is not only about managing uncertainty and learning from successes; it is also about learning from failures. The CEO of an innovative engineering company with stellar performance at one time argued, "if we want to grow beyond our existing business model, we need to learn to defend the solutions that we conquered. We are very good at attacking, but we are not able to defend our positions." The company was set up for groundbreaking innovations, but the company failed to manage the incremental steps necessary to maintain a position once it had taken it. Breakthrough innovation needs to be followed by a constant flow of high-quality incremental innovation. It is great to break new ground, but the value of your innovation can quickly slip away to competitors if you can't defend it.

A lot of the frustration surrounding innovation efforts in companies is the result of hoping to get breakthrough ideas when structures and processes are largely set up for incremental innovation.

The last decade has seen different emphases on open and closed innovation. Some companies still believe in a closed model, but most organizations have embraced a more open model, in which internal resources and external networks are combined to optimize the innovation process. Open models are even more important for breakthrough innovations. For example, the model used in university research has always emphasized collaboration and the open exchange of ideas. Breakthrough innovations coming out of universities are the culmination of lots of small steps from different research groups across the globe. An old adage says, "Visionaries see more because they stand on the shoulders of giants," and open access to knowledge builds these giants. In that same spirit, companies like IBM, Nokia, and Sony have made their patents related to improving the environment available for free on the Eco-Patent Commons platform. People can use this intellectual property to come up with environmentally friendly innovations. Other initiatives, such as Green Xchange, intend to create communities for people to exchange ideas, knowledge, and patents concerning environmental innovations.[11] But the idea of open innovation isn't only about giving things away, or making things freely available—it's also about creating networks that work together to address bigger opportunities.

NOTES

1. R. Jana, "Inspiration from Emerging Economies," *Businessweek*, March 23, 2009.

2. J. Nocera, "How Not to Stay on Top," *The New York Times*, August 19, 2013.

3. For more on the concept of disruptive innovation and disruptive technology, see C. M. Christensen, *The Innovator's Dilemma: When New Technologies Cause Great Firms to Fail* (Boston: Harvard Business School Press, 1997).

4. J. Goldenberg, R. Horowitz, A. Levav, and D. Mazursky, "Finding Your Innovation Sweetspot," *Harvard Business Review* 3 (March 2010): 120–129.

5. For companies' potential reaction to these disruptions, see C. C. Markides and D. Oyon, "What to Do Against Disruptive Business Models (When and How to Play Two Games at Once)," *MIT Sloan Management Review* 4 (Summer 2010): 25–32.

6. This approach to thinking about innovation was originally formulated by Robert Shelton. See T. Davila, M. J. Epstein, and R. Shelton, *Making Innovation Work: How to Manage It, Measure It, and Profit from It* (Upper Saddle River, NJ: Prentice Hall, 2013).

7. Different companies and authors label this matrix using different terms. The y axis has been referred to as assets or technology and the x axis as markets or competitive impact. The distinction between incremental and breakthrough innovation and the differences in between have been referred to as core (similar to incremental), adjacent (incremental with a breakthrough component to it), and transformational (similar to breakthrough). Incremental has also been labeled sustaining innovation, and breakthrough has been labeled as radical, game changer, or emerging business areas. See B. Nagji and G. Tuff, "Managing Your Innovation Portfolio," *Harvard Business Review* 5 (May 2012): 68–74; M. W. Johnson and A. G. Lafley, *Seizing the White Space: Business Model Innovation for Growth and Renewal* (Boston: Harvard Business Press, 2010). For an in-depth analysis of business model innovation through adding novel activities, linking activities in novel ways, or changing who performs different activities, see R. Amit and C. Zott, "Creating Value through Business Model Innovation," *MIT Sloan Management Review* 3 (2012): 41–49.

8. D. K. Rigby, K. Gruver, and J. Allen, "Innovation in Turbulent Times," *Harvard Business Review* 6 (June 2009): 79–86. These authors further develop the idea of combining creativity and business at the leadership level.

9. Ibid.

10. C. Markides and P. A. Geroski, *Fast Second: How Smart Companies Bypass Radical Innovation to Enter and Dominate New Markets* (San Francisco: Jossey-Bass, 2004).

11. M. Tripsas, "Everybody in the Pool of Green Innovation," *The New York Times*, November 1, 2009.

READING 2: QUESTIONS FOR THOUGHT

- Why is it important for companies to consider both incremental and breakthrough innovations?

- What are some examples of incremental innovations? How did those innovations benefit the companies that produced them?

- What are some examples of breakthrough innovations? How did those innovations benefit the companies that produced them?

- Why are the skill sets to produce incremental innovations different than those necessary to produce breakthrough innovations?

DRIVING GROWTH THROUGH INNOVATION: HOW LEADING FIRMS ARE TRANSFORMING THEIR FUTURES

Robert Tucker is a leading consultant and speaker on the topic of business innovation. His best-selling book *Driving Growth Through Innovation: How Leading Firms Are Transforming Their Futures*, broke new ground when the first edition was published in 2003, as it clearly explained the need for a systematic process to approaching business innovation. Advising companies around the country and the world, Robert Tucker has been referred to as "America's Innovation Coach."

This next reading consists of the introduction to Mr. Tucker's book. In the introduction, Tucker lays out five best practices for driving growth through innovation. These best practices are drawn from extensive research Tucker and his team at the University of California at Santa Barbara have conducted, including interviews with many CEOs of large corporations.

A key theme from Tucker's book is that innovation is not something a company can simply wait to initiate when the need arises. Innovation must be approached as a top-down discipline that is implemented across the organization, leveraging a clear process and a continuous commitment. When companies have a process in place, they are in position to efficiently enable commercialization of new product and service ideas. Without an innovation process, great ideas may never make it to market as they get lost in the day-to-day shuffle of running the business.

INTRODUCTION TO DRIVING GROWTH THROUGH INNOVATION

HOW LEADING FIRMS ARE TRANSFORMING THEIR FUTURES

BY ROBERT B. TUCKER

Since the first edition of this book appeared in 2003, innovation has become topic A in management suites around the world and the subject of countless articles and conferences. Yet, if you're like so many managers I am in contact with each year, my guess is that you're probably not convinced that your firm's attempts to embrace innovation are nearly where they need to be to meet the competitive challenges you face, nor are they bringing you the revenue growth you seek.

You may question whether there are enough breakthrough ideas in your pipeline. Perhaps you see a new and dangerous competitor looming on the horizon with the potential to disrupt your business model. You may be concerned whether your company can meet the changing needs of your customers or whether you have individuals in your organization who have that entrepreneurial mindset—that seemingly innate ability to spot opportunities and seize the initiative to bring them to fruition. And you may be responding to a directive from your chief to double the size of your business unit or division in ... the next three years!

That's why I wrote this book—to help you and other key managers in your firm develop a game plan to tackle the issue of jump-starting growth. I've written *Driving Growth Through Innovation* from the perspective that you've been charged with rethinking and redesigning how innovation is accomplished in your firm. I'd like you to consider this book as your guide to the essential things you need to think about and to put in place. And think of me as your coach, your advisor, your consultant in this journey.

The strategies and best practices and methods in these pages are based on my two decades' experience working with companies to improve innovation. If you're open to learning from their experiences—from their failures and successes—I believe you will discover an approach that is right for your firm and will help you grow. I also believe you'll grow as an individual in the process of mastering innovation.

Over the years, I've witnessed companies and their people transform as they committed to new ways of doing innovation. I believe you will achieve results that will surprise even you, impress stockholders and stakeholders, delight your customers, and force competitors to react to your moves. But only if you begin this journey with pen in hand, ready and willing to make required changes.

You've probably seen how superficial, flavor-of-the-month initiatives seldom have lasting benefits. Nowhere is this more true than in the arena of innovation. Of late, as innovation has moved to the front burner, I have seen far too many companies try to make innovation one of their 13 pillars of success, or their eight essential priorities. This won't work; innovation is much more complicated than that, and the pull of today's business is simply too great when innovation is but an afterthought.

On the other hand, I also have the great privilege to work with firms and to research firms that are getting serious about innovation. These are the ones we'll explore and examine in the pages of this book.

I call these companies the Innovation Vanguard firms, and in the first edition of this book I wrote about the emerging best practices 23 of these firms were developing to make innovation an established practice.

In the early 2000s, when most companies were serving the gods of either cost cutting or acquisitions, these firms were already challenging assumptions about how to facilitate greater numbers of ideas to commercial reality and, in the process, figuring out how to do innovation differently in a new century. My team of researchers, most from the University of California, Santa Barbara, helped me study these companies and interview their CEOs and innovation champions.

Companies in the vanguard at the time included Whirlpool, Progressive Insurance, Citigroup, EDS, BMW, and many others. Since then, new companies, including Bank of America, Procter & Gamble, John Deere, and others, have embraced systematic innovation and have achieved tremendous results. In this newly updated edition, I have combined my original research (where it's still relevant) with new research into those companies that continue to push the envelope for change in their organizations.

BEST PRACTICES FOR DRIVING GROWTH THROUGH INNOVATION

1   Innovation must be approached as a disciplined process.

2   Innovation must be approached comprehensively.

3   Innovation must include an organized, systematic, and continual search for new opportunities.

4   Innovation must be directed from the top and involve the total enterprise.

5   Innovation must be customer-centered.

What I have discovered is that firms that achieve growth from their innovation practices are companies that encourage ideas from everybody and everywhere in the organization, not just from traditional sources. Because of the pace of change today, your next breakthrough idea could almost just as easily come from your logistics department brainstormers as from your R&D process, and it is as likely to be a "bottom-up" idea as it is top-down. Using unconventional methods, the Innovation Vanguard seek out the unmet and unarticulated needs of their customers and they teach themselves how to listen differently than everyone else. They master the art of gleaning insights into their customers, and in anticipating their needs and wants often before the customers themselves know what it is they will respond to. Vanguard firms also strive for a faster *throughput of ideas* from concept to commercialization. Because they have a "process for innovation" just like they have a process for everything else, they prototype and experiment with and explore ideas more quickly, assess feasibility more intelligently, and make proper resources available so that good ideas don't get lost in translation.

In examining the best practices of Vanguard companies, I have discovered five essential practices that undergird them all.

PRINCIPLE 1: INNOVATION MUST BE APPROACHED AS A DISCIPLINED PROCESS

In a cover story in *Inc. Magazine*, journalist John Grossman was allowed to participate in a new product brainstorming session at Eureka Ranch, a leading ideation center in Ohio. Grossman detailed how seven top managers from Celestial Seasonings tea company, then facing flattened sales and needing desperately to introduce new products, were guided through three days of non-stop sessions, all designed to come away with new ideas. But three years later, when one of my researchers followed up with the company to see which of the new products on the market came as a result of that session, we were surprised by the answer: zero. Huh? Not a single idea became a product that made it into the marketplace, we were told. A Celestial Seasonings spokesperson, who did the fact checking for us, explained it this way: "[It's] our corporate structure and management … it's hard to get ideas through an organization."

Truer words were never spoken. Companies often seek to promote creativity by, for example, sending their people to facilitated brainstorming sessions such as the one at Eureka Ranch, where companies hope their people will learn some new whiz-bang method of generating ideas. Nothing wrong with that; such sessions can be a nice diversion from the daily grind and are likely to produce lots of new possibilities. If nothing else, they can prove that you and your colleagues are capable of thinking out of the box, and that can be an empowering demonstration in itself. But just don't think anything is going to happen back at the office, because it likely won't. By the time Monday morning rolls around, that retreat will already seem like a fantasy. Why? Because innovation at your company is not a discipline, and ideas, no matter how exciting, get pummeled by the pressures of the present. You need an overarching process in order to be able to capitalize on ideation sessions, and that's where discipline comes in.

Sometimes managers will tell you that lack of creative ideas isn't the problem in their company. On the contrary, they're convinced that they have "too many creative ideas" rather than too few. But this, too, is symptomatic of the lack of a disciplined process. If there's no process in place to separate the winners from the duds, that's a destroyer right there. To a kid with a hammer, everything's a nail. To a brainstorm participant without criteria, every idea is fantastic.

If there's no selection team in place to prioritize and prune and harvest and nurture ideas on an ongoing basis, you have no process. If there are no resources and at least some funds available to people with ideas, you have an anti-innovation culture. And if important people in your firm aren't involved, if your chief isn't up to speed on the growing importance of innovation and isn't enthusiastic about the topic, you have no process and you have no discipline.

Vanguard firms know that *disciplined innovation* is not an oxymoron. Nor does having an innovation process mean, as some at first fear, that you set up a stifling bureaucratic system that exasperates imaginative people before they've even begun. On the contrary, as we'll see in the examples in the pages ahead, the important thing about a disciplined process, which is not always easy, is that it gives structure and freedom to your approach.

Innovation, even when practiced as a discipline, doesn't guarantee you'll get break-throughs—at least not right away. You can't schedule yourself to have a great big idea on Tuesday just because you need one, and then three more by the end of the week. Even with an innovation process, you'll still need to keep up the search. It's just that your process will ensure that you keep up the search quarter in and quarter out, through good times and bad, because that's exactly why you need a process: without one, you are liable not to get around to it.

Like all disciplines, you'll get better with practice, and your practice will evolve. When you come right down to it, the only thing that separates your firm from competitors is the strength of your innovation process: the ideas, knowledge, commitment, and *innovation skills* of your people. So the discipline part is about empowering people with the tools to show them how to generate ideas, and it's also about empowering them in how to *think through their ideas* to know which ones are aligned with the goals of the business and the criteria management has laid out. Once you've done that, you'll have a much better idea which ones should be pursued and how to take ideas forward. Teaching the discipline of innovation involves showing people how to champion and communicate their ideas, how to find resources, and how to overcome obstacles and collaborate and persist when the going gets tough.

You won't stop experiencing "failures," because failure is an inevitable part of innovation. You'll simply make less obvious mistakes and your "failures" will propel you forward faster. And while lack of discipline pretty much guarantees failure, practicing innovation as a discipline almost guarantees a higher batting average of hits—ideas that bring greater value to customers and thereby build your top and bottom lines.

PRINCIPLE 2: INNOVATION MUST BE APPROACHED COMPREHENSIVELY

Innovation can't be confined to one department or to an elite group of specialist performers who will be responsible for making new ideas happen. This sounds great to the uninitiated, yet is one of the most common temptations for organizations and their leaders just becoming interested in the discipline. Simply put: they'd like to confine the messiness and the presumed chaos associated with innovation to a specific group and a specific place, hermetically sealed off from the rest of the work force. "Maybe we should start a skunk works to … ," while tasking the rest of the organization to keep producing operational excellence.

Vanguard firms realize, based on experience, that while it may sound good in theory, such compartmentalization doesn't work. All too often, rejection of the new product or service or process or strategy ideas begins immediately when the special team is assembled and others wonder why they weren't chosen or how this new approach will impact their work. And pity the ideas that do emerge needing adoption because they will be subverted, pummeled, and rejected faster than a snow-cone melts in Phoenix in midsummer! If the entire organization doesn't have a stake in an idea's success, you'd be amazed at the speed with which the idea will die.

My strong recommendation is that innovation must be part of every business unit and every executive's job description. In turn, the search for new ideas must permeate the company and encompass new products, services, processes, strategies, business models, distribution methods, and markets. If you can cause this to happen (and you can), you will have succeeded in making innovation part of the DNA of your entire organization and you will be said to be comprehensive in your approach.

In the Vanguard companies, one thing you notice is that responsibility for results has been diffused throughout not just business units such as new product development or marketing, but to each and every functional department, whether purchasing, operations, transportation, finance, or human resources.

To empower such widespread responsibility won't happen just because you announce that this broad participation is sought. So then, what does motivate managers and leaders across the organization to embrace innovation broadly and give it ongoing priority? Metrics.

The adage "that which gets measured gets improved" is just as true when it comes to broadening and motivating the scope of from *where* you seek big ideas as from *whom* you are getting them.

The most common innovation metric, one everybody is familiar with, is the one where you keep tabs on percentage of revenues derived from new products you've introduced in the past four or five years. 3M invented this metric and in sharing it saw it widely adopted and widely quoted. But because it only measures new product innovation, it is not nearly enough. In subsequent chapters we'll return to this topic and I'll show you some additional ways to gauge progress, or lack thereof, from all areas.

PRINCIPLE 3: INNOVATION MUST INCLUDE AN ORGANIZED, SYSTEMATIC, AND CONTINUAL SEARCH FOR NEW OPPORTUNITIES

Given the torrid pace of change, the rapid commoditization of products and services and even business models, organizations that rely on today's ideas, today's products, and today's assumptions are clearly vulnerable. This is precisely why firms that make innovation a disciplined process have specific systems and practices in place that help them at the so-called "front end" of the innovation process to bring future growth engines into focus.

Vanguard firms scan the horizon for impending threats, potential discontinuities, and, most of all, for emerging growth opportunities. They are seeking to spot where "we can use new technologies to disrupt an existing industry," in the words of one executive we'll hear from later. They are disciplined and regularly ask searching questions such as: What do these developments mean to us? How might we take advantage of them? What threats must we respond to now if we are to turn this change into an opportunity?

Innovation-disciplined companies promote a deeper understanding of social, demographic, and technological changes in a continual, systematic search for tomorrow's opportunities. And they use novel methodologies such as ethnography and archetype research and customer case research to gain richer insights into consumer behavior, which thereby gives them an edge in exploring implications and opportunities hidden in such trends.

PRINCIPLE 4: INNOVATION MUST BE DIRECTED FROM THE TOP AND INVOLVE THE TOTAL ENTERPRISE

After observing dozens of companies' efforts to build innovation capability, there's one success factor you can count on and it's this: the leader is engaged; the leadership team is involved; the top team, including the CEO, has bought in! I believe innovation must be directed and supported from the very top of the organization and ultimately involve your total enterprise. You and your fellow managers, indeed your company, will be tempted to make innovation one of seven or ten or even more top priorities. You and your colleagues will hope that this will be enough to make lasting change and to move the growth needle. You will be tempted to rationalize the lack of understanding or support for what you clearly see as the way forward and hope that you can inspire top team participation at a later stage—after you've shown early wins and fast results. Resist all these temptations, and do it right. Here's what I mean:

Because of its complexity, innovation needs to be *the top priority* of senior management in your company while a new approach is conceived and implemented. The top team must take the lead and establish innovation goals. The top team must figure out how to involve people in contributing ideas and break down the silos that prevent collaboration and experimentation. And the top team is the one that needs to establish milestones and metrics to gauge progress along the way.

Even with the surge in interest in innovation in this decade, the majority of companies still have no way to motivate their people to generate new ideas, and no way to gather those ideas up even if they did.

Worse, there's a prevailing assumption in many companies that mid-level managers and even rank-and-file employees cannot come up with powerful, growth-producing, potential breakthrough ideas. And still others will tell you flat out that they don't want their people to get any ideas; they just want them to execute, do what they were hired to do, and leave well enough alone.

Not the Vanguards. They are over this conceit. Not all ideas will be useful. Some will be redundant, self-serving, and trivial. But firms that practice innovation as a discipline, those that invest in building innovation capability, often use what are now commonly called "idea management systems" to capture ideas. They have discovered that this dormant creative potential can be awakened, managed, and translated into a new funnel for capturing value.

PRINCIPLE 5: INNOVATION MUST BE CUSTOMER-CENTERED

Innovation-adept firms live and breathe the customer. They recognize that customers are fickle and difficult to please and can sometimes lead you astray if you listen to them blindly, or if you ask them, in focus groups, what they are likely to respond to if you build it. But they don't let that stop them from being customer-centered.

In fact, the ever-evolving discipline of innovation now says that simply listening to customers in traditional ways—make that surveys and focus groups—is likely to give you only incremental ideas. The seminal work of Harvard's Clayton Christensen has also shown that you have to be *careful which customers you listen to.*

In fact, while listening is important, it's even more important to watch what they do, how they use your products and services to meet their needs in order to gain insights into what they will want next and what they'll respond to.

They also know that creating new, exceptional, and unique value propositions for their customers is the only route to success. And while you can fool some customers all the time, and all customers some of the time, ultimately, the reputation and acceptance of your products, services, and service offerings had better deliver.

READING 3: QUESTIONS FOR THOUGHT

- Why is it important for innovation to be approached as a disciplined process, as described by Tucker?
- Tucker believes that innovation should be a part of everyone's job. How do you think this approach could benefit organizations that you are a part of?
- How do you think an organization can benefit from a top-down approach to innovation?
- Tucker is an advocate of innovation being customer-centered. Why do you think this is so critical?

2

CREATING A CULTURE OF INNOVATION

In chapter 1, we learned why a focus on innovation is of critical importance to drive company growth and ensure long term survival. But, to be most effective, innovation activities must be accepted across an organization. This requires making efforts to create a culture of innovation. When everyone in the company understands and embraces innovative efforts, new ways of doing business are more readily accepted. And as we have seen, companies need to continually reevaluate how they do business in the present dynamic business environment. In this chapter, we will explore the characteristics that are most helpful in creating a culture of innovation.

THE CORPORATE CULTURE OF HOW

Every company has a distinct corporate culture that has evolved inside the organization and drives how work gets done. Successful innovation is most often achieved when there is a culture that allows it to happen. There are many company traits that can either promote or stifle innovation. And while there is no single magical formula for creating a culture that fosters innovation, there are clearly some traits that are helpful, if not required, to yield innovation success.

The next reading explores some of the traits that are most helpful in creating a culture that promotes innovation. Trust and openness appear to be two of the most important. These two company values, while admirable and certainly reasonable to expect in our society, are unfortunately often not present in corporate America.

Mutual trust throughout an organization is necessary in order to achieve a variety of positive behaviors, including collaboration and idea generation. If employees don't trust each other, or don't trust upper management, they are unlikely to share their ideas. They may fear their ideas will be rejected or that credit will not be given. Upper management in turn must trust that employees can make positive contributions even if they are not physically at their work stations all of the time. Enabling employees to have free time to think about business problems and work on ideas can lead to extraordinary value creation for the organization.

Openness is also necessary to allow a diverse group of employees to participate in innovation and ensure ideas are given a fair chance. Opening the opportunity to participate in innovation to the entire organization increases the chance that employees with a vision or passion for solving customer problems will have the opportunity to contribute ideas. And creating an environment in which ideas are shared, accepted, and cultivated rather than viewed with skepticism—or simply rejected—enables great ideas to flourish rather than flounder.

The reading is an excerpt from the book *The People Equation: Why Innovation Is People, Not Products* by Deborah Perry Piscione and David Crawley. Ms. Piscione is a best-selling author, speaker, and consultant. Mr. Crawley holds a PhD in Semiconductor Physics from Cambridge University.

THE CORPORATE CULTURE OF HOW

BY DEBORAH PERRY PISCIONE AND DAVID CRAWLEY

THE PEOPLE EQUATION PRESCRIPTION

A Corporate Culture of How refrains from placing judgment on the characteristics of people who are unlike you and embraces a plurality of differences. To do this, you need a method to inculcate this practice. Typically, in a hierarchical organization, you do this by creating a vision, mission, values, and strategy statement that would be directed by the top of the organization and promulgated throughout the hierarchy. In a Corporate Culture of How, you lead solely with your values—not through a traditional mission statement—and through informal norms that can be discussed and integrated continuously. Once those values are clearly understood and embraced, you can expect and enable the following:

Start from a place of trust until you have reason not to trust. We addressed the issue of trust in preceding chapters, and we can't underscore it enough. Trust is the one characteristic that will make or break an organization. Yet the importance of establishing trust is rarely practiced. We believe there is nothing more important than trust in a fluid economy.

When Deborah was teaching innovation process (and stressing the importance of trust) to a group of fifty manufacturing CEOs at an executive education program at Tecnológico de Monterrey in Lyon, Mexico, one of the participants said to Deborah, "We don't even trust one another in this room, so how do you expect us to collaborate?" Deborah responded by offering two choices: you can do nothing and continue to lose market share (in this case, it was shoe manufactures who were losing market share to the Chinese), or you can establish a new mindset for how people can work together. Pick one person and collaborate, starting from a place of trust (until you have reason not to), and be the model for others to follow.

Twenty percent participation. "It has been my observation that if you invite an entire business unit, division, or enterprise to innovate, at any one time, 20 percent of the people will be engaged in some form of innovation activity (e.g., thinking up new ideas, working on business cases, developing prototypes)," says Laszlo Gyorffy, a principal at Enterprise Development Group.[4] He continues, "While 20 percent may not sound like a lot, it is usually the amount of change that an enterprise can handle. I would also say the 20 percent number is fluid in terms of who are the people contributing. In other words, the percentage may stay the same, but different people participate at different times. I believe everyone has the potential to come up with a good idea." In many cases, an employee may think, "I may have a big idea and work on it from January to April this year, but then not take anything new on for months," according to Laszlo. With Laszlo's point in mind, we have found that there are serial "intrapreneurs" in most organizations. These are the people who see a problem or an opportunity and cannot help themselves, as they must solve the problem or capture the opportunity. These are the people who are always championing something and should be nurtured and supported in a way that they can safely carry out their ideas, free from the fear of being criticized, micromanaged, or let go. These are the core entrepreneurial, risk-taking types who provide consistent fuel to the company's innovation engine.

Twenty percent time. Allow people to step away a day a week or for 1.5 hours each day to explore and tinker with new ideas that may or may not have anything to do with their daily job. In a fluid economy, no one is immune from disruption and anyone can get into your line of business even though they may not currently be in your business. Your employees have to reflect on new ideas, incremental improvements, and perhaps the next big idea. In our anecdote about Apple in the preceding chapter, it was not anticipated that a computer company would evolve into a consumer-electronics company, and it certainly was an unexpected surprise how well the iPod was adopted by consumers across the globe. Had Tony Fadell and his team not had the freedom and time to experiment, to test out numerous prototypes that failed and then won, we wouldn't be enjoying the iPod today. Encourage people to get out of the office, breathe fresh air, and spend time doing something they enjoy doing, but set up a process that will capture their ideas or improvements, such as Improvisational Innovation discussed in chapter 2.

Promote networking within and build on ideas. One of the greatest challenges of large organizations is the difficulty of having their employees network with other employees outside an employee's division or area of work. This is an enormous loss to everyone's potential because by cross-pollinating various skill sets and passions, there is a tremendous opportunity for people to learn from one another.

A Corporate Culture of How fosters an ideation process in which people who don't work together day to day should have the opportunity to come together and build on ideas. In Deborah's book *The Risk Factor*, she covered NetApp, a data-storage company that encouraged employees to think about new ideas and allowed them to bring their ideas to other divisions to seek ways to improve their ideas before they brought them to their own divisions for approval and budget.

The language of "Yes, and ..." Also in *The Risk Factor*, Deborah wrote about David running the robotics Hacker Dojo in Mountain View, California, where a group of robotics hobbyists gathered to build robots on the weekend. This all-volunteer group met on Saturdays and included a variety of interesting people: a former NASA scientist, a senior engineer who wrote some of the most difficult software present on some of the earliest computer workstations, a precocious software engineer who had already started his own consulting company before he had reached his teenage years, and, among many others, a retired Lockheed-Martin satellite guidance systems engineer. The team, while all enthusiastic, faced a significant challenge: robots, without a good guidance system, don't know where they are.

The retired Lockheed engineer had an idea for how to solve this problem. Satellites solve a similar problem by looking at patterns of stars. He reasoned that in the same way, the robot could look at lights on the ceiling and thereby figure out its location. After a couple of weeks of effort, the Lockheed engineer came back with some kind of light sensor mounted on a piece of wood, with part of a plastic bottle painted black attached to this setup. As David looked at the handiwork, he was thinking, "This is clearly never going to work," but instead of sharing this unhelpful immediate reaction, he thought about the concept of "Yes, and ... ," took a deep breath, and said: "Okay, so what's the next step?"

The engineer discarded the painted plastic bottle pretty quickly, but he just as quickly came up with a system based on off-the-shelf cameras. A few weeks later, David was watching in amazement as the Lockheed engineer was demonstrating a system that could provide centimeter-accurate feedback based on ceiling lights.

If humans are predisposed to respond negatively to innovative ideas—when the people putting forward those ideas are most vulnerable and most likely to be damaged by rejection. The emotion of denial—which often leads to "no"—can feel harsh to someone who has just put themselves in the vulnerable position of putting forward a new idea. The emotion of anger is necessarily threatening for someone who would otherwise continue to engage his or her whole cerebrum in a thoughtful process of envisioning a better future. Compromise can often be perceived as watering down a vigorous idea. Depression or other displays of negativity can only dampen the embers that may ignite a new idea. How is an innovation-oriented individual to respond? I call it the language of "Yes and...."

In the language of "Yes and ... ," when you are greeted with a new idea, you respond in the affirmative and then try to redirect or build on the idea in a way that makes it more productive for the organization. This does two things:

- It helps integrate the idea into your own thinking. The notion of "Yes and ..." is a useful device to force you to consider fully how you can make use of the idea. It doesn't eliminate the possibility of eventual rejection, but it allows you to direct the emotions of rejection toward analyzing the concept and trying to make it better.
- It encourages the suggestor to come up with a further, richer, more deeply held idea that can enable further progress.

What comes after "and ... ?" Your "and ..." should try to encapsulate any concerns that you have about the idea and suggest a next step that will enable the idea to move as far forward as it genuinely has legs to do so.

Innovation is a vulnerable place because it is intrinsically an uncertain place. As we've mentioned before, if you knew what the outcome would be, it wouldn't be innovation. Also, obvious solutions are clearly not game-changing innovations, and truly innovative solutions are not obvious. This combination means that the most natural reaction in the world is to say no, but this is also the response that is most destructive to stimulating further innovation.

"For an idea that does not at first seem insane, there is no hope."
—Albert Einstein

Innovation always requires exploring new and unproven territory. By its very definition, innovation implies driving into a space beyond which all previous innovators have gone. If one is innovative, one is always trying for something that has never been done—or trying something that others have attempted but failed. Frequently, the initial attempt of an idea is without merit, but in the act of trying, one might stimulate others to have ideas that are sometimes slightly more worthy than the initial concept. These ideas may give rise to other, still better ideas, and so it is often only through the vigorous pursuit of many unworthy ideas that a good idea is found. Even then, it is only with great fortune that you come across a successful idea that can really surpass all that has gone before. The process is risky, difficult, and fraught with dangers.

Given these overwhelming odds, what are the chances that someone who is attempting to come up with something new puts forth a new idea that is actually worthy? In addition, if the idea is truly innovative and truly reaches for areas that are uncharted, how is it possible to know definitively whether the idea is good or not? To quote Einstein, "For an idea that does not at first seem insane, there is no hope."

Those who engage in this process are necessarily going to put forward ideas that lack all merit, with the hope that they put forward ideas that merely seem at first to be stupid but have some grain of hope. It is very easy to criticize these ideas and pounce on the vulnerability that putting forward these ideas generates. But to do so would cause that individual to never take that type of risk again, and it will come across as a threat that shuts down open thinking, closing the cerebrum to the very best thinking.

NOTE

1. Laszlo Gyorffy, interview with the authors, February 28, 2016.

READING 4: QUESTIONS FOR THOUGHT

- How do you think the suggestions in the reading would work in organizations that you are a part of or have been a part of in the past?

- Envision you are with an organization that offered you "twenty percent time." How do you think this would benefit you personally? How do you think your "twenty percent time" contributions would benefit your organization?

- How do you think "Yes, and…" behavior could benefit you personally in your business and personal interactions?

INNOVATION MYTHS

Ram Charan is an adviser to many Fortune 500 CEOs, and his books on business management have sold over two million copies. Charan's book *Execution*, which appeared in 2002 and was coauthored with Larry Bossidy, was on the New York Times best seller list for three years.

In 2008, Ram Charan joined with A. G. Lafley, the former chairman and CEO of Proctor & Gamble, to write a book titled *The Game-Changer*, a guide for how leaders can drive innovation in their companies. Shortly after publishing the book, Charan and Lafley coauthored the following brief article that discusses various myths about innovation and offers advice on the company culture that is necessary to produce successful innovations.

One of the themes I try to promote in this book and in my class at the University of North Florida is that innovation is essential to company survival. Charan and Lafley support this point in their article, stating "the company that fails to innovate is on the road to obsolescence."

Among the myths that Charan and Lafley point out is the notion that innovation is all about new products. Understanding that innovation can pertain to services, programs, and processes as well as products is a powerful revelation. Innovation can benefit both external and internal customers, both in the near term and the distant future. The key is to have a process in place to seek out and understand customer problems (external and internal) and drive towards the implementation of solutions.

INNOVATION MYTHS

BY RAM CHARAN AND AG LAFLEY

It is really the game changer.

Innovation is shaping corporate life, helping leaders conceive previously unimagined strategic options. Most acquisitions, for example, are justified on the basis of cost and capital reduction: the merger of two pharmaceutical companies and the global rationalization of overhead and operations and the savings from combining two sales forces and R&D labs. *However, you can only buy earnings through acquisitions for so long; and cost-control is a defensive strategy.*

Innovation enables you to see many potential acquisitions through a different lens, looking at them not just from a cost perspective, but also as a means of accelerating profitable top-line revenue growth and enhancing capabilities. For example, the innovation capabilities of P&G were enhanced by its acquisition of Gillette. Its market-leading brands (such as Gillette, Venus, Oral B, and Duracell) are platforms for future innovations; and core technologies in blades and

Ram Charan and AG Lafley

Ram Charan and A. G. Lafley, "Innovation Myths," *Leadership Excellence*, vol. 25, no. 6, pp. 5-6. Copyright © 2008 by HR.com. Reprinted with permission. Provided by ProQuest LLC. All rights reserved.

razors, electronics, electromechanics, and power storage strengthen the technology portfolio from which P&G can innovate.

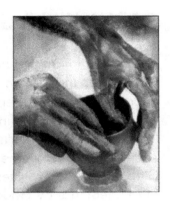

Innovation also provides an edge in entering new markets. In large part, it is P&G's revived innovation capacity that is enabling it to make inroads into developing markets, where growth is greater. Innovation puts companies on the offensive. Consider how Colgate and P&G, effective serial innovators, have innovated Unilever out of the U.S. oral-care market. The company that builds a culture of innovation is on the path to growth. The company that fails to innovate is on the road to obsolescence. The U.S. domestic automakers and major companies such as Firestone, Sony, and Kodak all used to be industry leaders, even dominators. But they all fell behind as their challengers innovated them into second place (or worse).

Peter Drucker once said that the purpose of a business enterprise is "to create a customer." Nokia became number one in India by using innovation to create 200 million customers. Through observing the unique needs of Indian customers, particularly in rural villages where most of the population resides, it segmented them in new ways and put new features on handsets relevant to their unique needs. In the process, it created an entirely new value chain at price points that give the company its desired gross margin. Innovation, thus, creates customers by attracting new users and building stronger loyalty among current ones. That's a lot in itself, but the value of innovation goes well beyond that. By putting innovation at the center of the business, from top to bottom, you can improve the numbers; at the same time, you discover a much better way of doing things—more productive, more responsive, more inclusive, even more fun. People want to be part of growth—not endless cost cutting.

A CULTURE OF INNOVATION

A culture of innovation is different from one that emphasizes mergers and acquisitions or cost-cutting. Innovation leaders have an entirely different set of skills, temperament, and psychology. The M&A leader is a deal-maker and transaction-oriented. Once one deal is done, he moves to the next. The innovation leader, while perhaps not a creative genius, is effective at evoking the skills of others needed to build an innovation culture. Collaboration is essential; failure is a regular visitor. Innovation leaders are comfortable with uncertainty and have an open mind; they are receptive to ideas from different disciplines. They have organized innovation into a disciplined process that is replicable. And, they have the tools and skills to pinpoint and manage the risks inherent in innovation. Not everyone has these attributes. But companies with a culture of innovation cultivate people who do.

DEBUNKING SEVEN MYTHS

The idea of innovation has become encrusted by myths. Here are seven:

Myth 1: Innovation is all about new products. New products are, of course, important but not the entire picture. When innovation is at the center of a company's way of doing things, it finds ways to innovate, not just in products but also in functions, logistics, business models, and processes. A process like Dell's supply chain management, a tool like the monetization of eyeballs at Google, a method like Toyota's Global Production System, a practice like Wal-Mart's inventory management, the use of mathematics by Google to change the game of the media and communications industries, or even a concept like Starbucks' reimagining of the coffee shop—these are all game-changing innovations. So was Alfred Sloan's structure that made GM the world's leading car company for decades, as was P&G's brand management model.

Myth 2: Innovation is only for geniuses like Chester Floyd Carlson (the inventor of photocopying) or Leonardo da Vinci: Throw some money at the oddballs in the R&D labs and hope something comes out. This is wrong. The notion that innovation occurs only when a lone genius or small team beaver-away in the metaphorical (or actual) garage leads to a destructive sense of resignation; it is fatal to the creation of an innovative enterprise. Of course, geniuses exist and, of course, they can contribute bottom-line-bending inventions. But companies that wait for "Eureka!" moments may well die waiting. And remember, while da Vinci designed a flying machine, it could not be built with the technology available at the time.

Myth 3: Innovation is for the future. True innovation matters for the present, not for centuries hence. Another genius, Thomas Edison, had the right idea: "Anything that won't sell, I don't want to invent. Its sale is proof of utility, and utility is success," he told his associates in perhaps his most important invention—the commercial laboratory. "We can't be like those German professors who spend their lives studying the fuzz on a bee," he said.

Myth 4: Innovation is a one-time event. Generating ideas is important, but it's pointless unless there is a repeatable process in place to turn inspiration into financial performance. We see innovation as a social process. To succeed, leaders need to see innovation not as something special that only special people can do, but as something that can become routine and methodical, taking advantage of the capabilities of ordinary people, especially knowledge workers. It is easy to put it off because you are rewarded for today's results, because you don't know where to find ideas, because innovation is risky, or because it is not easily measured. But these are excuses, not reasons. We have both practiced innovation as a process that all leaders can use and improve. It involves more people, and is more manageable and predictable than most people think.

Myth 5: Innovations happen in isolated silos or think tanks. Making innovation routine involves people. In real life, ideas great or good do not seamlessly work their way from silo to silo. No, from the instant someone devises a solution or a product, its journey to the market (or oblivion) is a matter of making connections, again and again. Managing these interactions is the crux of building an innovation organization. Innovation is a social process, and this process can only happen when people do that simple, profound thing—connect to share problems, opportunities, and learning. Anyone can innovate, but few can innovate alone.

Myth 6: Innovation can't be planned. You as a leader can map, systematize, manage, measure, and improve this social process to produce a steady stream of innovations—and the occasional blockbuster. Innovation is not a mystical act; it is a journey that can be plotted, and done over and over again. It takes time and steady leadership, and can require changing everything from budget and strategy to capital allocation and promotions. It requires putting the customer front and center, and opening up the R&D process to outside sources, including competitors. But it can be done.

Myth 7: Innovation happens in large, well-financed companies. Size doesn't matter. Innovation can happen in companies as large as P&G, Best Buy, GE, Honeywell, DuPont, and HP and as small as my father's shoe shop in Hapur, India. When I was nine years old, we targeted a line of shoes at the "rich people" largely associated with the local grain trading exchange. We became number one in town in less than two years, and the profits from this innovation funded my formal education.

A.G. Lafley is chairman and CEO of P&G, one of the most admired companies and a developer of business leaders. Ram Charan is coauthor of Execution. *Visit www.ram-charan.com. They are coauthors of* The Game Changer *(Crown Business).*

ACTION: Make innovation your game changer.

READING 5: QUESTIONS FOR THOUGHT

- Based on your personal experience in organizations you have been a part of, which of the seven myths do you feel has the most impact?

- The article makes the point that innovation is not just about new products but also about how the company functions and finds new ways of doing business. How might this notion help an organization that you are a part of to improve how they operate?

- Do you feel that the organizations you have been a part of exhibit a culture of innovation? Why or why not?

3

IDENTIFYING CUSTOMER NEEDS FOR INNOVATION

In my college class I tell students that the most important part of the innovation process is identifying customer needs. Successful innovations must solve for customer problems. Sometimes these are easily recognizable problems that customers can readily articulate. Solving for these types of customer problems usually results in incremental innovations. However, in many cases customers have latent problems that they can't articulate or don't even recognize. Solving for these problems can result in breakthrough innovations. But, identifying these types of problems is a challenge. In this chapter we will explore different methods of identifying customer needs that are essential for innovators to be familiar with to guide their innovation efforts.

THREE STEPS TO BETTER INSIGHTS FOR INNOVATION

In the next reading, Peter Mulford begins with the assertion that "effective innovation requires good insights." This simple statement captures the essence of how great innovations get their start. Too often companies jump straight to idea generation without first conducting sufficient research—or any research at all—to identify customer needs, wants, and desires. Without a deep understanding of the customer problem you are trying to solve, you cannot generate an effective solution. Students in my class often hear me say that customer research must be at the foundation of any innovation effort and that the most important phase of the innovation process is understanding customer problems.

In this short but extremely insightful article, Mulford, a partner in the global consulting firm BTS, succinctly describes the importance of conducting proper customer research at the beginning of the innovation process. Mulford points out the pitfalls that companies can and have experienced when they do not spend the necessary time and resources to probe their customer data and properly frame the problem. Mulford also advocates what he refers to as the "ALOE" tools, which stands for asking, listening, observing, and empathizing, that enable you to drill down and determine the "why" behind customer attitudes and behavior.

Customers should be at the forefront of the innovation process. If we do not have a customer in mind and a customer problem at hand, then innovation efforts are essentially running blind. I hope this reading and the subsequent readings in this chapter will drive home this point and provide you with specific insights and tools that can be used to achieve the objective of understanding customer needs for innovation.

THREE STEPS TO BETTER INSIGHTS FOR INNOVATION

BY PETER MULFORD

FIRMS TEND TO BE DATA RICH, BUT INSIGHT POOR. TO GENERATE BETTER IDEAS—AND INCREASE THE ODDS OF LAUNCHING BETTER INNOVATIONS—CONVERT THE DATA INTO INSIGHTS FIRST.

Effective innovation requires good insights. From CEOs searching for the next product innovation to ad sales teams looking to impress clients, managers everywhere are looking for better ways to gather, interpret, and leverage data and knowledge to develop and launch better innovations.

Advances in technology for data aggregation and analytics, as well as cognitive and machine learning, have given would-be innovators access to a tremendous—and swelling—amount of data. The problem is that time-pressured managers often rush from data to action based on what the data say without probing deeply to determine what the data *mean*. As a consequence, they can miss valuable insights and opportunities or, worse, make decisions based on incorrect interpretations.

It needn't be this way. My organization has studied and observed firsthand how teams at private and Fortune 100 firms around the world convert knowledge to insights. As well, we've seen what happens when teams skip this step. This experience has helped us formulate three practical steps that managers, and the librarians who support them, can take to develop better insights when innovating or making big decisions.

The main idea is to probe and discover the deeper "why beneath the why" that describes the data in question. So the next time you or your team are seeking to leverage data to enhance decision making, consider following these three steps:

Start with the "three W's" to frame the human problem you are trying to solve. A common reason that innovation efforts fail is that they are often developed from the inside out. That is, they start by "ideating" a new technology, product, or solution, then look outside the firm for a customer problem to solve. Teams that innovate this way are frequently working on the wrong problem or even no problem at all—indeed, the annals of innovation history are littered with examples of failed innovations that began this way.

Consider the case of a heart monitoring device developed by a tech start-up in Silicon Valley. The team spent several months building the prototype solution, which was successful from a technical perspective. The problem? Only when they brought customers in to try the solution, late in the process, did they realize the product likely wouldn't sell. It was subsequently scrapped. The company founder later admitted, "The failure I had was asking them last, when *we should* have asked them first. *We* could have learned that painful lesson so much faster and so much cheaper."

People leading innovation efforts should, therefore, create a mindset in which their teams start by identifying the customer problem they are trying to solve. The three W's framework is a simple tool to apply to this end. It says that, for any innovative effort, teams should explore and answer the following questions:

1   Who is the person or people for whom we are innovating?

2   What is the need or want they are trying to fill?

3   Why do they have that particular need or want?

The three W's are an approach to framing the problem and finding the solution. The data generated using this framework can first be

PETER MULFORD is an executive vice president and global partner at BTS, a professional services firm that provides strategy execution, leadership development, and sales transformation services to businesses. He has more than 17 years of experience in management consulting and has advised numerous global firms on developing business acumen and innovation capability, including Coca-Cola, Sony, Hewlett Packard. Barclays Bank. Toyota, and McDonalds. Prior to joining BTS, he lived in Tokyo, where he worked for Aswa Ltd., a Japanese consultancy, and advised German firms on their Japanese market strategy.

applied to help develop an understanding of the real nature of the customer's needs and wants as well as the "why" underlying those needs and wants. A deeper understanding of the "what" and "why" will, in turn, improve the quality of both the ideation efforts that follow and the experiments that innovators run later. By relentlessly asking and exploring these three questions, the team will dramatically improve the odds of success by ensuring it is working on a problem the customer actually cares about.

Use ALOE tools to uncover the "why." A key problem with data is that it often fails to reveal the deeper "why" required for great innovation. Consider the "Pepsi Challenge" campaign of the late 1970s. The campaign produced data demonstrating that consumers preferred the taste of Pepsi over Coke in blind taste tests conducted in public arenas. Coke responded by launching "New Coke," only to relaunch the original formula less than three months later after consumers responded angrily to the move. Six months after the relaunch. Coke's sales were increasing at twice the rate of Pepsi's.

What had happened? The research and data used by the Coca-Cola team failed to identify the deeper "why" underpinning consumer behavior. As Donald Keough, a former president of Coca-Cola, noted. "All the time and money and skill poured into consumer research on the new Coca-Cola could not reveal the deep and abiding emotional attachment to original Coca-Cola felt by so many people."

Managers can get to the "why beneath the why" hidden in customer data by using ALOE tools. Specifically, they should use tools intended for *asking, listening, observing,* and *empathizing.*

ALOE tools include advanced interviewing skills, such as the following:

1 The ROPE method (results, opportunity, problems, and execution);

2 So-called "design thinking" tools such as empathy maps and customer journey mapping; and

3 Other problem re-framing techniques such as the outcome expectation map and issue trees.

ALOE tools work because they help you probe beneath the data and reveal the customer's emotions, thoughts, and motivations so you can better determine the "what" to solve for him or her. These techniques are particularly useful for surfacing insights when you are innovating products that are radically different. This is because consumers tend to have a limited awareness of their real preferences with respect to radical innovation, which mitigates the effectiveness of traditional marketing data collected from customer surveys and focus groups.

Change the angle of inquiry to bust biases. Decades of psychological research have demonstrated that people readily fall prey to biases and patterns of "group think." These biases and patterns can retard efforts to glean fresh insights from data. One way to address this problem is to change the angle of inquiry, which requires forcing your team to evaluate data from new and unexpected perspectives.

In practice, this means crafting a series of questions your team can use to probe available data from different angles. For example, a media and entertainment firm looking to develop a better user experience might change the angle of inquiry from "Why are consumers cutting the cord?" to "What's the biggest avoidable pain point our cable customers endure?" Similarly, an athletic apparel retailer might shift from "What SKUs are selling above plan in Store X" to "Why is a given SKU selling in Store X, but not in Store Y?"

With the amount of data available to leaders growing by the minute, the temptation to leap from data to innovation is strong. By resisting this temptation and using techniques to generate insights before leaping into action, managers can improve the quality of the ideas they generate and the innovation experiments they launch.

NOTE

ROPE is a question technique developed by Richard Hodge and Lou Schacter. For more information, read *The Mind of The Customer: How Great Companies have Reinvented their Sales Process to Accelerate their Customers' Success.*

READING 6: QUESTIONS FOR THOUGHT

- How do you think that organizations you are currently or have previously been a part of could benefit from spending more time to develop insights about their customers?

- Conduct a thought exercise by applying the three Ws framework to an organization you are currently or have previously been a part of.

- Continue with the thought exercise and apply the ALOE tools to uncover more depth regarding why customers might have the need you identified. Imagine that you are observing customers as they use a product or service and asking them questions to better understand their needs.

ALLOWING YOUR CUSTOMERS TO NAVIGATE

Understanding customer problems and obtaining customer feedback on potential solutions is an essential part of the innovation process. Companies that are diligent about including customers in the innovation process in this manner dramatically improve their chance of success when launching new products and services.

The following reading is a short excerpt from the book *First and Fast: Outpace Your Competitors, Lead Your Markets, and Accelerate Growth* by Stuart Cross. Mr. Cross is a consultant, business coach, and speaker based in the United Kingdom.

In this reading, Cross explains why it is essential to talk to the right customers, in the right place and with the right stimulus, to garner the feedback necessary for successful business innovation. Cross's suggestions amount to a cutting-edge view of how customer research can be done more effectively and efficiently to support innovation. As we will see later in the chapter on design thinking, Cross's assertion that consumer research should be conducted with prototypes, not concepts, represents the latest thinking in this area. This displays the value of learning from practitioners such as Cross as opposed to solely relying on the leading theorists and philosophers about innovation.

ALLOWING YOUR CUSTOMERS TO NAVIGATE

BY **STUART CROSS**

HOW TO WORK WITH CUSTOMERS TO ACCELERATE INNOVATION

Winning the race to develop and offer new solutions for customers is at the heart of 21st-century business success. And, just as we need to think differently about how companies organize internally to meet this challenge, we also need to think differently about how we engage and work with customers. Here are six ways that you can get better and faster insights from your customers so that you become the fastest, and ultimately the first, in your market.

1   **Talk to the Right Customers.** As we've already discussed, not all customers are the same. When dealing with new products and services, you need to talk to customers who are more accepting and welcoming of innovations. From Figure 7.1, it is the early adopters,

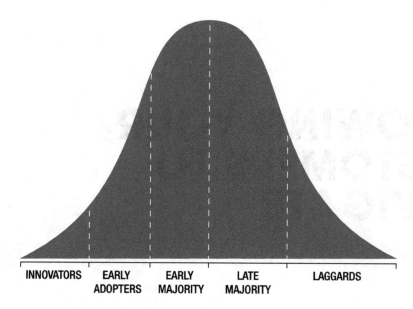

| INNOVATORS | EARLY ADOPTERS | EARLY MAJORITY | LATE MAJORITY | LAGGARDS |

Figure 7.1. The customer diffusion curve

in particular, that can often give the best indication of likely success. Innovators are likely to respond positively to anything that's new, but "early adopters" are more discerning and will take more convincing of your product's benefits before giving you a positive response.

In short, the right customers to engage to drive your innovation process are not necessarily representative of your existing customer base as a whole. Instead, they are the ones who are best placed to understand what you're trying to achieve. They can act, in many ways, as a glimpse into the future, as the majority of customers may catch up with their tastes within the next year or two. These customers can also influence the mass-market consumers, as they are likely to be bloggers, opinion formers, and recommenders to more conservative buyers.

2 **Use the Right Environment.** Too much research takes place on the end of a phone line or e-mail connection or in faceless meeting rooms. If you're a retailer, test your latest retail thinking in a store. If you're a restaurant, talk to your customers as they're eating a meal or at home making plans for the next meal out. The managers at Marriott hotels, for instance, realized that they were over-investing in their lobbies when they observed that guests seldom used the sofas or chairs that were freely available in these areas. When they engaged with their customers, they understood that waiting around in hotel lobbies was not something that people wanted to be seen doing. As a result, the development team spent more effort creating a database of

recommended places to visit at each hotel, as that was something that their guests really valued. In other words, by focusing their research in real hotels, Marriott's managers were able to identify insights that customers would never have raised in a typical focus group conference room workshop.

3   **Prototypes, Not Concepts.** Focusing on your customers' actual decisions, rather than their unreliable predictions about those potential decisions, means that you should use prototypes in your research whenever possible. They then have the chance to play with the product or experience the service, rather than simply giving you reactions to what is likely to be an abstract concept. As we discussed earlier, Steve Jobs didn't necessarily ask customers what they wanted, but he strongly believed in going back to customers with prototypes and models to check that his new idea was likely to fit with what customers needed. Critically, the prototype does not need to be particularly advanced for it to help customers make the mental leap from an abstract notion to a concrete idea. For example, I once ran an idea generation workshop with a foot care company and we ended the day discussing some of our best ideas with a panel of target customers. One of the ideas we came up with was an exfoliating sock. The customers were having trouble understanding the concept, so one of the managers got hold of a normal sock and added some exfoliating lotion to the inside of it. He told the focus group that the product wouldn't be as "oily" as this prototype but that it would provide an exfoliating effect. One or two of the customers tried the sock on and instantly gave more vivid and richer feedback on what it would take to make it attractive enough for them to consider buying.

4   **The Power of Instant Feedback.** The use of a focus group at the end of an idea-generation workshop is an example of instant feedback. It provides far greater momentum into any new product or service development process than waiting weeks for more formal research. Critical to its success is that the developers need to be involved in the feedback process. That way the development team isn't relying on researcher's interpretations and reformulations of customers' responses, but they can actually witness user responses themselves, providing them with richer, more visceral and quicker information to use in the next stage of the development process. I have worked with the new offer development team of several retailers, for instance, where we have simply created an idea and implemented an initial, rapidly prototyped solution in-store and then observed shoppers to see if and how they interact with our new solution. The results are virtually immediate. If the first few shoppers fail to interact with a new display, no amount of waiting is likely to change that pattern. As a result, setting up prototypes in a way that gives you instant feedback can act as a huge accelerator on your new offer development process.

5   **Exploit Technology.** The use of technology can help you develop your ideas faster, but also get faster and better feedback and insights from your customers. In the digital world, for example, it is possible to rapidly develop prototype websites and apps that you can share with a sample of customers to gain views and check your thinking. Some major consumer goods companies that I work with have an entire virtual store that, with the aid of special goggles, people can shop and interact with prototyped virtual displays. These research centers can cost millions of dollars to develop, but you don't need to invest so much to exploit technology effectively. You can now ask your customers to use the video recorders on their smart phones to create a video diary of their thoughts and ideas, or to create a real-time video of their entire customer experience. Online questionnaires and customer panels can also enable you to gain rapid feedback on their thoughts and the use of social networks or group messenger apps can enable customers to share, pool, and develop insights and ideas with the development team.

6   **Co-creation Between Customers and Executives.** Not only can customers provide feedback on your ideas, but they can also become involved in their development. This happens most rapidly and most effectively when they are done alongside the development team. At one client, a customer development team worked with a small group of customers and one or two senior executives over a period of a few weeks to collectively develop some new product and service ideas. In the initial workshop, the customer group was dismissive of the team's concepts, complaining that they were insufficiently distinctive and were, in essence, me-too ideas. The development team went away and came back with more radical and distinctive ideas. These led to more constructive discussions in the subsequent meetings, and within four weeks, full-scale prototypes had been developed for wider and more detailed testing.

All six of these ideas are about getting your customers far more closely integrated with your innovation and product development processes and creating faster feedback loops so that you can refine and develop your ideas at pace. In some cases, this may take several months of work, but in others, as we have seen, you can reduce the development phase to a matter of days, enabling you to get ahead of your rivals and be the innovation leader of your market.

READING 7: QUESTIONS FOR THOUGHT

- Think about a company you are familiar with or one that you have worked at. If you were innovating for that company, who would be the right types of customers to talk to as you seek to gather customer insights for new products and services?

- Continuing with the same exercise above, what would be the right environment in which to talk to the customers?

- What are some of the benefits that you think companies can gain by applying the suggestions from the reading around seeking instant customer feedback by testing prototypes?

FINDING THE RIGHT JOB FOR YOUR PRODUCT

In chapter 1, I introduced you to Harvard professor Clayton Christensen and in the introduction to the first reading, I cited his seminal book, *The Innovator's Dilemma*. The dilemma centers around the notion that brilliant business managers, making what seem to be all the right business decisions, can unwittingly steer their companies to ruin when facing a disruptive innovation. The first reading in this book, "The Great Disruption," demonstrates the dilemma with several examples.

A few years after the publication of *The Innovator's Dilemma*, Christensen published a follow-up book, *The Innovator's Solution*. In this book, Christensen describes what business leaders and managers can do to avoid being disrupted and to increase the chance that their organizations can create disruptive innovations themselves.

One of the suggestions Christensen puts forth in the book is the "jobs-to-be-done" theory. Jobs-to-be-done is a powerful framework that enables innovators and marketers to better understand customer needs and behavior. The theory purports that people "hire" products and services to get tasks done. For example, people hire a hamburger to do the job of providing a quick and tasty meal that can be eaten on the go. And they hire a bar of soap to do the job of cleaning their hands and body.

Several years after the publication of *The Innovator's Solution*, Christensen, along with Scott Anthony, Gerald Berstell, and Denise Nitterhouse, published the article in our next reading, titled "Finding the Right Job for Your Product." This insightful article summarizes the jobs-to-be-done approach. By analyzing consumer behavior in the jobs-to-be-done framework, we can gain clarity around customer needs and more readily identify customer problems for innovators to solve.

Scott Anthony is a senior partner at the consulting firm Innosight and the author of many articles in the *Harvard Business Review*. In 2017, Anthony was a recipient of Thinkers50 Award. This award salutes the world's leading thinkers on management. Gerald Berstell is the president of Innovation Research where he has been conducting research to aid the innovation process for over thirty years. He holds a MBA from Harvard Business School. Denise Nitterhouse holds a doctorate of business administration from Harvard Business School.

FINDING THE RIGHT JOB FOR YOUR PRODUCT

BY **CLAYTON CHRISTENSEN, SCOTT D. ANTHONY, GERALD BERSTELL, AND DENISE NITTERHOUSE**

Most companies segment their markets by customer demographics or product characteristics and differentiate their offerings by adding features and functions. But the consumer has a different view of the marketplace. He simply has a job to be done and is seeking to "hire" the best product or service to do it. Marketers must adopt that perspective.

The market segmentation scheme that a company chooses to adopt is a decision of vast consequence. It determines what that company decides to produce, how it will take those products to market, who it believes its competitors to be and how large it believes its market opportunities to be. Yet many managers give little thought to whether their segmentation of the market is leading their marketing efforts in the right direction. Most companies segment along lines defined by the characteristics of their products (category or price) or customers (age, gender, marital status and income level). Some business-to-business companies slice their markets by industry; others by size of business. The problem with such segmentation schemes is that they are static. Customers' buying behaviors change far more often than their demographics, psychographics or attitudes. Demographic data cannot explain why a man takes a date to a movie on one night but orders in pizza to watch a DVD from Netflix Inc. the next.

Product and customer characteristics are poor indicators of customer behavior, because from the customer's perspective that is not how markets are structured. Customers' purchase decisions don't necessarily conform to those of the "average" customer in their demographic; nor do they confine the search for solutions within a product category. Rather, customers just find themselves needing to get things done. When customers find that they need to get a job done, they "hire" products or services to do the job. This means that marketers need to understand the jobs that arise in customers' lives for which their products might be hired. Most of the "home runs" of marketing history were hit by marketers who saw the world this way. The "strike outs" of marketing history, in contrast, generally have been the result of focusing on developing products with better features and functions or of attempting to decipher what the average customer in a demographic wants.

This article has three purposes: The first is to describe the benefits that executives can reap when they segment their markets by job. The second is to describe the methods that those involved in marketing and new-product development can use to identify the job-based structure of a market. And, finally, the third is to show how the details of business plans become coherent when innovators understand the job to be done.

HIRING MILKSHAKES

A "job" is the fundamental problem a customer needs to resolve in a given situation. To illustrate how much clearer the path to successful innovation can be when marketers segment by job, consider an example from the fast-food industry, where companies historically have segmented their markets along the traditional boundaries of product and customer categories.

When a fast-food restaurant resolved to improve sales of its milkshake,[1] its marketers first defined the market segment by product—milkshakes—and then segmented it further by profiling the customer most likely to buy a milkshake. Next, they invited people who fit this profile to evaluate the product. Would making the shakes thicker, more chocolaty, cheaper or chunkier satisfy them more? The panelists gave clear feedback, but the consequent improvements to the product had no impact on sales.

Then a new researcher spent a day in a restaurant documenting when each milkshake was bought, what other products the customers purchased, whether they were alone or with a group and whether they consumed it on the premises or drove off with it. He was surprised to find that 40% of all milkshakes were purchased in the early morning. These early-morning customers almost always were alone, they did not buy anything else and they consumed the milkshakes in their cars.

The researcher then returned to interview the morning customers as they left the restaurant, each with a milkshake in hand, and essentially asked (but in language that they would understand), "Excuse me, but could you please tell me what job you were needing to get done for yourself when you came here to hire that milkshake?" Most of them, it turned out, bought their shakes for similar reasons: They faced a long, boring commute and needed something to keep that extra hand busy and to make the commute more interesting. They weren't yet hungry but knew that they'd be hungry by 10 a.m.; they wanted to consume something now that would stave off hunger until noon. And they faced constraints: They were in a hurry, they were wearing work clothes and they had, at most, one free hand.

When the researcher asked what other products the customers might hire to do this job, it turned out the milkshake did the job better than any of its competitors. Bagels were dry; with cream cheese or jam, they resulted in sticky fingers and gooey steering wheels. Donuts didn't carry people past the 10 a.m. hunger attack. Bananas didn't last long enough to solve the boring-commute problem. In contrast, it took 20 minutes to suck a viscous milkshake through a thin straw, hands remained clean and stomachs were satisfied until lunch. It didn't matter that the milkshake wasn't a particularly healthful food because that wasn't the job it was being hired to do.

Once it was understood which jobs the customers were trying to do, it became very clear which attributes of the milkshake would do the job even better and which improvements were irrelevant. How could they better tackle the boring-commute job? Make the shake even thicker, so it would last longer, and swirl in tiny chunks of fruit—not to make it healthy, because customers didn't hire the milkshake to become healthy. But adding the fruit could make the commute more interesting—drivers would occasionally suck chunks into their mouths, adding a dimension of unpredictability and anticipation to their monotonous morning routine. Just as important, they could move the dispensing machine in front of the counter and sell customers a prepaid swipe card so that they could dash in, gas up, and go without getting stuck in the drive-through lane.

Understanding the job and improving the product on dimensions of the experience so that it does the job better would cause the company's milkshakes to gain share against the real competition—not just competing chains' milkshakes but donuts, bagels, bananas and boredom. This would grow the category, which brings us to an important point: Job-defined markets are generally much larger than product category–defined markets. Marketers who are stuck in the mental trap that equates market size with product categories don't understand who they are competing against from the customer's point of view.

CARS OR OFFICES ON WHEELS?

Automakers and their market analysts segment their markets into product categories such as subcompacts, compacts, mid-size and full-size sedans; SUVs and minivans; light versus full-size trucks; sports cars and luxury cars. They segment their customers along extraordinarily sophisticated demographic and psychographic dimensions as well. Yet the failure of these practices is glaring, because these segmentation schemes don't reflect the jobs that customers hire a car to do. Millions, for example, hire a car primarily to be a mobile office. Most models sell fewer than 100,000 units per year, and their makers struggle to sustain premium pricing for any of the features that add cost to their cars. And yet, no company has designed a car that is optimized to do the mobile-office job that these millions of people need it to do. If the job were the unit of analysis for carmakers, it's easy to see how they could differentiate a family of products in ways that mattered for those who hire a car to be their mobile office. The same customers who resist premium prices for features that are irrelevant to this job gladly would pay for electrical outlets, wireless access to the corporate customer relationship management database, a hands-free phone, a big-screen BlackBerry, docking stations, fold-out desks and organizing systems—all of which could differentiate the car on dimensions that would merit premium pricing.[2] After test-driving model after model, many buyers who need to do this job conclude that there is little differentiation across the products in this market. But the products are consummately differentiable.

THE JOB OF DIFFERENTIATION

One of the most powerful benefits of segmenting markets by job and then creating products or services to do a job perfectly is that it helps companies escape the traditional *positioning paradigm* in which so many are trapped. The positioning paradigm posits that products in most markets can be mapped on a couple of axes, along which competitors have sought to differentiate themselves. In furniture retailing, for example, breadth of selection might be the metric on one axis, and quality of furniture might be measured on the other. The relative position of various automakers' products can be similarly mapped. One axis might be product category (compact, mid-size, SUV, etc.), while the other might map the degree of luxury in interior features and décor. Differentiation-conscious marketers within the conventional positioning paradigm search for a vacant spot on such maps into which they can position new products.

The problem with the positioning paradigm is that even when marketers find open spaces into which unique products can be slotted, customers often don't value the differentiation, and competitors find it easy to copy. The starting point on such maps of differentiation typically is occupied by products that have only the basic functions that customers need. "Disruptive" companies in that minimalist position then move "up-market" in pursuit of profit, copying features and functions of competitors' higher-priced products. When this happens, features that once defined a differentiated, augmented product become expected in all products. This forces marketers to search for yet more "unique" features with which to augment their offering.[3] A punishing fact of life on this treadmill is that when once-unique features of an augmented product become commonly expected, companies are saddled with the costs of providing those features but cannot sustain premium pricing for offering them. The root reason for this entrapment is the pervasive practice of positioning products in categories that are defined by the properties of products, so that "better" is achieved by copying features and stretching functionality.

When a company begins to view market structure by job, however, it can break away from the traditional treadmill of positioning and differentiate itself on dimensions of performance that are salient to jobs that customers need to get done. This differentiation seems to stick much longer. In furniture retailing, for example, most companies have been trapped in the traditional positioning paradigm whose axes variously measure breadth of selection, style and quality/price. However, it seems there are at least two fundamentally different jobs that arise in customers' lives. One happens in the lives of people who have graduated from their starter home and now need to equip their longer-term residence with furniture they will keep for the rest of their lives. Retailers that customers hire to do this job indeed must offer broad selection and enduring style and quality. Their customers are quite willing to wait the two to three months often required for delivery of such furniture. The other job arises among customers who have just moved into a bare apartment or starter home.

When the once-unique features of an augmented product become commonly expected, companies are saddled with the costs of providing those features but cannot sustain premium pricing.

The jobs that customers are trying to get done cannot be deciphered from purchased databases, but rather from watching, participating, writing and thinking.

The market position of IKEA International A/S is based on this latter job. Its in-stock, take-it-home-and-assemble-it-yourself kits are seen as valuable features by its customers, not as inadequacies that are tolerated in order to get discount pricing because they need furniture now. Those customers also value IKEA's racks of kitchen utensils, linens and other home decorations, because the job is to outfit and decorate the dwelling. To accommodate the many customers who are young couples, instore child care is a crucial aid in getting the job done. Without this package, IKEA could only help customers do a piece of their job. For its customers, the IKEA experience is delightfully different from a visit to a retailer that is trapped in the traditional positioning paradigm, attempting to appeal to a lower-income "demographic" by selling lower-quality furniture.[4]

Sometimes the job a customer needs done is "aspirational." The need to feel a certain way—perhaps macho, pampered or prestigious—arises in many of our lives on occasion. In such situations it often is the brand itself, more than the functional dimensions of the product, that does the job. When we find ourselves needing to do one of these jobs, we can hire a branded product—Gucci, Louis Vuitton, Virgin and so on—the very purpose of which is to provide such experiences.

THE REAL COMPETITION: OTHER JOB CANDIDATES

Although most marketers view their competitors as those who make the same category of products, this is generally only a small subset of the "job candidates" that customers consider hiring. Consider, for example, a job that arises millions of times on morning subway trains and buses. Crowded commuters want to pass the time productively. A free, single-section, easily folded newspaper called *Metro* has been positioned for this job and is read daily by tens of millions of people. It does not simply compete against the major metropolitan dailies; it competes against conversation with strangers, paperback novels, iPods, mobile phones, BlackBerries and boredom.

Automakers are not competing only with other automakers to fill the "my-car-is-my-office" job. They are competing against companies that help people be productive when they're not in home or company workspaces; such companies are Starbucks Corp.; Franklin Covey Co., a developer of time-management and productivity seminars and products, headquartered in Salt Lake City, Utah; Research in Motion Ltd., developer of the BlackBerry and e-mail products, based in Waterloo, Ontario; and mobile-phone service providers. Even as automakers struggle to sustain premium prices for the feature-laden cars they introduce every year, customers whose cars are their primary offices show a remarkable willingness to pay very high prices for the services that carmakers aren't offering, just to help them get this job done.

Because segmenting by job clarifies who the other job candidates really are, it helps marketers to compare the strengths and weaknesses of each of the products that compete, in the customer's mind, for the job and to derive the attributes and experiences that would be required to do the job perfectly. Marketers who segment by product and customer category just can't see as clearly the competition that comes from outside their product category and therefore are not in an informed position to compete effectively.

DOING THE JOB OF FINDING THE JOB

How can marketers figure out the jobs-to-be-done segmentation scheme in their markets? The jobs that customers are trying to get done cannot be deciphered from purchased databases in the comfort of marketers' offices. It requires watching, participating, writing and thinking. It entails knowing where to look, what to look for, how to look for it and how to interpret what you find.

Where to Look There is a hierarchy that consists of places where researchers who are seeking opportunities to generate new growth might look for jobs that customers need doing. The first step in the hierarchy is the current customer base. Peter Drucker got it right: "The customer rarely buys what the business thinks it sells him."[5] Companies almost always find that their customers are using their product for different jobs than the company had intended. Often they learn that the product does one of these quite well, but they see customers force-fitting it for other jobs, putting up with its inefficiencies because it's their only option. Such situations are opportunities to modify the product and its marketing mix so that it can compete more effectively and gain share against job candidates in other product categories.

In the second step of the hierarchy are people who could be your customers but are instead buying competing products to get their jobs done. Subtle differences that seem inconsequential when comparing products within a category can be very important when the job is the unit of analysis. The third step in the hierarchy of growth opportunities is exploring disruption. Disruptions take off when "nonconsumers" are trying to get the job done and simply are constrained from good solutions by the complexity and cost of existing products.

When the customer is a business. If your customer is a business, the job it needs to do is generally obvious: Make money. Selling a product to an organization that helps it make more money in the way it is structured to do so is a great way to justify premium pricing. This often isn't as easy as it seems, however, because most employees in customer companies have a limited, local understanding rather than a companywide perspective about how money is made.

Hill-Rom Co., a medical equipment company in Batesville, Indiana, grew its share of the hospital bed market by figuring out how to understand what drove its customers' profitability even more astutely than the customers did. Like most companies, Hill-Rom employees made contact with its customers' employees at many levels. Its senior executives visited with the senior hospital administrators, the company deployed its market researchers to work as orderlies on hospital wards, salespeople called on purchasing people, service technicians interacted with hospitals' maintenance staffs and employees in the financial departments of each company negotiated on how and when to pay for their purchases of beds. Unlike most companies, however, Hill-Rom convened regular meetings of all employees who had contact with specific customers' employees in order to piece together an insightful view of the levers the company could affect that would improve its customers' profitability.

One key insight from these meetings was that nurses, who account for a significant share of hospitals' operating costs and whose interactions with patients strongly influence perceptions of the quality of care, were spending inordinate time on tasks unrelated to nursing—picking up things from the floor that patients had dropped and solving television problems, for example. By adding features and functions to their beds that obviated many non-nursing tasks, Hill-Rom differentiated its beds in ways that helped hospitals make more money. Hospitals readily paid premium prices to get those improvements. These insights did not come from segmenting markets by small, medium and large hospitals. They came from understanding the job—the levers that drive hospitals' profitability.[6]

As Hill-Rom discovered, developing a multidimensional perspective on a corporate customer's profit engine pays off. A question to a person involved in a business-to-business purchasing process is as simple as, "How did you decide that you were paying an acceptable price for this purchase?" and can yield useful insights about the levers that drive the customer's profit engine.

When the customer is an individual. Understanding the jobs-based structure of markets where the user is an individual entails different techniques than when the customer is an organization. The research methods that work best depend upon the customer's position along a spectrum. One extreme comprises situations where the job is "knowable," such as with milkshakes and mobile-office automobiles, in which commonly available products are being employed every day, and yet suppliers haven't deciphered what customers are really hiring their products to do. At the other extreme are ill-defined situations in which neither the company nor the customer can articulate the job to be done.

How to Look Marketers seeking to understand the jobs-based structure of individual customer markets must act like investigative reporters who have a set of tools at their disposal that includes surveys, interviews, observations, participation and experimentation.

Interviews and surveys. When the job is knowable, researchers actually can use relatively conventional market-research tools such as customer interviews and surveys. Although skillful use of these tools is important, even more crucial is defining the unit of analysis to which the tools should be applied. The objective is always to understand the situation, not the customer. This is a critical distinction. Some marketers with whom we've discussed this concept have asked, "How does your notion differ from 'needs-based' segmentation?" The difference is the unit of analysis. The problem with focusing on customer needs is that a customer finds herself needing different things at different times. In contrast, the situation, or the job, is a simpler, more stable point of focus because it exists independently—disembodied, as it were—from the customer. Although there may be a correlation between customers with particular characteristics and the propensity to purchase particular products, it is the job that causes the purchase to occur.

Another reason it is so important to understand the situation that precipitated purchase is that this yields insight not just into the functional dimensions of the job to be done but into the emotional factors as well: fear, fatigue or frustration; anxiety or anger; panic, pride or pain; and so on. Products don't engender emotions. Situations do. Hence, to provide the set of functional, emotional and social experiences in purchase and

> The problem with focusing on customer needs is that a customer needs different things at different times. The job is a more stable focus because it exists independently from the customer.

use that are required to do the job completely, it is the situation rather than the customer that must be the fundamental unit of marketing analysis.

Observation. In the middle of the spectrum between "knowable" and "ill-defined" are instances in which customers know what jobs they need done, but there is no product or service designed to do it yet. In such instances, customers engage in compensating behaviors to "make do" with what's available. Marketers can sometimes identify these compensating behaviors simply by observing the consumer in context. Such observation is particularly critical when a new technology is developed, often for a purpose in another industry, and marketers are searching for opportunities to import it into other jobs. Sony Corp.'s legendary cofounder Akio Morita was in such a situation. The transistor had been developed by Bell Laboratories—an innovator in telecommunications equipment, based in Murray Hill, New Jersey—for telecommunications. Where else could it be used? Morita had a policy of never relying on quantitative market data to guide new-product development as he led the company between 1950 and 1980, because data doesn't exist for new applications of a technology. Instead, he and his associates just watched what people were trying to do and tried to imagine how applying the company's electronics miniaturization technology could make it easier and more affordable for more customers to do those jobs. Morita's success rate for new products was much higher than the 25% success rate for products whose launch is guided by more quantitatively sophisticated market-research methods.[7]

Empathic observation of compensating behaviors. When the situation is particularly murky, marketers will need to participate in the particular context themselves in order to peel away the compensating behaviors and work-arounds that mask the underlying job needing to be done. Hill-Rom used the technique of *empathic discovery*[8] to understand how the work of individual nurses affected hospital economics as its market researchers worked as hospital orderlies. This method also enabled The Procter & Gamble Co.'s marketers to see that using a dustpan was compensating behavior, leading to the development of its Swiffer floor-cleaning system.

Sometimes compensating behaviors with a job lurking beneath them quite literally knock on the door, enshrouded within an idea for a new product or service. As an example, an inventor approached the Big Idea Group of Manchester, New Hampshire, a developer of new products, with a card game he had created. The chief executive officer of BIG, Mike Collins, sensed from his experience that the game wouldn't sell. Instead of sending the inventor away, however, he asked, "What caused you to develop this game?" The inventor had a ready answer: "I have three young children and a demanding job. By the time I get home from work and we finish dinner, it's 8 o'clock and the kids need to go to bed—but I want to have a fun experience with them. What am I going to do? Set up Monopoly or Risk? I need some fun games that we can set up, play and put away in 15 minutes. There just isn't a game designed to do this."

Bingo. Though his solution to the job was mediocre, the valuable insight was the job itself—something that arises in the lives of millions of busy parents every evening. It was then a straightforward job for a team of experienced game developers to work with this man to create a very successful line of "12 Minute Games" that are now sold nationwide. Marketers who frame their role as searching for good product ideas generally are not nearly as productive as those who are searching for jobs.

The intuition that comes from living with the problem is a key reason why many of the most successful software products are developed by people who had been on the "user end," living with or working around the inadequacies of prior products. It is the organizing concept behind MIT professor Eric von Hippel's highly successful *lead user* methodology.[9]

Coevolution. In some situations, marketers and engineers have a sense that a new technology has the potential to unleash new applications, but potential customers cannot even articulate what jobs they might want done if technology were to make it possible. In these situations, the company and its customers must discover the product and the job together. This requires that the company get into the market quickly with a very flexible product and discover, along with customers, value-adding ways to use it. For example, in the late 1990s, the emerging technology of *telematics* presented a number of intriguing potential applications: It conceivably could give drivers maps to their destinations, inform them about shops in the area that sold products they might want to buy, help police find vehicles in case of theft or accident, enable hands-free telephone calling, collect and interpret data on engine wear and on and on. Though many automakers were paralyzed by their inability to know exactly what applications and features consumers would want, General Motors Corp. got into the market quickly with OnStar, an in-vehicle safety and security system that is a flexible, configurable product platform with a minimal fixed cost. OnStar's marketers then paid careful attention to the circumstances their customers were in when they signed up for the service and those they were in when they used the service. After a couple of years of coevolution, a major job had become clear: "I want peace of mind that if something unfortunate happens, my loved ones and I will be taken care of." By focusing on doing that job, OnStar has become a highly profitable, rapidly growing differentiated service that GM provides to millions of its customers.

In many ways, coevolution is as much an "innovation process" as it is a research method. It creates its own data. When it is undertaken, interviews, observation and empathic participation all can be used to figure out the job.

Synthesizing Insights At this point, the written and electronic records from the customer interactions described above—be they interviews, surveys, observation, participation or coevolution—need to be distilled into a "situation case" that describes the situation the customer found herself in when the product was hired or used.[10] A situation case begins with a description of the chronological trail of events, experiences and thought processes that led to the purchase decision. Good situation case researchers work like investigative reporters or detectives tracking down the whole story behind the specific events of purchase and use. They build their cases through a combination of the methods summarized above, often discovering the unexpected.

Generally, about 25 situation cases constitute critical mass. These cases then can be grouped by the similarity of the situations described. The result often is that most of the cases fall into a glaringly large group that represents a significant job that lots of people have. There usually are a few smaller groups of cases and a few "outliers." For each group, a summary then can be distilled describing the job the customers in those cases were trying to get done when they hired the product and how frequently the job seems to arise in the lives of those customers.

Once defined, this helps the researchers to understand what other "job candidates" were considered as potential hires. This defines the real competition in the customer's mind. They can then describe the "hiring criteria" that were used when comparing the candidates. These are the experiences, features and functions that constituted the basis for hiring one product over another. This analysis can be included in the summary and is often best constructed as a table, with the job candidates listed in the left column and the required experiences in purchase and use arrayed across the top. Each box of the resulting grid will contain descriptions of how well each competing product provides each experience.

From these can be gleaned the next element of the summary: an assessment of the deficiencies and constraints that future product and service innovations need to alleviate in order to grow the market—a collection of "help wanted" signs posted by customers, as it were. This not only provides the agenda for future new-product development projects but also gives a sense for whether competitors can more readily eliminate those constraints. Glaring "help wanted" signs signal significant opportunity. If there aren't significant "help wanted" signs, it's a signal that the products of one or more competitors already are doing that job well.

Purchased databases and customer questionnaires can be used to segment markets by product and customer characteristics and to define new products with better attributes than existing ones. But they cannot yield differentiating insights about the job-based structure of a market. This understanding can only emerge from techniques like those described above.

CONFIGURING THE MARKETING MIX AND BUSINESS PLAN

Entrepreneurship researcher Amar Bhide once surveyed about 400 entrepreneurs,[11] about half of whose ventures had failed. Of those who had succeeded, 93% reported that the strategy that led to their success was largely different from what they originally had planned. Indeed, most successful new ventures iterate toward or converge upon a viable strategy. It is rare to get it all right at the outset. In a similar vein, about 75% of all new products and services that established companies introduce into their markets fail to reach viable, profitable scale and are withdrawn.[12] In many of these instances, the managers killed underachieving products without ever understanding what their real job potential was. Situation case studies enable managers to see that a product in crisis may be a product that is valued in ways other than originally foreseen and may signal different opportunities for success.

Though our research on this issue is still in process, it appears that the precipitating event that allows the winning strategy of an emerging company to coalesce is the clarification of a job that customers need to get done for which its product is being hired. It is only when the job is well-understood that the business model and the products and services required to do it perfectly become clear. Then, and only then, can the company "take off."[13]

Once a job is clarified, the business-planning process should delineate the functional, emotional and social experiences that the customer will require in purchase, use and after-sale follow-through. The "Four Ps" of marketing—Promotion, Product, Price and Place—offer a useful way to structure the business plan to ensure success. Forensic analyses of new-product failures often reveal that marketers have cobbled these four factors together in inconsistent ways. As the examples below illustrate, understanding the product's job and its real competitors makes it much easier to get the Four Ps right.

Promotion: Communicating to Those Who Need to Do the Job
When a product does a job well, it unlocks the potential for marketers to create a *purpose brand*. A purpose brand links customers' realization that they need to do a job with a product that was designed to do it.

Coevolution is as much an innovation process as it is a research method. It creates its own data. Interviews, observation and empathic participation all can be used to figure out the job.

During the early years after a product's launch, when volumes are small, word-of-mouth advertising is far more cost-effective than media advertising. Positive word-of-mouth advertising only can be achieved after customers have used a product that did the job well. A very long list of powerful brands, including FedEx, Starbucks, Google, Black-Berry, craigslist.org, QuickBooks, TurboTax and OnStar, were built in just this way with minimal advertising at the outset. Because each is associated with a clear purpose, these brands pop into customers' minds when they need to do the jobs that these products and services were optimized to do. Our ongoing research into the history of today's valuable brands suggests that almost all of them took root as a purpose brand.[14]

A clear purpose brand acts as a two-sided compass. On one side, it guides customers to the right products. The other side guides the company's product designers, marketers and advertisers, giving them a sense of "true north" as they develop and market new and improved versions of their products. A good purpose brand clarifies which features and functions are relevant to the job and which "improvements" will prove irrelevant. The price premium that the brand commands is the wage that customers are willing to pay the brand for providing this guidance on both sides of the compass.

Without a specific purpose for their product, marketing executives must attempt brand building through expensive advertising. The high fixed cost of building new brands through advertising deters many companies from attempts to build new brands at all, so they acquire and consolidate brands instead. Managers ensnare themselves in this trap because of the way they have been taught to segment markets.

Positioning products to do specific jobs also helps companies target their advertising more efficiently. When a chain of scuba-diving shops marketed its diving classes and products to a "demographic"—primarily people who subscribed to scuba-diving magazines and who lived in ZIP codes near their stores—it struggled to succeed. When the company decided to find out what situations its customers had found themselves in when they decided to "hire" its scuba classes, it realized that many of them were engaged couples planning wedding trips to tropical climes, suggesting that the company should be buying mailing lists from *Brides* instead of *Dive* magazine.

Products That Do the Job Perfectly When marketers segment by product or customer characteristics, they frequently find themselves offering features or improving on dimensions of performance that are irrelevant to the job. For example, as digital photography threatened Eastman Kodak Co. with disruption in the early 1990s, Kodak's executives—having framed their market around photography—began to prepare the company for this transition by investing billions of dollars in a megapixel and megazoom digital imaging race that it was not well-positioned to win. In about the year 2000, however, Kodak executives realized that while some customers hired their cameras for the job of preserving high-quality images for posterity, a much larger group sought simply to entertain themselves, to share fun moments with family and friends. The result was the Kodak EASYSHARE camera, an affordable product with a great purpose brand. Understanding the job for which the product was meant to be hired allowed Kodak to eschew the expensive improvements that didn't matter in favor of relatively simple ones that did. By making it simple to attach images to e-mail, Kodak's product easily proved itself to be better than enclosures in first-class mail, phone calls with no images and cumbersome up- and downloading procedures. Kodak's share of the U.S. digital camera market grew from 8% to 28%.[15]

Is the Price Right? Unless marketers understand what other job candidates they're competing against from the customer's perspective, they cannot ensure that the price—the third element of the marketing mix—is right. They cannot know whether their offering is over- or underpriced. For example, to carry out its mission of educating people about the city's rich architectural heritage, the nonprofit Chicago Architecture Foundation started conducting boat tours that passed by the architectural masterpieces lining the Chicago River. Their initial target customers were "affluent people with high education levels and a strong interest in architecture," and they advertised in media serving that demographic. After the boat tour's lackluster first season, a researcher joined a cruise the next spring and asked passengers why they were taking the cruise. A surprising number were doing it to entertain visitors from out of town. Architecture, as it turns out, was a minor part of the cruise's appeal to this audience. CAF found that its cruise was actually less expensive than many alternative ways one could entertain visitors, and it was able to boost prices accordingly.

Placement When marketers have defined the set of experiences in purchase and use that need to be provided in order to do the job perfectly, the necessary product placement becomes obvious. Recall that to optimally do the job of making the morning commute interesting, the milkshake-dispensing machine had to be placed in front of the counter and equipped with a prepaid swipe-card system. Instant service was an important experience to offer customers hurriedly heading for work. This had not been clear to the managers when they had classified the milkshake as simply another item on the menu.

Consider another illustration. A maker of boxed drinks, whose products were a mixture of 40% fruit juice and 60% flavored sugar water,

A purpose brand links customers' realization that they need to do a job with a product that was designed to do it. It clarifies which features and functions are relevant to the job and which are not.

had placed its products in the boxed drink section of supermarkets, juxtaposed with competing products that were 100% fruit juice. Though the pure juice products were much more expensive, sales of the juice/water drinks were languishing. When interviewed about their purchases, customers, who were mostly parents, revealed that the job they were trying to get done had a functional dimension—to put a healthy drink in their children's school lunches—and an emotional dimension—to feel like they were taking good care of their children. When pitted against the job candidates that contained 100% juice, the mixture drink simply wasn't qualified; it rarely got hired. The company then had its drink placed in another location in the supermarket, in snack foods, and sales improved markedly. When compared to the job candidates in the snack aisle, a drink that had 40% real fruit juice solved the emotional component of the "good parent" job much better than the competing candidates.

SIZING UP THE SITUATION

The logic of segmenting markets by job is not new; many marketers will say that they already know many of the concepts. In fact, marketing guru Ted Levitt taught us 30 years ago that customers "don't want a quarter-inch drill. They want a quarter-inch hole!"[16] If that logic seems compelling, then why are product categories and customer categories the default modes of segmentation in nearly all companies? A core reason why marketers in most companies say one thing (that they know markets ought to be segmented by job) and yet do another (they segment by product and customer category) is rooted in the easy availability of the latter sort of data.[17]

The good news is that when companies understand who they are up against in the mind of the customer, they can piece together the real size of the market in which they compete. Because job candidates are drawn from many product categories, the salient size of most markets is usually much larger than is calculated by summing the sales within a product category, meaning that potential for growth is greater. Indeed, many mature products on the trajectory of sustaining improvement that seem to have been commoditized—products for which improved performance does not result in improved pricing or market share—actually turn out to be immature, not-good-enough products with lots of scope for differentiation and premium pricing once the job and its associated hiring criteria are understood.

In our studies of the factors that make innovation a high-risk, high-expense proposition, we have concluded that working to understand the job to be done is one of the most important ways to limit both risk and expense. Quite possibly, the root reason why innovation is so failure-ridden is not that the outcomes are intrinsically unpredictable but rather that some of the fundamental paradigms of marketing that we follow in segmenting markets, building brands and understanding customers are broken. The odds of getting it right will be much higher when we frame the market's structure to mirror the ways that customers experience life.

ACKNOWLEDGMENTS

We thank Bob Leahey of InfoTrends Research Group Inc., Armando Luna of Blue Cross and Blue Shield of Florida Inc., Emily Sawtell of The McGraw Hill Cos. and Steven Wunker of Innosight LLC for their comments on drafts of this paper. We also thank Rick Pedi and Bob Moesta of Pedi, Moesta & Associates Inc. for allowing us to use disguised insights and examples from their work with these ideas.

NOTES

1. The descriptions of the product and company in this example have been disguised.

2. There are other job segments in the auto industry. The key reason why DaimlerChrysler AG's early minivans were such a hit with customers was, we believe, that they were positioned on a job that arose in the lives of families—to interact easily and safely with each other while traveling together from here to there. Creating a job-focused product does not guarantee a perpetual monopoly, of course, and other automakers ultimately introduced their own minivans. It is noteworthy, however, that it took competitors years to introduce performance-competitive minivans. Because they were organized by product category rather than job, the minivans just didn't fit with the way they were structured or thought about in the market. As a result, Chrysler's market-share leadership persisted for over a decade. Another job that people hire a car to do is to express care and love for a spouse or a child. No car has the features and associated services bundled with it to do this job well.

3. See T. Levitt, "Marketing Success Through Differentiation—of Anything," Harvard Business Review 58 (January-February 1980): 2-9 for a classic description of the augmented product concept. Harvard Business School professor Youngme Moon has written and taught extensively about the concepts in this section, and we thank her for "augmenting" our own understanding of this phenomenon through her articles, cases and teaching notes.

4. IKEA founder Ingvar Kamprad had a partial, intuitive sense of what some fraction of furniture buyers needed to do when they walked into a store. As he and his associates started the company and tried to help their customers, understanding of the job coalesced piece by piece. IKEA executives probably do not articulate their strategy as being focused on this job—most likely this insight resides in a tacit, cultural understanding. Our hope is that by articulating this model of jobs-to-be-done segmentation and illustrating it with companies like IKEA, whose strategies de facto mirror this model, we might help students and managers who weren't blessed with the intuition (and luck) of Kamprad to deliberately find opportunities such as these.

5. P.F. Drucker, "Managing For Results" (New York: Harper & Row, 1964), 94.

6. These methods are recounted in C.M. Christensen, "Hospital Equipment Corporation," Harvard Business School case no. 9-697-086 (Boston: Harvard Business School Publishing, 1997).

7. This information was provided by Michael Schulhof, former Sony board member and CEO of Sony Corp. of America for 20 years, during an interview in New York City in 2001.

8. Leonard, William J. Abernathy Professor of Business Administration Emerita at Harvard Business School, called this method empathic design. See D. Leonard and J. Rayport, "Spark Innovation Through Empathic Design," Harvard Business Review 75 (November-December 1997): 102–113.

9. See E. von Hippel, "Democratizing Innovation" (Cambridge, Massachusetts: The MIT Press, 2006). This is the latest in a stream of insightful work from von Hippel.

10. The customer case-research method is described in detail in two articles by G. Berstell and D. Nitterhouse: "Looking 'Outside the Box:' Customer Cases Help Researchers Predict the Unpredictable," Marketing Research 9, no. 2 (summer 1997): 5–13, describes the research process; and "Asking All the Right Questions: Exploring Customer Purchase Stories Can Yield Surprising Insights," Marketing Research 13, no. 3 (fall 2001): 14–20, lays out the questions and interviewing approaches that customer case researchers use to develop case studies.

11. A. Bhide, "The Origin and Evolution of New Businesses" (New York: Oxford University Press, 2000).

12. For one such estimate, see D. Leonard-Barton, "Wellsprings of Knowledge" (Boston: Harvard Business School Press, 1995).

13. In many ways, this is a key message of high-tech marketing consultant Geoffrey A. Moore's books. He contends that instead of selling a "product" at the outset, emerging companies need to find a customer who will pay a lot of money to the company to solve a critical problem for him. Then, and only then, does it have the privilege of "crossing the chasm." In addition to his landmark book, "Crossing the Chasm: Selling High-Tech Products to Mainstream Customers" (New York: HarperBusiness, 1999), Moore's other book that describes this most clearly is "Living On the Fault Line: Managing For Shareholder Value in Any Economy" (New York: CollinsBusiness, 2000).

14. This branding dimension of the jobs-do-be-done theory is described more fully in C.M. Christensen, S. Cook and T. Hall, "Marketing Malpractice: The Cause and the Cure," Harvard Business Review 83 (December 2005): 74–83.

15. Unfortunately, subsequent to the educational experiences that in 1999 to 2000 enabled Kodak's management team to take the digital business in this direction, Antonio Perez was brought in as the new chief executive officer after the retirement of CEO Dan Carp. With a more conventional mindset and no understanding of the problem of disruption, Perez combined Kodak's film and consumer digital businesses into a single business unit. By 2006, the company's share had dropped to an unprofitable 12%.

16. T. Levitt, "Marketing Myopia," Harvard Business Review 53 (September-October 1975): 26–180.

17. We thank our friend Armando Luna, vice president of corporate marketing for Blue Cross and Blue Shield of Florida, for teaching us about the origins of market-segmentation theory, which we summarize here in our own language: The theory of market segmentation has its roots in economic theory relating to monopolistic competition; see W. Alderson, "Marketing Behavior and Executive Action" (Homewood, Illinois: Irwin, 1957); and H.J. Claycamp and W.F. Massy, "A Theory of Market Segmentation," Journal of Marketing Research 5, no. 4 (November 1968): 388–394. The concepts of product differentiation and differential advantage emerged from this background and underpinned early market-segmentation theory. Because most economists' analytical tools consist of techniques for analyzing large data sets, market researchers with this training spent their careers trying to show relationships between the attributes of customers and their buying behaviors. They would conclude that the variables or characteristics in the regression equations whose coefficients were statistically significant comprised the salient boundaries for dividing consumers into groups. The availability of data and the tools of analysis, in other words, shaped the insights to be sought. In the process, many marketers have forgotten what the theory of market segmentation was based upon from the beginning: that different people have varying needs that change from time to time.

READING 8: QUESTIONS FOR THOUGHT

- Think about a product or service that you frequently use. What are the "jobs-to-be-done" that you have for that product or service?

- In the reading, it is noted that often a product or service is not competing directly against other similar products or services but instead against other methods of completing the "job." Think again about the product or service you frequently use. What are some competing methods of getting the job done that are not direct product or service substitutes?

- Imagine you are in the customer research department of the company that produces the product or service you frequently use. What methods do you think would work to identify the jobs-to-be-done for the company's top customers?

- Why might it be beneficial for a company to segment customers based on jobs-to-be-done rather than based on product or service usage?

4

GENERATING IDEAS TO SOLVE FOR CUSTOMER PROBLEMS

Once you have developed deep insights into the problems that customers need to solve and the outcomes they are seeking, the next step is to generate ideas for solutions. Sometimes, when great research has been conducted, ideas will simply flow naturally. But most often idea generation requires creating an environment that is conducive to sharing and building ideas. In addition, by leveraging various creative exercises, individuals and groups can more readily develop new ideas. Idea generation also benefits from diversity, as people with different backgrounds, experiences, and perspectives will often identify new ideas or build upon existing ideas in ways that a more limited group may not. In this chapter we will explore how to create the optimal conditions for productive idea generation.

IDEA GENERATION

Once you have sufficiently analyzed the customer, developed deep insights, and properly framed the problem and opportunity, you are ready to begin generating ideas. Idea generation is an essential and fun part of the innovation process. However, without the proper environment to encourage people to share ideas and allow those ideas to be nurtured, companies run the risk of missing out on potential innovations. A facilitator who understands the delicate nature of idea generation and is adept at creating the atmosphere conducive to drawing out and cultivating ideas from employees can be helpful at this stage in laying the groundwork for breakthrough innovations.

The following reading is the first of two installments from the book *The Idea Agent: The Handbook on Creative Processes* by Jonas Michanek and Andréas Breiler. In this reading, the authors provide a set of simple creative "do's and don'ts" that facilitators often use to enable the conditions for ideas to be put forth and flourish.

Jonas Michanek is a serial entrepreneur, speaker, and author on innovation. Andréas Breiler is the global manager of business development for IKEA.

IDEA GENERATION

BY JONAS MICHANEK AND ANDRÉAS BREILER

THE RULES OF CREATIVE CHAOS

Idea generation is the essential phase of idea management. It is during this phase that primary idea production takes place and it's here that most of the creative groundwork is laid. There's been much careless talk in many contexts about creative chaos and how complete freedom is the path to success, but even if chaos and freedom are important ingredients, planning an underlying structure is an absolute minimum in a result-oriented process. Like a football quarterback, a brilliant idea usually needs a team and a game plan to succeed. Creativity is often considered a phenomenon for which laws and frameworks don't exist, but the truth is that even in this area a few guidelines will certainly help.

Before starting the idea generation phase, it's worth introducing your creative team to the following principles for the **DOs** and the **DON'Ts** of idea generation.

CREATIVE DOS

COME FLY WITH ME

Letting go of inhibitions is crucial in all idea processes. In the end, it's those off-the-wall ideas that will help you develop the new approaches and perspectives that can lead to the novel and fascinating. Encourage team members to develop each other's ideas and apply them as springboards to the next level of team energy and a rewarding result.

GENERATE AN IDEA POOL

It must be rather obvious by now that it's quantity rather than quality that is the primary focus during the idea generation phase. At the start of the idea process, it's important to generate as many ideas as possible in as many categories as possible so that you can establish an idea pool for further development. Try to estimate in advance how many ideas you want to produce so that the team has a clear and definite goal that can be achieved and measured up to. Every new idea contains the seeds for hundreds more!

WRITE EVERYTHING DOWN/VISUALIZE THE IDEAS

While the stream of ideas is flowing freely, it's easy to forget to document what is being said—to actually preserve the idea capital that's being generated. Make sure that everyone has access to paper, Post-its and pens so that thoughts are written down and not overlooked. If you don't appoint a team member as secretary—which is frequently a misuse of resources anyway—then you should point out that each team member is responsible for their own ideas. It doesn't matter if some ideas are duplicated. And ideas don't need to be recorded in detail during the idea generation phase itself, just a few key phrases will do. The Idea Agent must then ensure that time is allocated after the exercise for team members to revise what they've written so that it can be understood by the others.

QUANTITY IS QUALITY

The importance of mass idea production cannot be overemphasized. A majority of surveys indicate similar results—only a few ideas per idea generation session will have real impact and the more ideas produced the greater the chances of a revolutionary result. The research results presented below are based on statistics from the software company Imaginatik Inc, who develop idea management programs.

2%–3% high impact, high-quality concepts

10%–25% ideas worth developing

20%–45% ideas that have already been generated or implemented

5%–10% duplicates

15%–30% "non-ideas" such as expressions, observations and requests

JUST SHOOT!

In the world of psychoanalysis they often talk about "thought control," in other words the mental policeman that sits in our head stopping us from saying something dumb, a form of self-censorship whose laws are founded on many years of learning and experience of social rules and norms. Try to encourage team members to give their mental police time off during the idea process and emphasize the importance of expressing ideas verbally as soon as they spring to mind. Be spontaneous, impulsive and speak before you think for a change!

CREATIVE DON'TS

CRITICIZING AND ASSESSING

To start putting down another person's ideas as early as the idea generation phase is devastating to the creative process. This is the most common of all the diseases in the category "ideophobia". Idea assessment will follow the process right through to realization, but it should never take place during idea generation. Criticism diverts the mind into counterproductive lines of thought and blocks ideas of all kinds from emerging. The Norwegian consultancy firm Stig og Stein has a good rule that will help avoid negative criticism: every time you feel the urge to say "No…" or "But…", you should force yourself to say "Yes, and…" then enrich the idea that you're about to criticize.

THE BOSS ALWAYS KNOWS BEST

In many organizations—especially those founded on an authoritarian hierarchy—it is frequently the boss's thoughts and ideas that count. The point of most meetings is to tell the boss what they want to hear. In an idea generation session this is always fatal. Persistent political correctness and trying to please will not benefit the development of any organization in the long term. This is why you should have a word with the boss about his or her place in the team during the idea management process. Should he or she participate or not? If she does take part, it should be on the understanding that it's on an equal footing with the rest of the team and that she might even consider toning down her role to allow the other team members more creative space.

TAKING TURNS TO EXPRESS YOURSELF

Democracy is a great institution but it doesn't work especially well in idea generation. Being too polite or putting up your hand and waiting patiently to get a word in will completely stymie that all-important creative spontaneity. When you're spouting ideas, the laws of anarchic freedom must apply. It's OK to interrupt your colleagues.

ONLY THE EXPERTS ARE ALLOWED TO CONTRIBUTE

Particularly in knowledge-intensive development processes, it is standard practice always to consult experts for advice and to carry out a thorough analysis that will help to find desired answers. But if you're keen to create truly revolutionary ideas, it's very unlikely that you will succeed if you put 10 like-minded business developers from the same unit on the job. You should obviously listen to the advice of experts and use analysis for input during need presentations, but when the idea generation process is in full swing, everyone should be given the opportunity to speak their minds. Laymen, customers or consumers can all make a worthwhile contribution by re-asking basic questions or thinking outside the self-imposed boundaries of the subject specialist.

SCORNING OFF-BEAT IDEAS

How many times have we endured the experience of a really negative person making faces at every idea we come up with? If this type of character is given too much space during idea generation, the entire creative process will grind to halt since the team will be too afraid of making a slip up and being subjected to a look that brands them as a prize jerk. As an Idea Agent, it's very important to keep tendencies like this in check, to encourage wacky ideas and to help negative personalities understand that this type of body language isn't welcome. In the idea generation phase, it's uncool to be boring and hip to be a bit of a nut!

ANALYZING AND INTELLECTUALIZING

In creative contexts, no idea needs to be well thought out before it's expressed. Anything is possible at the start of the process. In due course, all ideas will be developed, screened and assessed using every feasible and unfeasible criteria, but at the start of the process there are no limits. In other words, try not to get caught up in your thoughts because you're uncertain that your solution is practical or because there is no established market research that indicates that the idea might work. Dare to be a visionary!

READING 9: QUESTIONS FOR THOUGHT

- The article asserts that group idea generation requires a set of carefully crafted guidelines for success. Why do you think these guidelines are so important?

- Have you ever participated in a formal or informal brainstorming session? How do you think the guidelines in the reading could have helped create a more optimal environment for idea generation?

- Have you ever been afraid to share an idea or found yourself editing your thoughts before speaking about an idea? How might a brainstorming session that follows all the guidelines in the reading make you feel about sharing ideas?

- The reading makes a strong point about not judging ideas during the idea generation process. Why do you suppose that judging or criticizing ideas at this stage is so emphatically opposed?

IDEA GENERATION TOOLS

In the last reading, we introduced some simple rules to create the proper environment for idea generation to take place. But it is not enough to simply create the environment. Blue sky, open-ended brainstorming often fails to generate great ideas because most people find it difficult to simply come up with ideas without any parameters in which to guide their thought process. The notion of thinking "outside the box" has actually been debunked by several authors and researchers who have demonstrated that people think best when they are given a specific pattern or method or "new box" in which to think. Thus, the notion of thinking inside new boxes has been put forth by some innovation consultants.

To generate lots of great ideas, brainstorming facilitators often make use of a variety of creative exercises to stimulate idea generation. Most people think best when given a specific task. Creative exercises that provide specific parameters to frame people's thinking can often yield many more fruitful ideas in a brainstorming session than simple open-ended calls for ideas on a topic.

This reading features the second of the two installments from the book *The Idea Agent: The Handbook on Creative Processes* by Jonas Michanek and Andrea Breiler. In this reading, Michanek and Breiler provide six distinct creative methods that can help make a brainstorming session dynamic, fun, and productive.

IDEA GENERATION TOOLS

BY JONAS MICHANEK AND ANDRÉAS BREILER

NEGATIVE IDEA GENERATION

Turning commonly accepted wisdoms on their heads is one of the most powerful tools in creative management. One approach to viewing something from a new angle can be to reverse your perspective from the positive to the negative. The principle of Negative Idea Generation is that sometimes it's both easier and more fun to knock down, beat up and backbite than it is to build up. Put simply, some people find it easier to generate negative ideas—ideas that are a bit more frivolous and work against the grain—than positive ones. Negative Idea Generation is also an excellent method for idea generation in large groups. You should play high-energy music in the background during this exercise.

STEP BY STEP

1   Define a positive focus area that's fun and inspiring and that you can "turn on its head" and into a negative.

    For example: How can we get baby boomers to invest in newly built condo-miniums one sunny day 10 years from now?

2   Split your team into groups of six to eight around each table so that the groups can see each other. If there are several groups, you can have different focus areas without disturbing the process.

3   Explain the exercise to the groups. Tell each group to "reverse" the positive focus area for about five minutes and create a negative-sounding focus area. This can be done in various ways, but it's important to retain the essential elements of the original focus area to achieve a satisfactory result.

    For example: How can we get baby boomers not to invest in our real estate one rainy Monday 10 years from now?

    Then give each team member a sheet of A4 paper—either a grid like the one on the next page or plain white, and ask them to draw a large cross on it. In the top left-hand corner they should indicate the positive focus area and in the bottom right the negative one.

4   Now encourage the groups to generate ideas for about 15 minutes based on the negative focus area that they've created. The more off-the-wall the ideas are the better—tell team members to really make the most of their chance to play devil's advocate.

    Ask team members to write down their solutions to the negative issue in the field in the bottom right of the page.

5   You should wind up the generation of negative solutions when an acceptable number of ideas has been generated. Now take about 15 minutes to trans-form the negative ideas into positive equivalents that relate to the positive focus area. It should be quite easy to reverse some of the negative ideas directly into positives while others will generate a whole new range of possibilities. Ask your team not to make their transformations from negatives to positives too simple! Then make sure that they write their ideas in the field in the bottom left of the page.

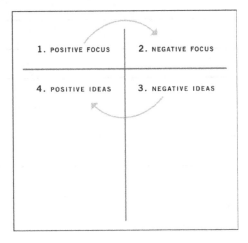

SITUATION

Negative Idea Generation is useful when working in groups of over 10 people. You can manage a process with a very large number of participants by splitting them into groups of 6–8 people. The method is also practical when the team includes a large number of negative personalities. Allow them to say "no" for about half an hour and the climate will improve.

RESULT

Lots of fun and high spirits, but also ideas that range from the excessively logical to the really wild.

PARTICIPANTS

6–100.

TIMEFRAME

30–60 minutes.

ENVIRONMENT

A large room with separate tables seating 6–8 people.

MATERIALS

Paper and pens. Use a template during the process like the one in the illustration on the previous page.

_____

_____

_____

_____

_____

_____

_____

_____

_____

_____

_____

_____

THE DREAM TRIP

Dreaming and visualizing can be a good technique for generating new ideas. The power of imagination is a very useful means of breaking free from the inhibitions in which common sense and habit have often chained us. The Dream Trip utilizes this to help create ideas and to encourage a visionary climate in the team. The method is best used in the initial phases of idea generation when there is a broad or loosely defined focus area.

STEP BY STEP

1   Make sure you prepare the Dream Trip thoroughly before you start. The method can be based on several scenarios with different ulterior motives. Choose one from these three examples that suits your purpose best.

   a.   Imagine that you're standing somewhere in the future reading a newspaper. There's a report on the front page with a large photo describing how you managed to find the perfect solution to the focus area and what the result was. As you're reading the report, you notice that everything you dreamed about and that you thought was virtually impossible has been achieved. What is it that you created? How exactly did you create it?

   b.   Imagine that you're taking a trip to a place in the future unrelated to the focus area. This could be a trip to the zoo; you could be catapulted into an episode of *Star Wars*, or just browsing round a big city. Then let your team "introduce" the focus area into your dream scenario and see what solutions develop.

   c.   Take a trip to the future and a place where the solution to your issue already exists. What can you see around you? Who's there and what are they doing? What feelings do the images you see generate? How do events unfold? What are the solutions in this world?

Try to dream your way through the imaginative journey and then write down a few key words from your story.

2   Introduce the focus area and answer any questions. Then ask team members to shut their eyes and listen to the start of the Dream Trip. Begin describing the scenario that team members find themselves in. Talk slowly and pause regularly so that they have time to form their own images and visualize their

own fantasy world. If you have music that you think might suit the mood, play it.

3   When team members have been visualizing for about five to 10 minutes, ask them to open their eyes, reconnect with the focus area and write down the ideas that they envisioned.

4   When they've written down their ideas, they should describe their experiences to each other—in small groups or as a team. It's essential to allow them the space to explore each other's thoughts so that they can develop new ideas from the visions that are being described. Ask them to enrich each other's ideas and to generate new ones as they take turns to present, and remind them to write everything down.

5   Allow team members some alone time after this process to generate new ideas or enrich the ones that they heard during the exercise.

SITUATION
When you're looking for ideas "on a higher plane" or if you want the team to develop broader visions.

RESULT
Visionary ideas that sometimes need a short process of individual enrichment.

PARTICIPANTS
Most suitable for team members that can visualize individually. The method can be used with up to 15 people.

TIMEFRAME
45 minutes.

ENVIRONMENT
In an inspirational room. Accessorize the room to suit the selected Dream Trip and enhance the experience.

MATERIALS
Paper and pens.

VISUAL CONFETTI

Some people are inspired by words and verbal forms of expression, others by images, colors and shapes. Visual Confetti is an associative method that applies the visual in creating new ideas. It involves compiling a collection of images such as spectacular abstract motifs, or photos of objects with a relation to the focus area.

There are quite a few variations on this exercise. Your images don't need to be projected on a wall and can be used in smaller sizes if more convenient. You can show them in bunches, or individually as in the example below. You can also develop the method by asking your team to describe the smells, sounds and other impressions that they associate with the images, and this information along with the images themselves will enable them to generate ideas.

STEP BY STEP

1 Compile about 30 images that you think are inspiring or relevant to the focus area. They could be of the Great Wall of China, a Van Gogh painting, a spider monkey in the Amazon jungle or even a competitor's product.

2 Ask your team to sit in front of you in a semi-circle and make sure that they all have a pile of Post-its and a pen. Introduce the focus area. Stand next to the image projected, facing the team, so that you can talk to them while they're viewing the images.

3 Show the first image then read out the focus area and ask the team to look at the image for inspiration.

   For example: If the focus area is "How can we get Generation X to buy our white goods?", the Idea Agent should say: "In relation to this image: How can we get Generation X to buy our white goods?"

Anyone who has an idea should say it out loud and then write it down on a Post-it. And one idea per Post-it is the rule. It's important that you coach the team by continually spurring them on with praise and encouragement. As soon as you notice that they're getting a bit passive, it's time to change image.

4 When an acceptable number of ideas has been generated or energy levels are flagging, you should wind up the exercise.

SITUATION
Visual Confetti is designed for people who think in images. The method is useful when alternated with exercises that are more verbally based.

RESULT
Tangible ideas with a wide range that can be enriched both in written and graphic form.

PARTICIPANTS
1–800.

TIMEFRAME
45 minutes.

ENVIRONMENT
As bright as possible, but not so bright that the team can't make out the projections.

MATERIALS
A projector, images in digital or physical form, pens and paper. Allow team members to document their ideas as both images and text.

_____

_____

_____

_____

_____

_____

_____

_____

_____

_____

_____

_____

_____

MERLIN

Merlin was the wizard in the legend of King Arthur and the Knights of the Round Table. According to legend, he was the greatest, most powerful wizard in all the land, and so, of course, are you and your team in this exercise. Merlin's magical powers could be channeled in four ways, to enlarge, to shrink, to make vanish and to reverse. But you can always dream up your own variations—for example, the world's cheapest, the world's most expensive, the world's smallest and the world's craziest. When applying the Merlin method, it's very important to think about the types of idea you are interested in generating and how the central issue should be formulated.

STEP BY STEP

1   Introduce the central issue.

2   Now demonstrate your first magic trick, preferably with a clear example.

   For example: "What would happen if we took our existing products and made them incredibly small? Well, you could put them in your handbag, you could stick them in your computer, you could swallow them…"

3   After about 10 minutes, you should conjure up a new perspective and then continue like this until all perspectives have been covered.

4   Wind up the exercise by allowing team members to write down their ideas while enriching them with information and substance.

 SITUATION
The method is very suitable for advancing and refining existing products. It might be a little tricky to start with this method from scratch.

RESULT
Good ideas with different perspectives. They will often be exaggerated but that's fine. It's much simpler to bring them down to earth than the other way round.

 **PARTICIPANTS**
5–12.

TIMEFRAME
Allow about 6–10 minutes per perspective, a short introduction and 5–10 minutes to write down ideas = 30–50 minutes in all.

ENVIRONMENT
Anywhere.

MATERIALS
Post-its, pens or large sheets of paper to illustrate your ideas while you're generating.

_____

_____

_____

_____

_____

_____

_____

_____

_____

_____

YOUR CREATIVE IDOL

Your Creative Idol involves mentally dressing up as a few incredibly creative people that you admire. How would Elvis have solved the challenge that's facing us, or what "glasses" would Leonardo da Vinci have worn to find new ideas around the focus area? You can use a famous person that you've chosen yourself, or some of your team's creative idols. Like What If?, this method has a bit of a role-play feel to it, though with Your Creative Idol, team members are more active in choosing the people that they can identify with.

STEP BY STEP

1   Introduce the method (not the central issue) and then suggest a few people whose creativity should be described. You can mix stereotypes and famous

people with powerful public images. Impressions will be enhanced if you use photos of the various personalities. You'll get lots of laughs if these images don't only include portraits of famous creators but also pictures of people who look rather boring.

2   Then either split your team into small groups of two to four people or let them work individually. Give them 10 minutes to describe how their "idol" would be able to solve the issue and how their creativity works.

3   Introduce the central issue and let your team ask any questions they have.

4   Ask them to take on the role of their creative idols and solve the problem the way their idols would. Make sure that lots of solutions are generated.

5   To encourage a more dynamic mood, it can be good to rearrange the groups and ask them to work with someone new so that they can test a new role.

6   A final presentation during which both personalities and ideas are demonstrated is always a fun way to wind up this method.

SITUATION
When team members have worked with an issue for a long time and need some distance from their usual approach. Or just an original idea generation method.

RESULT
Relatively tangible ideas and concepts from a range of perspectives.

PARTICIPANTS
6–30.

TIMEFRAME
This method can last anything from 30–40 minutes up to several hours. Just make sure it stays interesting and that the groups are constantly thrashing out ideas. When energy levels start to drop, you should rearrange the groups or wind up the exercise.

ENVIRONMENT
A room for each group to stop them from eavesdropping on each other.

MATERIALS

Paper and pens. It's also an advantage if there are nice, large color images of the people being described, as back up if nothing else.

_____

_____

_____

_____

_____

_____

_____

_____

_____

_____

TRIZ

TRIZ or TIPS (acronym for "Theory of Inventive Problem Solving"), is a method created by the Russian Genrich Altshuller. There is a lot written about TRIZ, as the methodology is comprehensive, but in brief it is a system for technical problem solving. Altshuller analyzed thousands of patents and technological innovations and found that there were clear commonalities that could be summed up in 40 so-called innovative principles. The TRIZ methodology in its simplest form may be used to develop technical products. When you have stated your problem in the need phase, you can use the 40 principles as a sounding board to see if they can create new solutions. The following describes how to use TRIZ in an easy way, which can be tough enough for those who do not have an engineering background. If you want to use TRIZ in a more sophisticated form of computations and calculations, you need to hire specialists in the Triz methodology.

Some examples of innovative principles:
Some more, some less. What happens if you add or subtract substances in the product?
Asymmetry. What happens if you change symmetric parts of the product into asymmetric?
Flexible membranes and thin layers. What happens if you replace traditional or rigid parts with flexible parts?

Thermal expansion. What happens if you use the effect of expansion of different materials at different temperatures?

Hollow materials. What happens if you use hollow or porous elements (shells or add ons)?

Horizontal motion. What happens if we limit or alter the horizontal movement?

Powerful oxides. What happens if you replace the air with an oxygen-rich, or similar, solution?

Separation. What happens if you separate the various elements or characteristics of the elements?

STEP BY STEP

1. Before the assignment, you as an Idea Agent should discuss with the need owner which innovative principles you believe are relevant to work with on the specific need. Print the principles you will use in a clear and visible format and describe them in a simple way as shown above.

2. Tell participants about the technical challenge or problem that you are facing.

3. Make a number of stations on the tables. On each station you put out a printed sheet of one innovative principle. That is, one principle per station. Place Post-its on each station.

4. Let the participants go to a station in pairs. Ask them to think briefly about the innovative principle before them and then, with the principle as a basis, find new solutions to the issue. They then to write down ideas on Post-it notes while talking and before they leave every station.

5. Tell the participants to shift to the next station after about five minutes and go in their pairs to a new station.

6. Continue until all pairs have been at all stations or until you feel that the groups need a pause (usually after about 30 minutes).

SITUATION
Good for technical needs. TRIZ does not always create clear answers but it is a way of using a systematic scientific base in order to seek inspiration to new solutions and ideas.

RESULT
Few, but some concrete ideas and suggestions.

PARTICIPANTS
2–15 technicians. TRIZ is difficult to run without participants with an engineering background.

TIMEFRAME
30–60 minutes.

 MATERIALS
Printouts with the innovative principles. Post-it notes and pens.

ENVIRONMENT
Preferably a room where you can build a lot of small stations for two people to work at.

READING 10: QUESTIONS FOR THOUGHT

- The reading describes six idea generation exercises. Which one do you personally think would work best for you? Why do you think it would work for you?

- Idea generation exercises should ideally be fun for all those who participate in them. Which of the six exercises do you think a group of your colleagues would enjoy the most? Why?

- Can you think of any other idea generation exercises that would be helpful in producing ideas? How would your idea generation exercise work?

CREATIVE CONNECTIONS: HOW COMPANIES INNOVATE BY CRAFTING NEW LINKS BETWEEN ATTRIBUTES AND

LESS IS MORE: HOW INDUSTRY GIANTS LIKE APPLE AND PHILIPS REALLY INNOVATE

Idea generation is one of the great mysteries of the human experience. All technological progress begins with ideas for how to solve problems or do things in a new and better way. Unfortunately, many people believe the myth that you must be a special creative individual in order to generate great ideas. But this could not be farther from the truth. All people are endowed with the ability to think creatively. The key is to understand and apply methods for creative thinking. Some people who seem to be creative thinkers may just naturally leverage creative methods as their normal way of thinking. But for most of us, we need to learn and practice creative thinking techniques.

The authors of the next two readings, professors Jacob Goldenberg and Rom Schrift, are proponents of the idea that creative thinking can be taught. The following two readings demonstrate a few of the techniques used in Systematic Inventive Thinking (SIT) to generate new and novel ideas.

Students can learn to generate ideas for new products, services, and business models by applying the SIT techniques in these two articles. As Goldenberg and Schrift have espoused in their other writings, it's not enough just to learn the techniques; you must practice them in order to gain the most benefit. Athletes conduct sport-specific drills to embed the muscle memory necessary to become adept at their sport. Similarly, to become a creative thinker and generator of great ideas requires practice at using creative techniques. By consistently applying the SIT techniques in these two readings, as well as other creative thinking techniques that are put forth in this chapter, anyone can expect to improve their ability to develop good ideas.

Jacob Goldenberg is a professor of marketing at the Arison School of Business Administration at the Interdisciplinary Center at Hertzelia and a visiting professor at Columbia Business School. Goldenberg was the editor-in-chief of the *International Journal of Research in Marketing* and now is an area editor for the *Journal of Marketing Research* and the *Journal of Marketing*. He received his PhD from the Hebrew University of Jerusalem.

Rom Y. Schrift is an assistant professor of marketing at the Wharton School, University of Pennsylvania. He earned his PhD in marketing and master's in philosophy from Columbia University Business School.

CREATIVE CONNECTIONS

HOW COMPANIES INNOVATE BY CRAFTING NEW LINKS BETWEEN ATTRIBUTES

BY JACOB GOLDENBERG AND ROM Y. SCHRIFT

THE ART OF CHANGING DEPENDENCIES

There are many methods available to managers pursuing new product and service ideas, including brainstorming and customer-driven, outcome-driven, or design-driven innovation. Unfortunately, few of these approaches have a track record of success, and new ideas frequently die even before implementation.

Market research suggests that many new product innovations actually come about by identifying and reenvisioning attribute dependencies, as illustrated by the following marketing success stories.

SNAPCHAT'S IN THE MOMENT EXPERIENCE

In September 2011, Snap Inc. launched Snapchat, a photo-sharing app where images shared with a selected contact would expire after a set number of seconds. Snapchat was highly successful, and in December 2012 the company expanded its offerings to include video-sharing capabilities. Snapchat Stories, increasing the expiration time to 24 hours and extending a user's share list to all Snapchat "friends" was introduced in October 2013; Discover, expanding the content universe to include content from top-rated media companies was launched in January 2015; and Spectacles, allowing a user to record personal video through special glasses that synced with the user's phone. All product expansions included a timing-out feature, retaining the "in the moment" experience. Snapchat boasted 166 million daily users in May 2017.

"SLOW DOWN GPS" APP WITH CHILD-VOICE NAVIGATION

If P & C Insurance of Sweden wanted to generate a higher preference for its brand and increase traffic safety. Research showed that 65% of Scandinavian drivers admitted to speeding in areas frequented by children.[1] If created a GPS navigation app where the voice giving directions switched from an adult's to a child's when the driver neared schools, parks, playgrounds, and other places where children gathered. Since the human brain is hardwired to pay close attention to children's high-pitched voices, the altered audio made drivers become aware of their surroundings quickly and slow down. If's lifesaving "Slow Down GPS" became the second-most downloaded navigation app in Scandinavia in 2015. The brand's "like" ratings jumped to an all-time high of 73%. The app won the Best of Global Digital Marketing Award for November 2015[2] and a Gold Cannes Lion Award in 2016[3] (see Exhibit 11.1).

NESTEA ICED TEA'S WINTER COLLECTION

The original NESTEA iced tea beverage was launched to help consumers cool off during hot summer weather. NESTEA's parent company, Beverage Partners Worldwide, wanted the brand to take on market-leader Lipton, so NESTEA began exploring new ways to expand. Seasonality had long been the key factor in driving sales in the category. The consulting firm SIT worked with NESTEA managers to increase sales during cold-weather months and developed flavors that tasted good when prepared hot as well as cold. Iced Green Tea, Iced Blackcurrant, and Iced Lemon became key ingredients in hot toddy recipes promoted during the winter holidays. The ad campaign resulted in higher iced tea sales in winter, and the firm captured greater market share[4] (see Exhibit 11.2).

COORS LIGHT BEER COLD-ACTIVATED LABEL

Coors Light needed to stand out from the crowd in the highly competitive US beer market. In 2007 they found a thermoactivated ink to use on Coors Light cans and bottles. The ink printed in white but turned bright blue when chilled to 44 degrees Fahrenheit, considered to be beer's optimal drinking temperature. A new label was designed, featuring a mountain image that changed from snow white to "ice blue" when chilled. This became a strong visual reminder for customers, signaling them at point of sale to buy and drink Coors at peak coolness. The firm's successful "Cold-Activated" campaign drove up sales, and by 2009 Coors Light was the #2 brand of light beer in the United States.[5] (see Exhibit 11.3).

GYM-PACT: MEMBERS PAY MORE IF THEY *DON'T* EXERCISE

Most fitness organizations generate profits by selling memberships to customers who pay upfront but who do not exercise regularly. Launched in 2010, Gym-Pact used a different model: the company offered memberships to Planet Fitness and other facilities and penalized participants $25 if they didn't go to the gym to work out.[6] The service used a mobile app that allowed users to set personal exercise goals and confirm compliance by checking in at gym locations via GPS. Penalties for missing workouts and rewards for meeting goals were paid via PayPal at the end of each month. Gym-Pact received $2.35 million in funding by 2014.[7]

THE COMMON STRUCTURE: ATTRIBUTE DEPENDENCY

Although the examples above represent ideas coming from different industries and product categories, all share a similar underlying structure. In each case the innovation involved either dissolving an established link between product attributes or creating new dependencies between attributes. Snapchat created a link to the immediacy—and in some cases the exclusivity—of social media by limiting the period that images could be viewed. With If's "Slow Down GPS," the type of voice (child vs. adult) providing driving instructions depended on the location of the car. NESTEA dissolved the link between seasonality and sales for its tea brand. Coors reinforced its link to cool refreshment by introducing a cold-activated visual cue in its packaging. Gym-Pact introduced a system that linked positive exercise behavior to monetary benefit by charging users more when they missed workouts.

Thus, all of these ideas can be mapped back to a creative approach called Attribute Dependency, a replicable template for generating original ideas that is part of the process known as Systematic Innovative Thinking (SIT).[8]

See Exhibit 11.4 for additional Attribute Dependency success stories.

SIT INNOVATION TEMPLATES

A study of past product launches in multiple industries revealed that 70% of successful innovations had followed a set of similar templates.[9] These patterns were analyzed by the consulting firm SIT, which found that they fell into five different types that became known as the SIT Innovation Templates. Each offered a blueprint that could be followed by management for developing new products.

The SIT templates are unique in that they approach the task of creative ideation from the perspective of the product rather than from that of the customer or the marketplace:

> Templates represent replicable patterns that are generalizable across variables and products…. Because the operation of templates involves the manipulation of product attributes, rather than market parameters, they can be used in considering new market needs…. The added value of the template approach is that it draws on the identification of similar structures in former product changes and provides a different angle and sometimes more accessible resource for ideation, compared to the information obtained from the analysis of current market needs.[10]

See Exhibit 11.5 for the five SIT templates that guide creative thinking in different ways.

USING THE ATTRIBUTE DEPENDENCY TEMPLATE

A study that evaluated successful product launches found that 35% of them were based on creative ideas that follow the Attribute Dependency model.[11] The remainder of this case provides detailed instructions on how to use the Attribute Dependency template and spark innovation in virtually any organization.[a]

The Attribute Dependency method works by creating or changing a dependency between two attributes within a product or between attributes of a product and its environment. This can mean the creation or removal of existing symmetries; that is, altering existing product attributes so that as one changes, so does another. The template helps managers realign attribute relationships in unforeseen, fresh ways.

ATTRIBUTE DEFINITION

To use this template, it is important to know how to distinguish components from attributes. Components are the features of a product or service. For example, for a consumer product like toothpaste, the components are:

- the tube
- the cap
- the safety seal
- the paste
- the box used to package the product

Attributes are the variable characteristics of a component.[12] They can be either qualitative (e.g., in color, raw material, or classification) or quantitative. For example, the paste in toothpaste can vary by:

- taste (e.g., bitter, sweet)
- texture (e.g., gritty, smooth)
- color (e.g., blue, green)
- viscosity (e.g., runny, thick)
- amount of active and inactive ingredients (by percentage or total quantity)

See Exhibit 11.6 for further examples of attribute designation.

It is also important to recognize the difference between internal and external attributes. Internal attributes are those which are under a firm's control. For

---

a   Instructions for using the Subtraction Template can be found in Jacob Goldenberg, *Less Is More: How Industry Giants Like Apple and Phillips Really Innovate*, Columbia CaseWorks ID #170302 (New York, NY: Columbia University, 2016).

example, a toothpaste manufacturer has complete control over (and can vary) the product's taste, texture, color, and viscosity as well as the relative amounts of active vs. inactive ingredients it contains. Therefore, all of these are considered internal attributes. In contrast, external attributes are those outside the control of the firm. For example, a toothpaste manufacturer cannot control the time of day the product is used, the pH level in the user's mouth, or the temperature of the water used for brushing.

Similarly, the relevant attributes of Pinterest can be categorized as follows:[13]

Internal Attributes:

- size of board (number of pins)
- size of the displayed board
- number of boards
- description of board
- subject of pins
- number of likes
- number of re-pins
- number of guest pinners

External Attributes:

- time of posting, time since posting, etc.
- number or type of followers
- boards trending

STEP-BY-STEP GUIDELINES

Proper use of the Attribute Dependency template requires that managers follow a regimented process. Those who attentively implement each step given below will find that the procedure yields a wide array of viable new ideas.

1   **Pick one product or service** as the focus of the Attribute Dependency exercise. The iPhone will be used as an example here.

2   **Create a list of all of the product's components**. For example, the iPhone has a case, screen, battery, operating system, etc.

3   **Select one component and make a list of all its attributes**. For example, the iPhone's operating system can vary by carrier, data capacity, drain on battery life, etc.

4   **Organize the attribute list into two parts.** Start with the component's internal attributes and then identify the external attributes that are important for the component's use in the market. For example, the internal attributes of the iPhone's operating system include the selected carrier, data capacity, price, and range, while its external attributes include the location, time, and context of use and the task that the user wants the phone to complete.

5   **Use the list to create a table matrix** composed of rows and columns, where the rows designate all the internal and external attributes and the columns designate internal attributes only. This matrix becomes a visual tool to guide thinking about pairs of attributes. It helps to focus the creative process so that each combination can be considered as a place to potentially change attribute dependencies (see Exhibit 11.7).

6   **Examine and analyze each cell in the table individually**, working across the matrix. Visualize a new dependency and explore the benefits it might offer by asking:

   • Does this dependency already exist? If so, how does it work? Can the direction be reversed? What would that look like? Imagine breaking the dependency altogether. If this link disappeared completely, how would the product work?

   • If no dependency exists, try to envision one. How might these elements be linked so that as one changes, the other does as well? What would that look like?

Try to picture the new product. For each cell, come up with an abstract, conceptual product and then try to think of a problem that it can solve.

7   **Envision the types of users who might be interested in this new solution**. Consider who would pay for this product in its new configuration. Try to describe these new customers in detail since thinking about them and their particular needs may generate insights leading to ways to reconfigure the product further.

FUNCTION FOLLOWS FORM

The principle that "function follows form" is also fundamental to the success of the Attribute Dependency template. This principle is the opposite of the famous "form follows function" design theory, espoused by modernist architects, who said a building's shape should be based on its intended use.[14] In contrast, in "function follows form" thinking, a manager starts with an existing product, changes it using a template, articulates how this altered product looks and functions, and then asks, "how might this revised product offer a new benefit to a consumer?" Only after the new product idea is formed does the team examine the wide array of possible users in the marketplace who might want the new product.

The "function follows form" principle is grounded in psychological research that shows that "people are more likely to make creative discoveries when they analyze novel forms and then assess the benefits those may project, than by trying to create an optimal form based solely on the desired benefits."[15] For example, imagine being shown a baby's milk bottle and being told that it varies in color as the temperature of the milk changes. If asked "why would this be a useful kind of bottle?," most people immediately realize that it would help parents protect their babies from drinking milk that was too hot. Now imagine the opposite challenge, i.e., being asked "what can we do to prevent babies from being burned by drinking milk that is too hot?"[16] A myriad of ideas may emerge in response to that question. The optimal answer is not obvious; it might take a long time to realize that a temperature-sensitive, color-changing bottle was the best solution.

LESSONS FROM THE FIELD

As experienced users of the Attribute Dependency template across multiple product and service categories, we offer a few final pointers on how to effectively employ this tool from the SIT system to generate outstanding creative ideas.

PRICE IS AN AGILE ATTRIBUTE

The act of setting prices is largely an Attribute Dependency exercise since as the price of a product changes, its value to a customer changes too. Many attributes can be easily linked to price to generate new product or service ideas. Such attributes and associated innovations include the age of the customer (senior citizen discounts), quantity (bulk purchase discounts), risk (insurance policies), time of use (early bird dinner specials), and the customer's "needs state" (charging more for a bottle of water on a hot day).[17] When an analysis shows that price and another attribute correlate positively, consider flipping the direction of the relationship, as GymPact's innovative pricing structure, which creates a cost benefit for customers who actively exercise, does. This change can sometimes make price dependencies more acceptable to the consumer. For example, the owner of a gas station that charges one price for cash and another for credit can describe the attribute relationship either as charging customers more if they use a credit card or as giving customers a discount if they pay in cash. Innovative managers can think creatively about price relationships to easily alter attribute dependencies.

DEPENDENCIES CAN BE PASSIVE, ACTIVE, OR AUTOMATIC

In crafting creative connections between product or service attributes, consider how the dependency arises. In passive dependency, no one needs to take action to connect the two attributes. For example, a set of mixing bowls can be designed so that as volume varies, each bowl has a different color. This makes it easy for cooks to select a bowl of a particular size from a nested stack.

In active dependency, a third party has to do something to trigger the dependency between features. Happy Hour at a bar is an example of this. The dependent attributes are price and time. However, the bartender has to take action and charge different prices during the designated period to implement this change.

In automatic dependency, one attribute changes as the other does, without human intervention. For example, light-sensitive eye glasses darken when exposed to sunlight. The wearer does not have to take any action to activate the photo-sensitive coating. The lenses' color-changing attribute is embedded in the product.

CONCLUSION

The SIT templates' originators stress that "simply conceiving a creative idea is not enough. Creativity is the act of generating a novel idea and connecting that idea to something useful."[18] Using the Attribute Dependency and other templates carefully, the SIT process presents all managers with a tool kit for finding profitable innovations "inside the box."

EXHIBITS

Exhibit 11.1

"Slow Down GPS" App Images (If Insurance, Sweden)

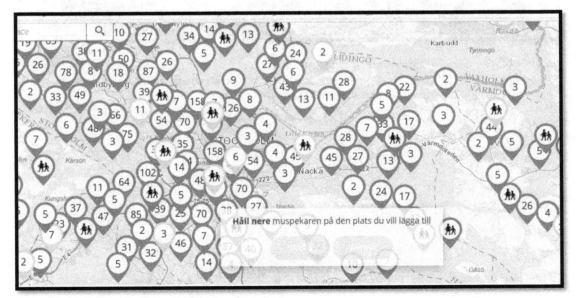

Source: "Slow Down GPS," If Insurance,
https://www.if.se/privat/forsakringar/bilforsakring/bilsakerhet/slow-down-gps.

Exhibit 11.2

NESTEA Iced Tea, Served Hot Ad Campaign

Source: Chris Whitehead, "Stay Warm and Toasty All Season Long with These NESTEA 'Winter Warm-Up' Recipes," Coca-Cola Canada, December 23, 2016, http://www.coca-cola.ca/stories/stay-warm-and-toasty-all-season-long-with-these-nestea-winter-warm-up-recipes.

Exhibit 11.3

Coors Light Label with Temperature-Sensitive Ink

Source: "Cold Activation," CTI, http://www.ctiinks.com/thermochromic-inks.

Source: Freddy J. Nager, "In the Can: Coors Campaign Leaves Us Cold," Atomic Tango, June 25, 2009, http://www.atomictango.com/marketing/coors-cold.

Exhibit 11.4

Additional Examples of Attribute Dependency Innovations

- **Domino's Pizza: "30 Minutes Delivery or It's Free" Service**
Domino's Pizza's 1973 ad campaign, "It's 30 Minutes or It's Free," promised that if a phone order for pizza didn't arrive within 30 minutes of the call, the customer was charged nothing. This innovative offer sparked Domino's rapid growth. The company became the fastest-growing quick service restaurant pizza firm in the United States by 1985.[19] (However, stories of traffic accidents caused by speeding delivery cars, supported by lawsuits won for people injured by Domino's drivers who were going too fast, caused management to suspend the effort in 1993.[20]) The new attribute dependency linked price to delivery time.

- **Rain-Activated Windshield Wipers**
Drizzling rain on a windshield can be a nuisance to drivers, causing frequent adjustments to the wiper settings to clear the windshield. The potential for driver distraction can be dangerous. The new Rainsense™ wiper system offered a solution. First installed by GM in its Cadillac, Suburban, and Escalade models, it used a sensor near the top center of the windshield to detect the amount of water on the windshield and control how frequently the wiper blades swept.[21] The system is now recommended by J.D. Power Car Ratings as a standard safety feature for all cars.[22] The new attribute dependency linked the presence and intensity of rain to wiper speed and frequency, making activation of windshield wipers automatic rather than driver controlled.

- **Worldmapper.org.**
Using this tool, the size of the nations on a world map can be adjusted according to the subject of interest (e.g., percentage of female managers in each country, amount of fruit exports, number of Internet users, etc.).[23] This use of an attribute dependency analysis allows users to visualize the world in many different ways.

Exhibit 11.5

How the Five SIT Innovation Templates Work

- **Subtraction:** something is removed from a product or service, usually a trait or component that was previously thought to be essential (e.g., removing the polymer from permanent marker inks to create dry-erase markers).

- **Division:** a component is separated from a product or service and placed somewhere else, where it becomes part of the product or service in a different configuration (e.g., changing a single, forged barbell into exercise weights that come with removable units, allowing exercisers to adjust workouts more easily).

- **Multiplication**: a feature is copied and duplicated within the product or service, yet changed in some way to provide a slightly different benefit (e.g., changing TVs so they offer a double picture-in-picture option, allowing simultaneous viewing of two channels so that, for example, a sports fan can watch one game, while tracking the score of another).

- **Task Unification**: two features are brought together in a product or service, unifying attributes that previously were thought to be unrelated in function (e.g., a facial moisturizer is reformulated to provide both hydration and sunscreen protection).

- **Attribute Dependency**: two attributes of a product or service become correlated with one another in a different way; when one attribute changes, so does the other (e.g., photo-sensitive eyeglass lenses darken as the wearer moves into bright sunlight and become clear again when the wearer moves into the shade).

Source: Drew Boyd and Jacob Goldenberg, *Inside the Box* (New York: Simon & Schuster, 2013), 5.

Exhibit 11.6

Examples of Components, Products, and Services and Their Associated Variable Attributes

COMPONENT, PRODUCT, OR SERVICE	ATTRIBUTES
Sugar in a cake	Type of sugar, total weight, amount in batter, amount in frosting
Baseball bat	Material, length, thickness, weight, hand-grip texture
Carpentry screws	Length, thickness, type of metal, width of head, shape of groove
Hat	Size, color, material, style, degree of water resistance
iPhone	Screen, case, battery, camera lens, operating system
Gym membership	Price, schedule, location, types of equipment, instructors' experience

Note: There are also a variety of external attributes that apply to products and services, depending on the marketplace, such as time of use (by hour of day, season, etc.), time of purchase, place of purchase, place of consumption or service delivery, season, weather, and temperature. Only the external attributes relevant to the product or service under SIT consideration should be taken into account.

Source: Jacob Goldenberg and David Mazursky, *Creativity in Product Innovation* (Cambrdige, UK: Cambridge University Press, 2002), 65.

Exhibit 11.7

Attribute Dependency Matrix and SIT Ideas for an iPhone Operating System*

INTERNAL ATTRIBUTES	CARRIER	CAPACITY	BATTERY LIFE	SOUND VOLUME	FUNCTION	RANGE	PHOTO QUALITY	LINKAGES	BROWSER TYPE	MUSIC SOURCE
CARRIER										
CAPACITY										
BATTERY LIFE										
SOUND VOLUME										
FUNCTION										
RANGE		7								
PHOTO QUALITY										
LINKAGES										
BROWSER TYPE							8			
MUSIC SOURCE										
EXTERNAL ATTRIBUTES										
LOCATION				3	10			5		9
TIME			6							
CONTEXT	1				2					
PRICE										
JOB TYPE					4					

Source: Innovation in Practice, www.innovationinpractice.com.

Note: Shaded cells are not used, as categories are redundant. The following ideas were crafted by using the matrix above to think about possible new or changed links. The number of each idea correlates with the cell indicated above:

1. Carrier Changes Depending on Context: Allow users to switch wireless carriers depending on whether phone calls are for business or personal; users preselect which numbers go through which carrier under iPhone contacts. This makes it easier for people to track phone expenses and for enterprises to monitor costs accurately.

2. Function Changes Depending on Context: Apps rearrange automatically, depending on the context (e.g., office or home). Geo-sensing tells the phone

where the user is, then reorders apps accordingly. In the office, top apps are business related (e.g., calendar, Notes, Slack). At home, top apps are recreational (e.g., Candy Crush, Snapchat, Facebook).

3   Volume Changes Depending on Location: The iPhone goes to silent mode automatically in quiet environments (e.g., conference rooms, churches, theaters) and switches to a louder mode in noisy environments (e.g., inside cars, grocery stores, ballparks).

4   Functions Tailored to Job: The iPhone is customized with apps depending on profession of the purchaser. For example, a health-care worker might buy an iPhone optimized for a hospital setting (e.g., with medical apps and preset security for access to patient records, location, medications, and infection risks).

5   Location Dictates Linkages: The user chooses Wi-Fi, carrier, email, and/or SMS depending on location to optimize costs. For example, Wi-Fi turns off for certain networks that are not protected, or the phone stays connected to the cellular network when needed, eliminating time lags and having to switch manually.

6   Battery Life Adjusts According to Time of Day: The iPhone automatically powers down features not needed during hours set by the user (e.g., at night, color screen turns black and white, Wi-Fi goes off, vibration function turns off).

7   Capacity Changes with Range: The iPhone can "borrow" data capacity from the optical disk space of a nearby linked Mac or PC, much like the MacBook Air does.

8   Photo Quality Varies by Browser: The iPhone allows user to vary the photo quality loaded into different browser types.

9   Music Source Changes with Location: The iPhone automatically picks up the music playing where the user is (e.g., in an airplane, restaurant, store, concert hall, or museum), in order to stream, amplify, or record it.

10 Shopping Process and Pay Function Change with Location: The iPhone "in-store shopping buddy" tells users in what order, by aisle, to get the items on their shopping list to save the most time. It guides the user to the fastest checkout line, knows how much the user is about to spend, and links directly to PayPal to complete the checkout process.

Source: Drew Boyd and Jacob Goldenberg, "The LAB: Innovating the iPhone Using Attribute Dependency," Innovation in Practice, September 28, 2008, http://www.innovationinpractice.com/innovation_in_practice/2008/09/the-lab-innovating-the-iphone-with-attribute-dependency-september-2008.html.

NOTES

1. "IF Insurance's Lifesaving GPS App from Sweden Wins the Best of Global Digital Marketing Awards in November and December," The Best of Global Digital Marketing, November–December 2015, http://www.best-marketing.eu/december-2015.

2. "IF Insurance's Lifesaving GPS App from Sweden Wins the Best of Global Digital Marketing Awards."

3. "Slow Down GPS, "Cannes Lion Award: 2016, http://www.canneslionsarchive.com/winners/entry/763252/slow-down-gps.

4. Drew Boyd and Jacob Goldenberg, Inside the Box (New York, NY: Simon & Schuster, 2013), 179.

5. Rick Lingle, "Coors' Label Shows Beer Tempertaure," Packaging World, June 11, 2007, https://www.packworld.com/coors-label-shows-beer-temperature-0; Stuart Elliott, "Coors Light Uses Cold to Turn Up Heat on Rivals," New York Times, April 27, 2009, http://www.nytimes.com/2009/04/27/business/media/27adnewsletter1.html.

6. Susan Johnston, "Harvard Grads Turn Gym Business Model on Its Head; Fitness Plan Members Pay More If They Don't Work Out," Boston Globe, January 24, 2011, http://archive.boston.com/business/articles/2011/01/24/gym_pact_bases_fees_on_members_ability_to_stick_to_their_workout_schedule.

7. Catherine Shu, "GymPact, the App That Pays You for Working Out, Relaunches as Pact with New Diet Features," TechCrunch, January 1, 2014, https://techcrunch.com/2014/01/01/pact.

8. Boyd and Goldenberg, Inside the Box, 159.

9. Jacob Goldenberg, Donald Lehman, and David Mazursky, "The Idea Itself and the Circumstances of Its Emergence as Predictors of New Product Success," Management Science, January 2001.

10. Jacob Goldenberg, David Mazursky, and Sorin Solomon, "Toward Identifying the Inventive Templates of New Products: A Channeled Ideation Approach," Journal of Market Research 36, no. 2 (May 1999): 200–201.

11. Boyd and Goldenberg, Inside the Box, 163.

12. Boyd and Goldenberg, Inside the Box, 124.

13. Drew Boyd, "Applying Attribute Dependency to Pinterest," September 9, 2013, http://drewboyd.com/inside-the-box-applying-attribute-dependency-to-pinterest/

14. Boyd and Goldenberg, Inside the Box, 10.

15. Jacob Goldenberg and David Mazursky, *Creativity in Product Innovation* (Cambridge, UK: Cambridge University Press, 2002), 83.

16. Boyd and Goldenberg, *Inside the Box*, 11.

17. "Innovation Sighting: The Attribute Dependency Technique in Pricing," Innovation in Practice, April 8, 2013, http://www.innovationinpractice.com/innovation_in_practice/2013/04/innovation-sighting-the-attribute-dependency-technique-in-pricing.html.

18. Boyd and Goldenberg, *Inside the Box*, 223.

19. "History," Domino's Pizza, https://biz.dominos.com/web/public/about-dominos/history.

20. Michael Janofsky, "Domino's Ends Fast-Pizza Pledge after Big Award to Crash Victim, *New York Times*, December 22, 1993, http://www.nytimes.com/1993/12/22/business/domino-s-ends-fast-pizza-pledge-after-big-award-to-crash-victim.html.

21. Michael Austin, "How It Works: Automatic Windshield Wipers," *Popular Mechanics*, April 4, 2014, http://www.popularmechanics.com/cars/a10323/how-it-works-automatic-windshield-wipers-16663151

22. Jeff Youngs, "Rain-Sensing Wipers," J.D. Power, February 24, 2012, http://www.jdpower.com/cars/articles/tips-advice/rain-sensing-wipers.

23. Danny Dorling, "Worldmapper: the Human Anatomy of a Small Planet," *PLOS /Medicine*, January 30, 2007, http://journals.plos.org/plosmedicine/article?id=10.1371/journal.pmed.0040001.

LESS IS MORE

HOW INDUSTRY GIANTS LIKE APPLE AND PHILIPS REALLY INNOVATE

BY **JACOB GOLDENBERG** AND
ROM Y. SCHRIFT

Creativity is more than just being different. Anybody can plan weird; that's easy. What's hard is to be as simple as Bach. Making the simple, awesomely simple, that's creativity.

—Charles Mingus (jazz composer and performer)

REVERSE ENGINEERING THE SUCCESS OF NEW PRODUCTS

Steve Jobs stood on stage at the January 2005 Macworld conference and launched into a presentation about how his company planned to kill the remaining competition in the MP3 player market.[1]

Apple's revolutionary iPod music device, introduced in 2001,[2] had reached 65% market share by 2004, up from 31% the year before.[3] The year-over-year growth was partly due to the release of the iPod mini—a smaller, cheaper, and more colorful version of the classic iPod model.[4] The goal now was to introduce yet another new product that would further expand the media player market as well as steal customers coming in at the market's lowest price point. "We want to make something that's even easier to use than the existing iPods," Jobs told the crowd before revealing images of Apple's latest device. "We want to bring even more people into the digital music revolution."[5]

The projection screen behind Jobs lit up with photos of the iPod shuffle. The ability to shuffle—to play songs from a user's music library at random—was one of many popular features of the original iPod. Now Apple had based an entire product around that single function. Smaller than a pack of gum and weighing less than four quarters, the iPod shuffle loosely resembled the original iPod but lacked two distinctive features: it had no display screen, and users weren't able to directly choose the song they wanted to listen to. Instead, up to 240 songs were loaded onto the device, and users hit the play button to either hear songs at random or launch a preselected playlist. The device had a control wheel similar to the original model's, but it allowed a user only to change the volume, replay the previous song, or skip to a new one. The cheapest version of the iPod shuffle held 120 songs and originally cost $99. The higher-priced version held 240 songs and cost $149. Both models were less expensive than the iPod mini ($199–$249)[6] and the standard iPod ($299–$399).[7] Competitors' products at that time ranged in price from $99 to $149, and some had less storage space.[8]

Conventional wisdom seemed to suggest that the iPod shuffle's design was inferior to other MP3 players' because of its limited features. As one tech blogger wrote, "I just don't see no screen at all as a feasible design … this seems like a recipe for a frustrating experience."[9] Yet later that month, gadget review site *CNET* praised the iPod shuffle for its simplicity and convenience and predicted that it would go on to be a hit.[10] The device drove iPod annual net sales from $1.3 billion to $4.5 billion that year[11] and lifted the product line's market share to 79% in 2006.[12]

"Winning over the teen demographic is critical … and Apple is clearly in the lead," wrote Piper Jaffray analyst Gene Munster a year after the iPod shuffle's release.[13] Munster surveyed 1,000 high school students about their intent to buy an MP3 player and predicted that iPod sales would continue to grow another 76% over the next 12 months.[14] But was Apple's new product intuition part of a systematic innovation process, or was it just coincidence?

INNOVATION TEMPLATES

Product innovation that addresses new market segments or steals market share from a competitor is a high-stakes and often frustrating process. For every 3,000 new product ideas that a company's R&D or marketing teams put forth, only two will go to market—and of those, only one will become a commercial success.[15] Furthermore, an estimated 46% of all resources that US firms allocate to new products are spent on those that fail.[16] When you consider that the world's top 1,000 companies spending the most on R&D dedicated a total of $680 billion—roughly 3.7% of revenue—to new product development in 2015,[17] it's not hard to see why companies might search for ways to become more efficient at this task.

Random thinking is often the standard when innovation teams aim to increase the fluency and number of ideas they create. The assumption is that the greater the number of concepts, the greater the probability of generating some worth pursuing. However, research has shown that complete randomness, disorganization, and lack of structure may paralyze creative efforts. By contrast, systematic creativity, which applies a framework to the generation of ideas, is reproducible, learnable, and more likely to generate results.[18]

Product and service innovation is an ideal area for managers to apply the principles of Systematic Inventive Thinking (SIT) in. By reverse engineering the evolution of systems that lead to breakthrough products such as the iPod shuffle, researchers have identified five distinct patterns or templates that are seen extremely frequently in products that go on to commercial success but rarely in those that fail: nearly 70% of successful new products exemplify one of these patterns, and less than 20% of failures contain them.[19] Each of the five templates—subtraction, task unification, division, multiplication, and attribute dependency—is a distinct way to describe how systems have successfully evolved over time.

In conjunction with the research in this area, the consulting firm SIT Systematic Inventive Thinking Ltd. converted each of these templates into actionable tools, i.e., a series of step-by-step instructions that ensure that the template will be incorporated into a new product, which will then have a greater chance of commercial success. This note will focus on the process and application of the subtraction tool.

THE SUBTRACTION TEMPLATE AND METHODOLOGY

Apple's iPod Shuffle is a good illustration of the logic behind the subtraction template.

The general idea of the subtraction template is that less is more and that value can be created by eliminating aspects of a product and reimagining the result for a new audience or new use. To apply the template, a product innovator would accordingly follow these steps:

1   List an existing product's internal components[a] (i.e., components within the manufacturer's control)

2   Identify each component's function in the product

3   Remove an *essential* component

4   Visualize the resulting form (what the potential product might look like)

5   Explore whether this new form meets known or latent consumer needs

6   Consider the feasibility of implementing the new product

7   Make necessary adaptations to overcome obvious challenges/concerns

Applying this method to developing a new product from the standard iPod, one could see how stripping away the device's screen and ability to select songs might lead to a prototype that resembled the iPod shuffle. In step five, in which one explores how this new form may address consumers' needs, one could clearly see how teenagers—a largely untapped customer base at the time the iPod shuffle was being developed— might have had a need for a pared down, easier to use, and less expensive version of the iPod. As a result, it would be easier to realize that the new design and lower price point had the potential to win over people who didn't typically purchase Apple products and possibly convert them into lifelong customers.

WHEN LESS BECOMES MORE: REINVENTING PHILIPS'S DVD PLAYER

In 2001 a product innovation team at Philips Consumer Electronics gathered in Eindhoven, Holland, to reinvent the DVD player.[20] At the time, first-generation DVD players were on the market from Philips, Sony, and Panasonic, but they looked no different than VCRs: they were big and bulky and often had a front-panel display

---

a   There are some instances where subtracting *external* components may also lead to interesting innovations; see Uber and Airbnb examples later in this case.

accompanied by rows of buttons. Since the new technology allowed for more options, these early DVD players included a wide array of functions and features.

Facilitated by a team from SIT Ltd., the multifunctional Philips team was trained to use the subtraction method to develop an improved DVD player. Table 1 provides a summary of the SIT moderator's prompts and the answers provided by the Philips team.

Table 12.1. The SIT Process as Applied to the Philips DVD Player

SIT PROMPT	SUMMARY OF DISCUSSION POINTS/CONCLUSIONS
What are the key components of the DVD player?	Front panel LCD screen, front control buttons, (for time-setting, recording, and play functions), clock, remote control, box frame, DVD slot
What is the functionality of each component?	Display screen: to view player control functions Buttons: to operate DVD Clock: to set time for recording Remote control: to operate DVD Box: to protect technology back end; box frame was sized to accommodate the large display screen (in fact, much of the box was hollow). Slot: to insert DVD into device
What if we removed the display screen?	Another place to view player control functions would be needed
What might be substituted for the display screen?	TV interface
Visualize the resulting form; what might this new DVD player look like?	Device with a much thinner box frame.
Are there any engineering obstacles to overcome if the display screen is removed? Are any adaptions of the current player needed?	Need to sync DVD operations with the TV screen; need to design a slimmer box
Are there any other components that can be removed? What about the array of buttons?	Can remove most buttons and rely on remote for interactivity
What needs might a more streamlined player meet for some consumers?	Reduces complexity of use; removes unnecessary features; creates an even thinner box.

KEY TAKEAWAYS

The Philips engineers didn't immediately realize that most people never even programmed the clock on a typical VCR display screen, so it didn't occur to them that additional functions and buttons might be unnecessary on a redesigned DVD player and in many cases would also put off customers who might be afraid to try the new technology because of its complexity. As suggested by usability expert Jakob Nielsen, every additional feature might be "one more thing to learn, one more thing to possibly misunderstand, and one more thing to search through when looking for the thing you want,"[21] inducing what some researchers have termed "feature fatigue."

When the team first tried to imagine a screenless DVD player, it was difficult for some of them to conceive of its value—mostly because they had never seen one before. When led by the SIT moderator, they came to recognize the limitations of fixed preconceptions. As Senior Philips Consultant for Market Intelligence Henk Speijer, who solicited SIT Ltd. to lead the ideation process, explained, "The difficult thing is that people believe that creativity is a personality trait of the best people in the company, but if you apply the right methods, like SIT, you generate many, many useful ideas."[22]

Once the Philips team engaged with the SIT moderator, they realized that the reason much of the player's bulky box frame was hollow was that it was sized to fit the large display screen. They were also able to imagine the player without a display panel when they realized that information about what the DVD player was doing could be displayed better on the connected television screen. In addition, as the team probed further, they came to see that many of the buttons on the company's early-model DVD players were redundant because they were also on the device's remote control. The team's final product, called the Slimline, was a trim, sleek DVD player with no visible buttons that soon became the industry standard as well as a product design archetype (dozens of devices thereafter were described as having a "slimline" design).[23]

See Figure 12.1 for examples of a traditional VCR player and a slimline DVD player.

EXAMPLES OF THE SUBTRACTION TEMPLATE

You know you have achieved perfection in design not when you have nothing more to add, but when you have nothing more to take away.

—Antoine de Saint-Exupéry (French writer, poet, and pioneering aviator)

Not all of the companies described here have used the subtraction *method* to create their successes. However, all of these innovators thought differently about already existing products, employing a "less is more" approach that led to the creation of

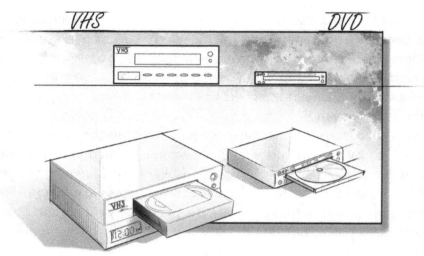

Figure 12.1. Traditional [VHS] Player and Philips Slimline Dvd Player

Source: Drew Boyd and Jacob Goldenberg, *Inside the Box: A Proven System of Creativity for Breakthrough Results* (New York, NY: Simon & Schuster, 2013), 53.

something new and valuable. In essence, all applied the subtraction *template* to their product development.

BETTY CROCKER CAKE MIXES

Although the subtraction template hadn't been identified yet when General Mills introduced a line of Betty Crocker instant cake mixes in the 1950s,[24] the company—probably as the result of good thinking and perhaps also of good instincts—achieved success using that template. Each mix contained all of the cake's ingredients, including milk and eggs, in powdered form. Users only had to add water, pour the mixture into a pan, put it in the oven, and bake it. However, despite the considerable time the product saved, it didn't sell well. Marketing executives surveyed users and reported that some said they felt guilty because they hadn't invested any time or effort in baking the cake and therefore had no "sense of ownership" of it.[25] General Mills addressed this by removing the powdered egg from the mix, in the hope that customers, who now had to beat an egg into the other ingredients, would feel more connected to the process of creating the cake.[26] The strategy worked, immediately changing the attitudes of consumers, and the mixes were a home run for General Mills

THE MANGO CELL PHONE

The development of Motorola's Mango cell phone in Israel in 1996 is another example of the subtraction template guiding a company's thinking in coming up with a new product that took advantage of a unique situation. Mobile phone prices and provider charges were still very high in 1996. Parents wanted to be able to contact their children but didn't want to give them the full freedom of a regular, full-use cell phone and potentially incur large charges making outgoing calls. Realizing this, the Mango team accordingly created a phone that accepted calls from any number but was only able to call one. The Mango was highly popular among parents, and within three months of its launch, it accounted for 46% of all cell phones sold in Israel during that period.[27] Within a year, it was named one of the top five best global marketing ideas by the American Marketing Association.[28]

APPLE

The Shuffle is just one example of Apple's "less is more" approach to product development. The company's use of the subtraction template is also evident in many other Apple products.

Before the company launched the iPhone in January 2007,[29] many of the best-selling smartphones and PDAs on the market included either an external QWERTY keyboard or a stylus. The iPhone did away with these features and instead incorporated a virtual QWERTY keyboard into its touch screen interface.[30] While Apple didn't invent the touch screen, the company's use of it nonetheless set the standard for that product category. The iPhone would eventually cannibalize the iPod and go on to become the company's best-selling product, accounting for 66% of revenue in 2015.[31]

In the fall of 2007, Apple launched the iPod touch,[32] which had all the features of iPhone, minus the phone function. The device was marketed heavily for children, teens, and students, prompting one gadget review site to call the device a "gateway drug" to the iPhone.[33] In 2007 net iPod revenue per unit sold rose 10%, to $164, which Apple attributed to the introduction of the iPod touch.[34]

In 2008 the company introduced the MacBook Air,[35] a pared-down version of the standard MacBook. By eliminating some of the original device's features, such as a DVD burner, Apple created a lighter, more portable computer.[36]

And when Apple rolled out the iPad in January 2010, it offered two versions of the product. One included a SIM card that allowed users to receive data service from a telecom provider, while the other did not.[37] Without the SIM card, there was no need for a data contract, which made that version of the product more attractive to some users.

Apple launched the App Store in January 2008,[38] which allowed users of the iPhone and the iPod touch to buy tools and applications for those devices. From an organizational perspective, the App Store allowed Apple to virtually subtract its R&D department and grow by outsourcing the development of new features to a large community of users. The store led to a surge in entrepreneurs who set out to build app-based businesses, and it quickly became the value engine of the smartphone platform, whose real value to customers was developed by the customers themselves. As with many successful revolutions, the change from the typical approach of having only the company develop a product's value to one in which customers develop the value jointly with the firm guided the innovative concept at the heart of the products—in this case, mobile platforms and smartphones. The company said that the App Store generated over $20 billion[39] in sales in calendar year 2015, and analysts estimated that about a third of that translated to income.[40]

A CAUTIONARY NOTE: SUBTRACTION IS NOT UNBUNDLING

It is very important to differentiate between the subtraction method and a well-known marketing technique called "unbundling." The unbundling approach proposes to eliminate some of the components of a product or to deliver a service in a way that detracts from its efficiency or quality and then charge less for it (creating an arguably "justified price discrimination"). This approach enlarges the target population for the product or service by appealing to a lower-income or price-sensitive segment. Offering a more modest version of a tour package (with cheaper hotels and charter flights) at a lower price or selling "do it yourself" furniture that is less expensive than fully assembled furniture are examples of such unbundling. Note that no new benefit other than lower cost is created by unbundling. With the subtraction method, on the other hand, there is always a new benefit connected with the new product or service itself. Because the additional benefit is presumed to attract a different target audience, the price of the new product or service may be the same or even greater than the cost of the original, despite the subtraction. For example, a beach chair with no legs might not necessarily cost less than a chair with legs—and in fact might even cost more since it better serves its intended use on the sand.

Although unbundling, like the subtraction method, can lead to successful new products and services, there is an important distinction to be made between the two approaches: The purpose of the subtraction method is to discover new value and develop creative ideas rather than to offer variations of established products or services.

THE SUBTRACTION METHOD: GIVING BIRTH TO NEW BUSINESS MODELS

In some cases, entire companies have been founded on the basis of business ideas that subtracted components of existing products or services in order to create new markets.

TWITTER

Twitter is an excellent example of the use of the subtraction template, whether its developers were consciously aware of it or not. Twitter's blogging platform eliminated free-flowing text—capping posts at a maximum of 140 characters—and produced viewer relationships that are not bidirectional by default, as they are in most other social networks. These constraints generated different blogging dynamics and attracted a different type of user, creating a community with an identity that is very distinct from, for example, Facebook's.

AIRBNB

Airbnb created a platform that matched guests with hosts, enabling the company's clients to use the space in people's homes, thus eliminating the guests' need for hotels. Airbnb reached $900 million in revenue in 2015, which put it above Choice Hotels International's $860 million and close to La Quinta Holdings' $1,030 million that year.

UBER

Uber launched in 2010 as an online service that connected potential riders with drivers from existing black car and limousine companies. However, by 2012 the company had expanded with UberX, an added service that eliminated the black car component and connected riders with Uber-approved drivers of everyday cars.[41] As a result, Uber's service become inexpensive enough to compete with taxi cabs and quickly grew to account for the bulk of the company's revenue stream. That growth helped Uber raise $258 million in Series C venture capital in 2013 and reach an estimated valuation of $3.5 billion, up from $60 million in 2011, after it had raised $11 million in a Series A fundraising round.[42]

NETFLIX

Netflix first eliminated the need for brick-and-mortar stores by offering a DVD-by-mail rental service and later eliminated the need for video discs by providing an Internet streaming service that allows users to watch video content that they don't own. Netflix's creative strategy has led to new products and rapid growth, prompting one industry observer to comment: "The word 'disruptive' is overused and has met its limits, but nothing better describes the likes of Uber and Amazon, that class of company that can justify millions of dollars spent in the name of growth. Netflix is certainly one of them."[43]

A SUBTRACTION EXERCISE

Most product development managers are trained to think in terms of adding new components or services, so eliminating them instead is perhaps a counterintuitive idea that will be best understood by experiencing the process oneself.

See the Appendix for an exercise that simulates the development process for a creative and lucrative product extension. *This exercise will prove most valuable when followed by an instructor debrief describing the real-world product that grew out of a similar exercise.*

Note: For additional information on subtraction method templates, see Drew Boyd and Jacob Goldenberg, *Inside the Box: A Proven System of Creativity for Breakthrough Results* (New York, NY: Simon & Schuster, 2013).

APPENDIX

EXERCISE: APPLYING THE SUBTRACTION METHOD

This exercise will lead you step by step in using the subtraction template to innovate a very basic product. Despite the template's simplicity, you will be able to see how you can easily come up with ideas like those that have enjoyed much real-world success.

1   Generate a list of the most common laundry detergent brands.

2   Identify the key component of laundry detergent.

3   Identify the function of that component.

4   Remove the component.

5   Visualize the resulting form of the product.

6   Consider whether there are needs that a detergent without the removed component might fulfill.

7   Consider whether there any obstacles to overcome in implementing the new product.

Bring these ideas to class or to your online forum and be prepared to discuss the possible new products that might emerge from this process. (Note: This exercise will prove most valuable when followed by an instructor debrief describing the real-world product that grew out of a similar exercise.)

NOTES

1. John Tso, "Macworld San Francisco 2005: The iPod Shuffle Introduction," You Tube video, 9:26, April 19, 2009, https://www.youtube.com/watch?v=12bjWBZKd30.

2. "Apple Press Info: iPod + iTunes Timeline," Apple, https://www.apple.com/pr/products/ipodhistory/.

3. Tso, "Macworld San Francisco 2005."

4. Laurie J. Flynn, "IPod Demand Leads Big Increase in Earnings for Apple," New York Times, July 15, 2004, http://www.nytimes.com/2004/07/15/business/ipod-demand-leads-big-increase-in-earnings-forapple.html.

5. Tso, "Macworld San Francisco 2005."

6. Apple, "Apple Unveils New iPod mini Starting at Just $199," press release, February 23, 2005, https://www.apple.com/pr/library/2005/02/23Apple-Unveils-New-iPod-mini-Starting-at-Just-199.html.

7. Apple, "Apple Introduces the New iPod," press release, July 19, 2004, https://www.apple.com/pr/library/2004/07/19Apple-Introduces-the-New-iPod.html.

8. Tso, "Macworld San Francisco 2005."

9. John Gruber, "Small, Cheap, and without a Display," *Daring Fireball*, January 16, 2005, http://daringfireball.net/2005/01/small_cheap_no_display.

10. James Kim, "Apple iPod Shuffle Review," *CNET*, January 25, 2005, http://www.cnet.com/products/apple-ipod-shuffle/.

11. Apple 10-K for fiscal year ended September 24, 2005, http://investor.apple.com/secfiling.cfm?filingid=1104659-05-58421&cik=320193.

12. "Apple's iPod Continues to Gain Market Share," *International Business Times*, October 4, 2006, http://www.ibtimes.com/apples-ipod-continues-gain-market-share-196689.

13. Gruber, "Small, Cheap, and without a Display."

14. Gruber, "Small, Cheap, and without a Display."

15. Greg A. Stevens and James Burley, "3,000 Raw Ideas = 1 Commercial Success!" *Research-Technology Management* 40, no. 3 (1997): 16–27, https://www.questia.com/library/journal/1P3-11645200/3-000-rawideas-equals-1-commercial-success.

16. Stevens and Burley, "3,000 Raw Ideas."

17. Barry Jaruzelski, "R&D Back on Track," *Strategy&* video, 3:02, October 27, 2015, http://www.strategyand.pwc.com/global/home/what-we-think/multimedia/video/mmvideo_display/back-on-track-video.

18. Jacob Goldenberg and David Mazursky, *Creativity in Product Innovation* (Cambridge, England: Cambridge University Press, 2002).

19. Jacob Goldenberg, Donald R. Lehmann, and David Mazursky, "The Idea Itself and the Circumstances of Its Emergence as Predictors of New Product Success," *Management Science* 47, no. 1 (2001): 69–84.

20. Drew Boyd and Jacob Goldenberg, *Inside the Box: A Proven System of Creativity for Breakthrough Results* (New York, NY: Simon & Schuster, 2013).

21. Roland T. Rust, Debora Viana Thompson, and Rebecca Hamilton, "Defeating Feature Fatigue," *Harvard Business Review*, February 2006, https://hbr.org/2006/02/defeating-feature-fatigue.

22. David Rosenberg, "The Brainstormer," *Wall Street Journal Online*, May 13, 2002, http://www1.idc.ac.il/faculty/jgoldenberg/pdf/The%20brainstormer.pdf.

23. Boyd and Goldenberg, *Inside the Box*.

24. Stevens and Burley, "3,000 Raw Ideas."

25. Stevens and Burley, "3,000 Raw Ideas."

26. Stevens and Burley, "3,000 Raw Ideas."

27. Margo Sugarman, "Mango Benny Einhorn: [Tel Aviv, Israel]," *AdvertisingAge*, December 9, 1996, http://adage.com/article/news/mango-benny-einhorn-tel-aviv-israel/75381/.

28. Bernd Jöstingmeier and Heinz-Jürgen Boeddrich, eds., *Cross-Cultural Innovations: New Thoughts, Empirical Research, Practical Reports* (Munich, Germany: R. Oldenbourg, 2007), 110.

29. "Apple Press Info: iPod + iTunes Timeline."

30. Kent German and Donald Bell, "Apple iPhone Review," *CNET*, June 30, 2007, http://www.cnet.com/products/apple-iphone/.

31. Bloomberg data, accessed May 2016.

32. "Apple Press Info: iPod + iTunes Timeline."

33. Jason D. O'Grady, "The iPod Touch Is a Gateway Drug," *ZDNET*, September 25, 2012, http://www.zdnet.com/article/the-ipod-touch-is-a-gateway-drug/.

34. Apple 10-K for fiscal year ended September 25, 2010, 2005, http://investor.apple.com/secfiling.cfm?filingid=1193125-10-238044.

35. Apple, "Apple Introduces MacBook Air—The World's Thinnest Notebook," press release, January 15, 2008, https://www.apple.com/pr/library/2008/01/15Apple-Introduces-MacBook-Air-The-Worlds-Thinnest-Notebook.html.

36. Dan Ackerman, "Apple MacBook Air Review," *CNET*, January 24, 2008, http://www.cnet.com/products/apple-macbook-air/.

37. Apple, "Apple Launches iPad," press release, January 27, 2010, http://www.apple.com/pr/library/2010/01/27Apple-Launches-iPad.html.

38. Michael Arrington, "iPhone App Store has Launched (Updated)," *Tech Crunch*, July 10, 2008, http://techcrunch.com/2008/07/10/app-store-launches-upgrade-itunes-now/.

39. Apple, "Record-Breaking Holiday Season for the App Store," press release, January 6, 2010, http://www.apple.com/pr/library/2016/01/06Record-Breaking-Holiday-Season-for-the-App-Store.html.

40. Gregg Keizer, "Apple's Cut of 2015 App Store Revenue Tops $6B," *Computer World*, January 6, 2010, http://www.computerworld.com/article/3019716/apple-ios/apples-cut-of-2015-app-store-revenue-tops-6b.html.

41. Evan Rawley and Dan Wang, *Uber: Driving into Uncharted Territory*, Columbia CaseWorks case #160415 (New York, NY: Columbia University, March 29, 2016).

42. "Uber," *Crunch Base*, https://www.crunchbase.com/organization/uber#/entity.

43. George Salapa, "Why Netflix's Financials Are Better Than You Think," *Forbes*, January 25, 2016, http://www.forbes.com/sites/valleyvoices/2016/01/25/why-netflixs-financials-are-better-than-youthink/#6065378b.

READINGS 11 AND 12: QUESTIONS FOR THOUGHT

- What is the advantage of using the creative exercises in the two readings as opposed to free-form, blue sky brainstorming?

- Think about a product or service you use frequently. Identify the components, internal attributes, and external attributes for the product or service. Consider various pairs of attributes. Thinking about the pairings, try to identify how the attribute pairs might be dependent and what benefit that they might create for a customer.

- Why does "function follows form" make sense when generating ideas for new products and services?

- Consider another product or service you use frequently. Identify all the components. Imagine you cannot include one of the components. Think about a new product or service that would result from the old product or service minus the removed component. What might be the customer benefit of the new product or service?

DEVELOPING INNOVATIVE SOLUTIONS THROUGH INTERNAL CROWDSOURCING

In the past decade much has been written about the concept of open innovation. This newly adopted practice has historical roots. The notion of soliciting the "crowd" for ideas to solve problems has a famous origin with the 1714 Longitude Prize, the first-ever open innovation contest. The British parliament offered a prize of £20,000 for a solution to the vexing problem of identifying longitude for ships while at sea. The inability to calculate longitude at sea made seafaring particularly perilous and was responsible for the horrific shipwreck of a British fleet in 1707. Many of the greatest minds in history vied for the prize, including Isaac Newton and Edmund Halley. But the prize was ultimately won by an unknown clockmaker, John Harrison, who devised a solution based on the use of precise timing equipment that kept time on ships accurate relative to the time at which they set sail from England.

Open innovation, or crowdsourcing, is certainly a method of idea generation that innovators should consider leveraging, since great ideas can come from the most unlikely sources. However, in my experience, an even more fruitful source of ideas comes from internal crowdsourcing, the concept of allowing all employees the opportunity to submit ideas. The employee suggestion box of yesterday has now been upgraded by a budding industry of idea management software platforms. Many companies have implemented these platforms, enabling employees to submit ideas and review the ideas of others.

The next reading features a recent article that discusses best practices in the use of internal crowdsourcing to generate ideas. Internal crowdsourcing leverages the fact that your own employees are best equipped to devise solutions to customer problems that leverage the current or emerging capabilities of your organization. While outside experts or even consumers may suggest ideas, those externally sourced ideas often lack relevance or feasibility based on your organization's strategy and core competencies.

In the article, the authors note the barriers that exist in many companies to the effective use of internal crowdsourcing. They also offer a host of solutions to those barriers that can ensure internal crowdsourcing is used effectively.

Arvind Malhotra is the H. Allen Andrew Professor of Entrepreneurial Education at the University of North Carolina. Ann Majchrzak is the associates chair in business administration and a professor for the Marshall School of Business at the University of Southern California. Lâle Kesebi is the Chief Communications Officer and Head of Strategic Engagement at Li & Fung Limited, a global supply chain company based in Hong Kong with twenty-two thousand employees. Sean Looram is an executive vice president with Li & Fung Limited.

DEVELOPING INNOVATIVE SOLUTIONS THROUGH INTERNAL CROWDSOURCING

BY **ARVIND MALHOTRA, ANN MAJCHRZAK, LÂLE KESEBI, AND SEAN LOORAM**

Internal crowdsourcing, which enlists ideas from employees, is not as well-known as other forms of crowdsourcing. Managed well, however, it can open up rich new sources of innovation.

THE LEADING QUESTION

How can companies get the most benefit from crowd-sourcing within the organization?

FINDINGS

- Allow employees to participate anonymously.
- Take steps to make sure company experts don't exert their influence too heavily.
- Use platforms and processes that foster collaboration.

As organizations look for better solutions to their everyday problems, many are encouraging their employees to use their experiences to develop new ideas and play a more active role in the innovation process. Whether the issue involves improving hiring practices, deciding which new products or services to offer, or creating better forecasts, companies including AT&T Inc., Google Inc., and Deutsche Telekom AG have turned to what's known as internal crowdsourcing.[1]

Although external crowdsourcing, which involves soliciting ideas from consumers, suppliers, and anyone else who wants to participate, has been widely studied,[2] internal crowdsourcing, which seeks to channel the ideas and expertise of the company's own employees, is less well-understood. It allows employees to interact dynamically with coworkers in other locations, propose new ideas, and suggest new directions to management.

Because many large companies have pockets of expertise and knowledge scattered across different locations, we have found that harnessing the cognitive diversity within organizations can open up rich new sources of innovation. Internal crowdsourcing is a particularly effective way for companies to engage younger employees and people working on the front lines.[3]

We conducted a four-year study of how multiple companies used internal crowds that included frontline employees to find new solutions to business challenges. We observed internal crowdsourcing in practice, interviewed executives who sponsored internal crowdsourcing innovation challenges, and surveyed participants. We also participated in the design, implementation, and execution of internal crowdsourcing events at several companies. (See "About the Research.") In this article, we will examine the benefits of internal crowdsourcing, the roadblocks that stand in the way of successful initiatives, and ways crowdsourcing efforts can be designed to overcome those roadblocks.

THE BENEFITS OF INTERNAL CROWDSOURCING

Companies that employ external crowdsourcing need to confront several issues.[4] First, because many of the crowd participants aren't specifically familiar with the organization or the context in which it operates, a high percentage of the suggestions may not be easy to implement. The voice of the customer obtained through external crowd-sourcing may be very good at describing the pain points and needs but not necessarily good at figuring out how to solve the problems. Indeed, proposals often call for strategic assets that companies don't have and can't afford. What's more, external crowdsourcing can stir up intellectual property issues involving who owns the ideas.[5]

While internal crowds are typically not as diverse as external crowds (and therefore less apt to propose radically new ideas), they have more localized knowledge. This can help companies turn suggestions into workable actions better and faster. Employees, especially people working on the front lines, often have intimate knowledge about the kinds of changes that are feasible, given the company's circumstances and current assets. Many of the solutions can be formulated as patches and workarounds to satisfy particular needs, and solutions obtained through internal crowdsourcing can have a rapid impact in the marketplace. In addition, the intellectual property issues tend to be less complicated because employees, rather than outsiders, are the ones providing the ideas. (See "Comparing the Benefits of Internal vs. External Crowds.")

Internal crowdsourcing events enable employees to express their ideas. By organizing these events, companies can send the important message to employees that their knowledge is valuable and the company depends on it. With mechanisms to share their views and structure internal collaboration, employees can feel empowered and engaged in the company's innovation efforts. Research shows that employees working in collaborative environments tend to be more satisfied with the innovation process.[6] This can lead to higher employee morale and lower turnover.[7]

ROADBLOCKS TO SUCCESSFUL INTERNAL CROWDSOURCING

As fruitful as internal crowdsourcing can be, it's common for companies to hit roadblocks in reaping the full potential of internal crowds. In the course of our research, we have identified seven barriers that involve participation, collaboration, and implementation. They are:

1 Rather than encourage employees to think broadly and creatively, companies often ask employees to concentrate on incremental adjustments to processes and on improving existing products and services. In doing so, many employees become confused about the purpose of internal crowdsourcing and how it's different from other initiatives in the company, such as continuous quality improvement and business process reengineering.

2 Given their other work responsibilities, many employees don't have time to participate in crowdsourcing activities.

3   Employees may be hesitant to participate, particularly when managers and internal experts are part of the mix and are using their real identities. This dynamic may crowd out people who have knowledge that can lead to innovative solutions or who want to develop solutions by working with others in the crowd.

4   Most companies run their crowdsourcing initiatives using a competitive process. Rather than encouraging participants to work with others to create solutions together, some companies distribute rewards based on the ideas submitted by individuals.

5   Sometimes, the technology platforms themselves focus people on contributing ideas and not on developing solutions together.

6   After crowdsourcing events end, employees don't always receive sufficient information on what happened to ideas.

7   Over and above the lack of feedback, those who suggest solutions don't always get opportunities to develop their ideas into solutions.

ABOUT THE RESEARCH

This article is based on a four-year, multi-method research project with companies engaged in internal crowdsourcing. In one part of our research, we conducted in-depth analyses at three large organizations (one in health care, one in telecommunications, and one in retail), and we conducted interviews with the executives in charge of the internal crowdsourcing. At the health care organization we studied, the chief medical officer was in charge of engaging frontline employees in the internal crowdsourcing process; two of us provided guidance and oversaw the execution of the company's internal crowdsourcing effort. At the telecommunications company, we worked with a senior executive in charge of the internal crowdsourcing effort. At fashion and retail company Li & Fung Ltd., we had access to the ideas, documents, and thinking process behind the design of an internal crowdsourcing event.

In addition, we collected data related to platforms and the design of incentives for crowdsourcing challenges at seven other companies, which were identified through a university-affiliated innovation center. They included a distribution company, a Scandinavian telecommunications company, a U.S.-based telecommunications infrastructure company, a data storage and analytics company, a graphics design software company, an industrial products company, and an e-commerce platform provider. Our partner at each organization was either the chief innovation officer or the CEO.

COMPARING THE BENEFITS OF INTERNAL VS. EXTERNAL CROWDS

While internal crowds are typically not as diverse as external crowds, the solutions employees propose may be more readily implemented and can have a rapid impact in the marketplace.

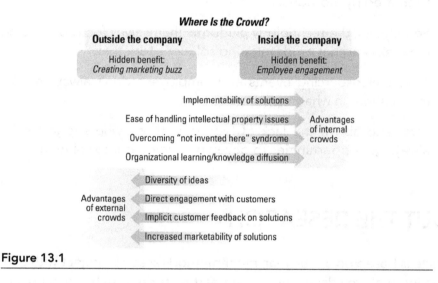

Figure 13.1

REMOVING THE ROADBLOCKS

In response to the roadblocks we have noted above, we have developed a set of seven action steps to help executives make their internal crowdsourcing efforts more effective. The first four steps should be considered either before or during a crowdsourcing event; the others are used once the event has occurred.

1. Keep the focus on innovation. It may be tempting to use internal crowdsourcing events to solicit ideas about short-term improvements. However, to get the most out of internal crowdsourcing, companies should resist this impulse and encourage employees to keep their focus on long-term opportunities. A large research and development (R&D) company we studied, for example, announced that it wanted employees to identify products and services that would be feasible in 2025. This encouraged employees to think more broadly than usual.

Other companies have defined challenges in a more open-ended way. A U.S. telecom infrastructure products and services provider presented its employees with a general question: "What are some strategies for our company to transition to a services-centric business to address new markets and new customers?" How questions are framed is a critical component of signaling and can influence how employees approach internal crowdsourcing initiatives.

Another critical aspect of establishing the grounds for creativity is to share with crowdsourcing participants the criteria that will be used to filter and select the best solutions. For example, an R&D-intensive company we studied disclosed the following parameters that its executives planned to use for selecting solutions: 50% would be weighted on crowd voting, 30% on novelty of the idea, and 20% on the potential to create new businesses. Fashion and retail company Li & Fung Ltd., based in Hong Kong, told employees that solutions from internal crowdsourcing would be picked based on six criteria: (1) ability to meet customers' unmet needs, (2) delighting the customer, (3) the solution's newness, (4) marketability, (5) commercial viability, and (6) scalability.

2. Give internal crowdsourcing participants slack time. One of the main reasons people participate in external crowdsourcing events is to have fun.[8] However, a critical difference between external and internal crowdsourcing is that many employees, particularly frontline employees, have very little discretionary time to participate. A managed health care company came up with a smart way to engage internal employees without undermining existing schedules. It notified supervisors of proposed dates for internal crowdsourcing events and asked them to select days when they could give employees some downtime. Once the dates were set, supervisors encouraged employees to participate in the internal crowdsourcing innovation challenges. We found that offering employees slack time to participate in internal crowdsourcing events can be a key factor in making the events successful, especially when the companies want the employees to work together to develop new solutions. When done well, internal crowdsourcing challenges not only produce ideas but also engage employees in a learning process.

3. Allow for anonymous participation. Difficulties can occur when participants in internal crowdsourcing use their organizational identities. Rather than freely promoting ideas that address the issues at hand, some individuals may feel compelled to defend their formal positions. Internal crowdsourcing participants should feel safe about contributing knowledge, regardless of their seniority or role in the company. One way to encourage this is to offer a degree of anonymity. Several of the companies we studied allowed employees to contribute their ideas anonymously, freeing them up to share knowledge that they might have kept to themselves if they felt pressured to advocate on behalf of the units they represented. Providing a psychologically safe environment leads to greater employee participation and collaboration, resulting in more effective innovations.[9] At Li & Fung, for example, almost 90% of the solutions the company received through internal crowdsourcing challenges were from junior to mid-level employees, and about 30% of the solutions were proposed by people working in support functions such as human resources, IT, and finance.

Participants who are forced to use their real names often feel exposed during internal crowd-sourcing challenges, especially if they are recognized internally as subject matter experts. With anonymity, they don't have to worry about how their ideas "look." This allows them to focus on learning and integrating the knowledge being shared.

4. Take steps to ensure that company experts don't exert their influence too heavily. Experts within a company may be inclined to wield their knowledge during the idea generation process, and this can be harmful. Although the voices of experts are often valuable, they can intimidate others in the company, who worry that they are out of place expressing ideas to a crowd that includes experts.

For internal crowdsourcing to produce innovative outcomes, efforts should be made to keep the process open to diverse perspectives. At an R&D-intensive company, the managers in charge of an internal crowdsourcing effort initially prohibited R&D employees from participating in a crowdsourcing event. The company changed its position when participants asked to see research evidence related to the question they were considering and specifically asked if they could hear from R&D experts.

A U.S. manufacturer, by contrast, determined that internal crowdsourcing participation by internal experts could be a strong plus. For its crowdsourcing initiative, the company asked some internal experts to serve as the moderators of crowd discussions. This involved teeing up questions to challenge the crowd to think of different ways to create new solutions. Among the questions the expert moderators asked: How could the idea be extended in new ways? How could we combine it with another idea? How could we differentiate it from other products on the market? How could we adapt the product to a different target audience?

There are benefits to both approaches. However, the decision to involve internal experts has a downside as well as an upside. Companies need to recognize that internal experts are often motivated to promote their own ideas. However, participants need to know that their suggestions will be highly valued. When engaging experts in an internal crowdsourcing event, companies should train them to operate as moderators and to do what they can to encourage others.

5. Use a collaborative process for internal crowd-sourcing. One of the secrets to unlocking the creative potential of internal crowds is recognizing that the goal isn't simply to generate winning ideas. It's also to build a system through which people within the organization share knowledge, learn from one another, and offer pertinent knowledge for use in new solutions.

We saw companies use one or both steps of a two-step process to foster collaboration in internal crowdsourcing innovation challenges. First, they asked people to share pertinent knowledge related to innovation opportunities. The emphasis here was on broad employee participation: asking people to share facts, examples, trade-offs, and even wild ideas. Then the companies asked people to help shape the knowledge into comprehensive solutions. The majority of the companies we studied relied heavily on the second approach.

However, some companies find it useful to use a hybrid, multistage approach whereby in initial stages the internal crowd shares raw ideas through a technology platform. Then, in the later stages, ad hoc teams are formed to pursue the most promising ideas further and develop them into comprehensive solutions. For example, Li & Fung asked employees from around the world to submit their ideas via a web-based platform. After that, a team of executives and internal experts selected the most promising ideas, based on preestablished criteria. Employees had opportunities to vote on the best ideas, narrowing the selections down to eight. In the final stage, teams composed of the idea originators and others who helped refine the ideas presented the solutions to a senior team that oversaw the internal crowdsourcing challenge. The top three teams were then asked to refine their solutions before traveling to corporate headquarters to present to a broader set of executives.

Companies that use a multistage process should provide incentives so that employees feel it's worth their while to follow the process and support the overall goal. If rewards go only to people who propose solid ideas, there can be negative consequences. People with half-baked ideas will submit them in hopes of winning, but those who don't have solid ideas (but might have input that could conceivably lead to important ideas) will hesitate to share their knowledge without incentives to do so. On the other hand, if incentives are offered only to good collaborators, there won't be incentives to contribute initial ideas that can lead to the development of comprehensive solutions. For these reasons, most of the companies we studied that succeeded with internal crowdsourcing offered different types of incentives. For example, a large industrial products company offered modest rewards ($50 gift cards) to both top idea contributors and collaborators. Top collaborators were determined by aggregating points for contributing new ideas, commenting on and refining other people's ideas, and combining multiple ideas into more robust solutions. They also received points based on their voting on other people's ideas.

We found that many participants lacked the time to engage fully in innovation activities. Instead, they logged on to the platform, took part in an innovation activity if it was easy to do so, and then left. We also found

Currently, there are a number of platforms available for crowdsourcing. Ironically, the technology platforms that are intended to help companies use internal crowdsourcing can cause roadblocks.

that crowd members responded in different ways to internal crowdsourcing platforms. Some responded to outcome-based incentives; others responded to process-based incentives. Regardless of how companies structure their internal crowdsourcing process, executives should remember that processes and incentives drive behavior.

6. Design platforms that facilitate shared development and evolution of solutions. Currently, there are a number of platforms available for crowdsourcing. Ironically, the technology platforms that are intended to help companies use internal crowdsourcing can cause roadblocks. In many cases, the platform makes it easy only for participants to submit their own ideas; it does little to connect individuals with ideas from other participants. The inability to see what other participants are suggesting can be a barrier to collaboration. Even if the platform allows for knowledge to be visible by others, it may allow for only limited interaction (for example, commenting or voting on others' contributions). Internal crowdsourcing platforms that support more innovative solutions use an implicit multistage process. The platforms encourage crowds to share knowledge (such as how other companies or other industries have solved similar problems) and then work that information into creative solutions. In particular, there are three features that we believe foster creativity in internal crowdsourcing: (1) knowledge sharing among the crowd across a variety of knowledge types (not just ideas); (2) the opportunity for coevolution of solutions by the crowd; and (3) the degree to which feedback from the crowd helps to refine ideas.

With these features in mind, we studied how companies used platforms to foster innovation in internal crowdsourcing challenges. The most popular platforms were online discussion forums and idea suggestion systems. When executives charged with innovation sought to engage individuals, they tended to use one of these platforms. However, such platforms do not explicitly encourage processes for groups to collaborate to create solutions together. Rather, they encourage individuals to post their ideas in the hope that other people will come in and refine the ideas. Although ideas can be refined after they have been posted, the platforms aren't designed to support and promote members of the crowd sharing knowledge that's relevant to the innovation opportunity. Online discussion forums also don't tend to make it easy for crowds to collaboratively piece together knowledge; even if some of the raw ideas have innovation potential, companies often need to wait until after the crowdsourcing event to sift through all the contributions, collect the innovation nuggets, and then work the ideas into comprehensive solutions. This post-crowdsourcing process can be onerous (particularly if the crowd generates thousands of potential innovation ideas). Given the time constraints and executives' predilections for picking solutions that leverage existing assets and capabilities, the executives in charge of sifting through and combining the ideas posted by the crowd may settle for less than optimal solutions.

While many companies use idea suggestion systems and online discussion forums, we found that some companies utilize co-creation platforms as a way to encourage greater crowd engagement and produce more innovative solutions from internal crowds. Such platforms explicitly encourage activities that go beyond the rudimentary activities of idea posting, commenting, and selecting. Typically, the first stage encourages people to share knowledge based on their rich and diverse experiences. This may include providing: (1) facts and established practices relevant to the opportunity; (2) examples of how other companies have addressed similar opportunities; (3) preliminary ideas that other people might build upon; and (4) insights about how to approach trade-offs not as compromises but as opportunities for innovation. The second stage then encourages people to integrate the knowledge into coherent solutions.

7. Be transparent about plans for follow-up post-crowdsourcing. Once employees have participated in internal crowdsourcing events, they want to know about the results. Which ideas were selected for further development and why? Will people be asked to develop some of the solutions more fully? Companies need to have procedures for how crowd-sourcing suggestions are handled. At the managed health care company, for example, the executives pledged to send out a detailed review of the crowd recommendations within one week of the completion of the internal crowdsourcing event. The project team committed to sending an email to all participants both announcing the winners and describing how the team planned to move ideas forward.

It's common for employees to be curious about how the ideas they submit are being viewed—and more specifically, who "owns" the solutions. In several settings, we found that crowdsourcing participants wanted to play a role in prototyping, testing, and implementing the ideas they proposed. A large international software company responds to this type of interest by inviting members of winning teams (both the initial proposers and collaborators) to participate in implementation efforts.

To maintain interest among employees whose suggested solutions are not selected for further development, companies should work to establish an atmosphere of openness and fairness. This can include providing opportunities for people to submit solutions more than once. One telecom company, for example, encourages employees whose solutions were not selected in the initial round to resubmit the ideas for consideration. The senior executive in charge of internal crowdsourcing sees this as a way to encourage participation and to demonstrate fairness.

Another way to demonstrate fairness is to commit to providing substantive feedback to employees who suggest solutions that are

Once employees have participated in internal crowdsourcing events, they want to know about the results. Which ideas were selected for further development and why?

not chosen. Although companies are accustomed to giving recognition to teams who submit winning solutions, they don't always offer clear criteria to guide the process or take the time to follow up with employees who don't win. But these efforts can pay big dividends in terms of driving future participation and generating better solutions later on. If internal crowdsourcing is to become an important mechanism for the organization's ongoing renewal, management needs to be serious about offering feedback.

In general, because roadblocks can surface at different points in the internal crowdsourcing process, the activity needs to be actively managed to ensure high levels of employee participation. However, it may be well worth the investment. The potential benefits of greater employee engagement are significant. A senior manager at an e-commerce solutions provider, for example, told us that during a 10-day crowdsourcing challenge, employees proposed more than 100 new solutions. Moreover, companies such as Li & Fung have noted that the level of employee participation in internal crowdsourcing events often goes well beyond what other collaboration mechanisms (such as virtual teams, face-to-face brainstorming, and innovation workshops) achieve. Despite its challenges, internal crowdsourcing can be used to unlock a company's innovation potential.

Arvind Malhotra is the H. Allen Andrew Professor of Entrepreneurial Education and professor of strategy and entrepreneurship at the University of North Carolina at Chapel Hill's Kenan-Flagler Business School. Ann Majchrzak is the USC Associates Chair in Business Administration and a professor of data sciences and operations at the University of Southern California's Marshall School of Business, in Los Angeles. Lâle Kesebi is the chief communications officer and head of strategic engagement at Li & Fung Ltd. Sean Looram is executive vice president at Li & Fung. Comment on this article at http://sloanreview.mit.edu/x/58423, or contact the authors at smrfeedback@ mit.edu.

NOTES

1. L. Myler, "AT&T's Innovation Pipeline Engages 130,000 Employees," Dec. 5, 2013, www.forbes.com; A. Ivanov, "Crowdsourcing vs. Employees: How to Benefit From Both," April 4, 2012, www.cmswire.com; R. Moussavian, "Work 4.0 Put in Practice," Aug. 24, 2016, www.telekom.com; and R. Singel, "Google Taps Employees to Crowdsource Its Venture Capital Arm," May 3, 2010, www.wired.com.

2. E. Bonabeau, "Decisions 2.0: The Power of Collective Intelligence," MIT Sloan Management Review 50, no. 2 (winter 2009): 45–52; and K.J. Boudreau and K.R. Lakhani, "Using the Crowd as an Innovation Partner," Harvard Business Review 91, no. 4 (April 2013): 60–69.

3. A. Siegel, "How Internal Crowdsourcing Will Transform the Way We Do Business," March 11, 2016, www.business2community.com; and H. Balmaekers, "The Crowd Within—Crowdsourced Innovation Inside Companies," March 23, 2016, www.intrapreneurshipconference.com.

4. A. Majchrzak and A. Malhotra, "Towards an Information Systems Perspective and Research Agenda on Crowd-sourcing for Innovation," Journal of Strategic Information Systems 22, no. 4 (December 2013): 257–268; and A. Malhotra and A. Majchrzak, "Managing Crowds in Innovation Challenges," California Management Review 56, no. 4 (summer 2014): 103–123.

5. M. Lieberstein and A. Tucker, "Crowdsourcing and Intellectual Property Issues," Association of Corporate Counsel, Aug. 29, 2012, www.acc.com.

6. S.G. Scott and R.A. Bruce, "Determinants of Innovative Behavior: A Path Model of Individual Innovation in the Workplace," Academy of Management Journal 37, no. 3 (June 1994): 580–607.

7. J. Baldoni, "Employee Engagement Does More Than Boost Productivity," Harvard Business Review, July 4, 2013, hbr.org.

8. D.C. Brabham, "Moving the Crowd at iStockphoto: The Composition of the Crowd and Motivations for Participation in a Crowdsourcing Application," First Monday 13, no. 6 (June 2, 2008).

9. M. Baer and M. Frese, "Innovation Is Not Enough: Climates for Initiative and Psychological Safety, Process Innovations, and Firm Performance," Journal of Organizational Behavior 24, no. 1 (February 2003): 45–68; M.A. West and W.M.M. Altink, "Innovation at Work: Individual, Group, Organizational, and Socio-Historical Perspectives," European Journal of Work and Organizational Psychology 5, no. 1 (1996): 3–11; and F. Yuan and R.W. Woodman, "Innovative Behavior in the Workplace: The Role of Performance and Image Outcome Expectations," Academy of Management Journal 53, no. 2 (April 2010): 323–342.

READING 13: QUESTIONS FOR THOUGHT

- What are some reasons why it might be beneficial to encourage internal crowd-sourcing in a large company?

- Among the suggestions for how to ensure a successful internal crowdsourcing program, which one do you think is the most important? Why?

- What is the difference between internal and external crowdsourcing? Why might a company want to use both?

5 EVALUATING IDEAS

The idea generation process often produces hundreds or even thousands of ideas. No organization can or even should try to implement all ideas. There needs to be an objective process to narrow down ideas and select the optimal ones to advance to the next steps in the innovation process.

There are many methods to evaluate ideas. The simplest is to conduct voting at the end of a brainstorming session. This serves a dual purpose of getting some initial feedback on what the group thinks about each idea as well as providing for closure at the end of a session after participants have spent a day generating ideas without judging them. Of course, simple voting is not the most scientific approach, and if the voting is done in the open, it often leads to group think as ideas that garner some initial votes tend to accumulate more votes since they become the "safe" option.

At the other end of the spectrum is a detailed business analysis of each idea including a high-level business case, a feasibility assessment, and possibly even formal consumer research to obtain feedback on the idea. This can be time-consuming and costly if it is conducted with a large number of ideas.

It is helpful therefore to have a set of tools that can be used to simply and efficiently evaluate ideas and select the optimal ones to consider for investment. This chapter provides some straight forward tools as well as an overall approach to evaluating ideas.

THE TOURNAMENT APPROACH TO IDEA EVALUATION

We learned in chapter 4 that one of the essential tenets for successful idea generation is to avoid criticizing or judging ideas. It is important to keep idea generation separate from idea evaluation to ensure we do not disturb the delicate creative process. Of course, once idea generation has formally ended, it is then necessary to have a method for evaluating ideas. The proper selection of the optimal ideas for design and development can be critical to the long-term success of an organization. When evaluating ideas, an organization is essentially deciding what ideas to invest in to ensure future survival.

During my professional career, I developed an Idea Tournament approach to evaluating ideas. The Idea Tournament puts all ideas, for a given objective, in direct competition with each other in an attempt to ensure the optimal ones are selected. The following reading presents my latest thinking on how to implement an Idea Tournament.

THE TOURNAMENT APPROACH TO IDEA EVALUATION

BY LEN FERMAN

Traditionally, the fun part of innovation is idea generation. This is the time innovators can think blue sky with no limits. This is when brainstorming facilitators drill into us that no idea is a bad idea, that we need to hear all your crazy ideas, and furthermore we are going to defer judgment on all the ideas. This is the part of the process in which we refer to Albert Einstein's famous quote: "If at first the idea is not absurd, then there is no hope for it."[1]

There does come a time, however, when it is necessary to judge ideas. After all, some ideas are not very good. And not every idea can or should be implemented. Even the largest organizations have resource limitations on what they can test and commercially rollout. As a result, there needs to be a process or an approach to evaluating ideas. We need to have in place a method for narrowing down and selecting which ideas will move forward in the innovation process.

Throughout my career as an innovator in large organizations, I grappled with the issue of how to ensure that idea evaluation was done well. Selecting the wrong ideas for design, testing, and rollout can have disastrous consequences. Stories of costly new product and service failures abound. Careers can be lost in the process. Customers ultimately lose out as well when the best ideas are mistakenly overlooked or discarded.

The problem is often that simply not enough attention is provided to putting an idea evaluation process in place. Generating ideas is fun. Evaluating ideas is tedious work, especially when there are hundreds or thousands of ideas to review. In some organizations, I have witnessed a decrease in company morale when ideas were solicited from employees, but inadequate resources were dedicated to idea evaluation. This inevitably leads to the perception that ideas are not fairly evaluated. Furthermore, if no feedback loop is provided to the submitter, it creates the employee view that the entire process was a waste. Even worse, employees may feel that their ideas are being adopted by the company without either compensation or recognition. When this occurs, employees become less likely to share ideas going forward, thus inhibiting future innovation.

This predicament led me to experiment with a new set of methods for evaluating ideas. I wanted to solve for the problems I saw in idea evaluation in which the process was laborious, conducted in isolation and secrecy, and ultimately led to questionable value in terms of the quality of ideas selected. In developing the present approach that I advocate, I had the assistance and inspiration of several colleagues at Bank of America including Tammy Kingston, Jason Burrell, Glenn Grossman, and John Tuders.

I was leading the front end of innovation at Bank of America, when I was tasked with managing an innovation challenge to generate and evaluate ideas that would provide value-added services to checking account customers. As checking accounts are a core business at the bank, this effort was going to involve a vast number of employees spanning a wide cross-functional team. As we looked for a theme for the challenge, we decided it would be fun and engaging to center it around the upcoming NCAA basketball tournament. March Madness is a captivating event that notoriously engages office employees in water cooler conversation about bracket predictions. Thus, the notion arose of an idea tournament in which the ideas generated during the ideation phase would be placed into competition against each other, complete with rankings and seedings. Idea competition would take place in an open environment with input broadly encouraged by employees and required from a core cross-functional group.

Subsequent research on this topic has led me to the work of professors Christian Terwiesch and Karl T. Ulrich of the Wharton School of Business at the University of Pennsylvania. Their 2009 book, *Innovation Tournaments: Creating and Selecting Exceptional Opportunities*, described the importance of innovation tournaments to generate and evaluate ideas.[2] In the book, they discuss various methods for screening and narrowing down ideas for selection.

While I wanted to have an objective process for idea selection that was grounded in sound methods, I also wanted to ensure that the process would be fun and engaging. It is important to engage a wide range of employees, especially those who will be involved in the downstream development and implementation phases. The pathway to a successful launch of the top ideas requires the acceptance of these downstream employees. I experienced the jolting resistance of the "not invented here syndrome" early in my career when trying to rollout new products and services that had been conceived and incubated in a vacuum by a small innovation team. I felt employee engagement on a wide scale was the solution to gaining internal acceptance of innovation efforts. As a result, I wanted to develop an idea tournament that captured the imagination of the participants and made them want to have meaningful engagement. This in turn would spur an appreciation and acceptance for whichever ideas became the tournament winners.

In the spirit of March Madness, I developed an approach in which there are multiple rounds. Over the years, I have continually revisited and evolved the approach. At present, I advocate ten rounds as follows:

Table 14.1.

ROUND	ACTIVITY
1	Cleaning, Dispositioning, and Internal Idea Evaluation
2	Idea Voting and Champions Draft
3	Idea Scoring
4	Consumer Quick Evaluation
5	Concept Writing
6	Concept Clarity Test
7	Concept Development with Consumers
8	Quantitative Concept Demand Test
9	Stakeholder Prioritization of Top Ideas
10	Final Stakeholder Review and Portfolio Selection

ROUND 1—CLEANING, DISPOSITIONING, AND INTERNAL IDEA EVALUATION

The first round of the idea tournament takes place immediately after the field has closed on idea generation. At this point, hundreds or thousands of ideas may have been generated through various methods. Often the ideas at this point are not consistently worded or not worded well, depending on how they were collected. I find that when conducting brainstorming sessions, for example, the ideas collected in group breakout sessions in which there is not a trained ideation scribe assigned can often be written up poorly. The problem also arises when conducting individual brainwriting exercises in which each person writes up their own ideas. Similarly, if an idea management system is being used to capture ideas from individual employees via the company intranet, there is again no control over the quality of the idea writing.

IDEA CLEANING

As a result, the first step in round 1 is simply to "clean" up the ideas. If there are more than two to three hundred ideas, I recommend a small team be assembled to conduct the cleanup. While this exercise can be slightly tedious, it is also a great opportunity to participate in an unheralded aspect of the innovation process. At this point, we are crafting fragments of ideas into well-written headline statements. The headlines, which are usually one-sentence descriptions of the idea, should ideally be in the ten- to twenty-word range. The task is to capture just the essence of the idea so that everyone in the company will understand it. If it's too short, it might not be properly understood. If it's too long, people will be less likely to read it, leading to the idea perhaps being discarded. When all the ideas are headlined properly, it makes the entire process run more efficiently since everyone can easily read and grasp the ideas quickly.

Here are some examples of properly and improperly worded idea headlines drawn from a brainstorming session I conducted on how to improve college campus life:

GOOD HEADLINES

1   App that enables reservations for premium parking spots on campus for two hours during classes

2   Provide Segways in the outer parking lot that students can ride to campus and return staff take back

3   Enable textbooks to be borrowed for short intervals during the semester

TOO SHORT / IDEA FRAGMENT (For each of the above ideas, I have suggested what the idea might have looked like if it was initially too short or simply a fragment.

These fragments must be developed into a headline since we have not captured the essence of the idea yet):

1. Reserve spots

2. Segways in parking lot

3. Borrowing books

In addition to writing the headlines, I strongly recommend both numbering and naming the ideas. A numbering system will help you to sort and keep track of the ideas. The numbering system might incorporate the source or type of idea as well. For example, when possible I always number ideas in a brainstorming session according to the creative exercise that was being used to generate ideas at a given point in the session. In this manner, I can track how well each exercise performed in generating quality ideas through the evaluation process. Naming is also important. By developing a one- to three-word name for the idea, we can more easily refer to the idea in subsequent conversations. This facilitates discussion of ideas without having to state the entire headline each time.

Continuing with the examples from above, here are some examples of idea names:

GOOD NAMES

1. Premium parking reservations

2. Segways

3. Textbook borrowing

Idea cleaning is also an opportunity to shape ideas and even add new ones (even though technically idea generation has closed). The fact is that many ideas we are working with at this point are fragments, as they were not properly headlined during the session or during intranet entry into an idea management system. The person or team cleaning the ideas must then determine what the idea submitter was attempting to convey. In cases where we can track directly back to the idea submitter, we could take the added step of contacting the submitter to clarify and help headline their idea. But often this is either not possible or impractical. Thus, the added role of the idea cleaner is to write up the idea as they see fit.

Sometimes the task of idea cleaning will enable you to visualize new ideas that did not come up during idea generation. The opportunity should then be taken to write up these additional ideas. Often there is an opportunity for great insights to come about at this stage when all of the ideas are being reviewed, and the myriad of possibilities for solving a challenge suddenly becomes clearer. It's not uncommon for this type of immersion in the ideas to yield an epiphany for an entirely new type of solution. Thus, the addition of a few more ideas should be encouraged at this point.

IDEA DISPOSITIONING

Once the ideas are clean, you can move on to dispositioning. Dispositioning is where the ideas are categorized in terms of which ones continue and which ones, for a variety of reasons, are not entered into the tournament (at least in their present form). Through this process of dispositioning, we identify the set of ideas that qualify for the tournament. It is not a requirement that every idea should be entered in the tournament. In any idea generation process, the resulting ideas—even if they have clean headlines—may not belong in the tournament for a variety of reasons.

Here is a list of the common dispositions I use in the exercise:

- PROCEED—These ideas enter the tournament.

Ideas with any of the following dispositions are not entered in the tournament:

- OFF STRATEGY—Ideas that don't fit with the challenge objective or don't fit overall company strategy.

- JUST DO IT—Ideas that do not require going through the innovation process. These might be quick fix items that can be easily implemented via business-as-usual processes. In the college campus brainstorming idea list, an example would be "fix the stop sign on Campus Drive." We don't need to take that idea through the innovation process. We simply ask maintenance to just do it.

- REFER—Ideas that fit strategy but belong in another department. Possible marketing promotions are an example of ideas that often receive this label.

- PREVIOUSLY TESTED or IN PROGRESS—Ideas that came up during ideation but upon further investigation are found to have been previously tested or to be presently in development. In large organizations this often happens as it is hard for everyone in an ideation session to know of everything that has been or is currently being tested.

- COMBINE—Ideas that are like other ideas in consideration and should be combined. For example, if two different subgroups of brainstorming participants generated the same idea, just worded differently, we would combine those into a single, well-headlined idea.

- IDEA FRAGMENT—Ideas that, despite the best effort to headline it or identify the original submitter, cannot be salvaged and therefore must be discarded. I view this as a failure in the idea generation process, as often these are ideas that someone put forth, but which simply did not get written up well. And after idea generation has closed, no one—sometimes not even the submitter—can recall the exact essence of the idea. The example above with the idea fragment that read "reserve spots" is a fragment because we don't know what the specific solution is that is being suggested. It has not answered how spots might be reserved.

While there are several dispositions that prevent ideas from entering the tournament, it is important to note that in this early part of the evaluation process the bias is for having ideas proceed. Thus, whenever there is doubt about an idea's disposition, I instruct the group to let the idea enter the tournament.

Once all ideas have been dispositioned, it is important to not simply discard the ideas that do not move forward. I advocate all ideas be entered into an idea archive. Ideally, the archive should include several fields so that information about each idea is available for future use. The fields I suggest are:

- Name of innovation challenge or challenge objective
- Disposition label
- Date idea was submitted
- Name of submitter
- Type of creative exercise used to generate idea
- Additional notes about the idea

A good idea archive can provide tremendous value over time. Foremost, it allows ideas that were dispositioned as off strategy to be revisited at some future time when the company strategy may have changed. In addition, it becomes a great source of ideas for future innovation challenges as the ideas may fit the new challenge objectives.

Combining ideas is another area that requires some special attention. Through the disposition process, we identify ideas that can be combined. But it is important to be careful to only combine ideas that truly are the same. If two ideas are similar but do in fact have some subtle differences, it may be best to leave them separate and give them both the label of proceed. Combining is only necessary at this point when the ideas truly are the same.

Here is an example of two ideas that, although they look similar, are in fact two separate ideas and should not be combined:

1   Provide Segways in the outer parking lot that students can ride to campus and return staff take back

2   Trolley cart service from the outer parking lot with students hired as drivers to offer more on-campus jobs

These two ideas seem similar because they both provide a solution for students to get from the outer parking lot to campus. But they are quite different solutions that should be both entered into the tournament to be evaluated.

Also, in the combination process, we want to make sure that each idea remains a single, distinct solution. We don't want one headline to offer two different solutions. In later rounds of the tournament, multiple ideas may get combined into a single concept, but at this point we want a slate of pure ideas that each offer a distinct solution.

INTERNAL IDEA EVALUATION

Now that we have a clean set of ideas ready to enter the tournament, an internal evaluation may be conducted on any ideas for which there is concern regarding whether they can technically proceed. This would include cases where there is a question regarding legal, compliance, or other issues that would take the idea off the plate (and send it to the archive). Since the bias is to let ideas proceed, this is not a thorough investigation of the idea but rather a quick check to see if the idea grossly violates any law or regulation or other barrier to potential implementation.

Now we have reached the end of round 1 and we have the tournament entrants available to share.

ROUND 2—IDEA VOTING AND CHAMPIONS DRAFT

In round 2 we share the cleaned set of ideas with a large cross-functional team. Often this will include everyone who participated in idea generation. This is the first opportunity to let the team judge the ideas. At this point, I like to allow the team to participate in two exercises: idea voting and the champions draft.

IDEA VOTING

Idea voting is just a simple voting process in which each team member can cast votes for a fixed number of ideas, usually ten or twenty at most. I always allow the opportunity for voters to spread their votes as they see fit. If a voter likes one idea more than any other, they can give that idea multiple votes as long as they don't use more than the total allotted votes. Oftentimes, an initial round of voting may have been conducted at the end of a brainstorming session. I like to provide that opportunity for closure and group satisfaction after a day-long session. But since those ideas are not cleaned and dispositioned, I always conduct the voting again through this round 2 exercise.

Note that it is also important to have a methodology in place in which the voting can be conducted blind to avoid bias and groupthink.

CHAMPIONS DRAFT

Voting can be very useful in identifying some early leading candidates. But I'm most concerned at this point about ideas that receive few or no votes. Several years ago, I realized that it was possible at this point to make a classic mistake in the tournament by losing a great idea very early on simply because the masses couldn't see the vision. As a solution, I added the champions draft in this round of the tournament. In the champions draft, I allow each person participating in the evaluation to champion one idea if they feel passionately about it. An idea that receives the champion label cannot be cut from tournament in the early rounds. This allows the person drafting the idea to have time to make the case for the idea and enable others to see the vision.

In adding the champions draft to the idea tournament, I was inspired by the book *Blink* by Malcolm Gladwell.[3] In *Blink*, Gladwell describes how experts in a field can often use a combination of their senses and experience to draw a correct conclusion without the need for empirical evidence. In this manner, I posit that employees in a company—especially those with a long tenure—may have a strong sense regarding the potential success for a new idea. And we don't want to lose that idea simply because the majority don't have that experience.

At the end of round 2, I typically will post the first set of idea rankings. This is another attempt to add to the spirit of the tournament approach and keep participants engaged and excited about the process. The rankings at this early stage are highly subjective and open to debate. But it is precisely that debate that I wish to foster. When participants come to work each day, I want them to be thinking about the idea tournament and how they can make the case for their favorite ideas.

In addition to posting the initial rankings, I also try to reduce the number of ideas in the tournament to about one hundred at the end of round 2. While the bias is still for ideas to proceed at this point, it is advisable to reduce to a more manageable set in advance of round 3. Thus, ideas with no votes and no champion label may be sent to the archive at the end of round 2. If you can not reduce to one hundred ideas at this point, that is okay; it simply means that you will have a larger task to conduct in round 3.

ROUND 3—IDEA SCORING

Round 3 is designed to be another fun and engaging exercise for a broad cross-functional group of employees. One or more exercises are introduced to the group that require employees to think about the ideas and rate them on various criteria. Ideally, the criteria are agreed upon prior to the exercise by either the cross-functional group or, even better, by senior stakeholders.

When referring to senior stakeholders I mean those senior leaders who have the authority to make the decisions on which ideas will be funded at the end of the tournament and move to the back end of innovation. Obtaining input on idea-scoring criteria is an excellent way to have a simple engagement point for the senior stakeholders at this early stage of the tournament.

The advantage of internal scoring exercises conducted by a broad cross-functional team is that they provide a way to help narrow down ideas which everyone views as an objective methodology. This helps foster acceptance for those ideas that proceed in the tournament.

The nature of the exercises can vary. I encourage innovators to explore different methods of scoring ideas or even create their own exercises. The next reading in this book provides two examples of scoring exercises that can be used. My personal favorite is the second exercise in the next reading which is titled, "Kesselring." I more commonly refer to this as an idea scoring matrix. I usually implement it by working with the team, or the senior stakeholders, to identify three to five criteria. My preference is to have at least one criteria focused on the customer experience, one focused on feasibility, and one focused on revenue generation. Other commonly used criteria would be cost, timing, "game-changing" potential, and ability to sustain a competitive advantage.

The key to making the exercises work is to have the individual employees conducting the scoring exercise to be fully engaged. To ensure engagement, I suggest making the scoring exercise easy to do and not too long. For example, you can offer an employee the opportunity to score twenty ideas as opposed to the daunting task of scoring one hundred or more. If they would like to score more, that is fine. But if you assign them too many, they may suffer from respondent fatigue. We want to make sure anyone participating in the exercise is giving it their full attention so that there is high data integrity.

Another way to conduct the scoring is to make it a group exercise, not an individual one. This has the benefit of making the exercise more enjoyable for the participants. It also enables debate about the scores, which is healthy at this point in the process.

It is also important to ensure the exercise is conducted in a standardized manner. When providing a rating score for an idea on a specific criterion, everyone should be applying the rating scale the same way. To help ensure standardization, I encourage those devising the exercise to be extremely explicit in defining the scales. If the highest score to be given is a 5, there must be a commonly applied definition of what constitutes a 5.

One more option when you have a large number of ideas to score is to divide the exercise by criteria. This enables you to assign subject matter experts to rate each idea by the criteria for which they are the authorities. For example, the customer experience team could rate each of the ideas on just the customer experience metric, while the operations team could rate each idea on just the feasibility metric.

During round 3, I will again post the top idea rankings and seek debate on the rankings. At the end of round 3, we will use the scoring exercise results and the debate on the rankings to narrow down the field again, usually to the fifty to seventy-five ideas range.

ROUND 4—CONSUMER QUICK EVALUATION

Round 4 is the first of several opportunities to partner with consumers in the tournament process. The consumer quick evaluation is just as it sounds. I take the headlined ideas and run them by consumers and essentially get a thumbs-up or thumbs-down rating. This is not a thorough evaluation of the idea; rather, it is just a way to get an additional data point on a large number of ideas at a relatively early stage in the tournament. A high rating will help keep an idea in the tournament. A low rating will give us data for consideration regarding whether the idea will make the cut for the next round.

Rarely have I ever implemented all of the consumer testing options in this and subsequent rounds, simply because they add time and cost to the tournament that few clients are willing to incur. However, that does not hold me back from recommending these steps. My belief is that consumers should be brought in at strategic points to provide input to the innovation process. Appropriate input from consumers is critical to ensuring success at launch when large amounts of money are being invested and the cost of failure is high. At this point, the expense of getting feedback from consumers is tiny by comparison, so skipping any of the consumer steps is shortsighted.

At the end of round 4, I am looking to cut the number of ideas remaining in the tournament to somewhere between twenty and fifty. The total number depends on the how much we are prepared to invest in the concepts in round 5.

ROUND 5—CONCEPT WRITING

Round 5 is a transformation point in the tournament. This is where ideas graduate to become concepts. A concept statement is a detailed description of the idea written in consumer language. The concept statement describes specifically how the idea works and demonstrates the benefit to the consumer. The ultimate purpose of the concept statement is to get detailed feedback from consumers to ensure we are on the right path and get an assessment of the potential demand for the new product or service.

Below is a whimsical concept I have written to provide an example of the format I like to use for drafting concept statements:

TIME CHANGER

Have you ever wished you could travel back in time and fix or change something?

Introducing Time Changer, the world's first personal time machine. Time Changer is an acceleration chamber that fits neatly underground in your backyard in just a twelve-foot-diameter space. It accelerates you faster than the speed of light, thus taking you back to the time of your choice. Now you can take back those words you wish you had not said to your ex-spouse. Or, invest in Apple stock before its 3000 percent increase.

So, don't waste time. Order your Time Changer and, today only, you'll receive $500 off installation. Or, wait until tomorrow and then you use your neighbor's Time Changer to go back in time and take advantage of this one-time offer!

Writing concept statements is an important task that must be done well. A poorly written concept statement will not resonate with consumers. As a result, I suggest hiring copywriters or leveraging the company's marketing or advertising department to write the concepts. Alternatively, creative individuals on the innovation team may be able to write the concepts.

Concept writing is also a time where the idea can be modified. Research on how the idea can be delivered may be done to ensure the concept makes sense and appeals to consumers, and thus some elements of design begin to enter the process. This is also an opportunity to combine two or three similar ideas into a single concept statement. This is only advisable if the ideas being combined are similar or complementary. We may also find that some ideas simply don't translate well into a concept. Thus, there is an opportunity to further reduce the field of ideas remaining in the tournament.

It is also advisable to create rapid prototypes at this stage if the cost of producing prototypes is low and it is feasible to test the prototypes with consumers. Rapid prototypes do not need to be actual working models of the new product or service. They can be as simple as an animated video that describes the concept or, for an online service, it could be a web page that enables consumers to have a limited interactive experience (but with no actual fulfillment taking place).

ROUND 6—CONCEPT CLARITY TESTING

Once concepts are written, it is critical to test the concepts for clarity. We must be confident that consumers will understand the concepts prior to the subsequent rounds where relatively expensive consumer research is conducted.

The simplest way to conduct the clarity test is to ask members of the cross-functional team to read the concepts and provide feedback. If our own employees don't understand the concept, then we know it requires a rewrite.

I also encourage team members to informally ask friends and family to review the concepts. If this raises intellectual property concerns, then nondisclosure agreements can be provided.

In addition, I encourage requesting senior stakeholders to review the concepts. This is the second time I generally seek to engage senior stakeholders in the tournament. And this is a critical stage. At this point, we have perhaps twenty to fifty concepts remaining in the tournament. If the number is on the lower side, it is certainly not too early in the process to start getting feedback from senior stake-holders. By asking them to review the concepts, we will find out if any concepts are considered off strategy and should not proceed in the tournament. Once again, the bias is always for ideas, and now concepts, to proceed, so it is important to share that spirit with the senior stakeholders. But a costly mistake can be avoided at this point if senior stakeholders have specific feedback regarding the nature or the removal of some concepts before investments are made in taking them to consumer research.

Finally, budget permitting, I recommend a brief round of online customer focus groups to allow consumers to read the concepts and ensure they are clear. This is not an in-depth review of the concepts, so several concepts can be shared in one online group. The output we are seeking is simply whether consumers understand the concept, and if not, what parts need to be clarified.

ROUND 7—CONCEPT DEVELOPMENT WITH CONSUMERS

In round 7 we seek to find out what consumers like and dislike about the concepts and where they see opportunities for improvement. We implement this as part of an iterative development process. Immediately after receiving initial consumer feedback, we modify the concepts and retest them with the next set of consumer focus groups and in-depth interviews. Often these cycles take place within the same day.

This is very similar to the build/test/refine/repeat approach popularized by design thinkers and lean innovation experts, notably Eric Reiss, author of *The Lean Startup*.[4] However, we are doing this with simple concept statements to gain some of the ben-efits of the design thinking/lean innovation process at an earlier, and less costly, stage of the innovation process.

One of the most exciting and fulfilling moments in my career at Bank of America came during a lengthy road trip testing new concepts. Traveling with a group of re-searchers, copywriters, and product development managers, we camped out in focus group facilities. In the course of many long days, we engaged consumers with our concept statements and then modified the concept statements between sessions. This iterative approach to building concepts with consumer feedback enabled us to transform one of the concepts by leveraging a fresh consumer insight we had gained. This led directly to a highly successful new service launch.

Concept development with consumers will also enable us to reduce the field in the tournament again. Concepts that simply don't resonate with consumers after multiple opportunities become candidates to cut and send to the archive. And this becomes a subject for debate as the rankings are updated and the top concepts begin to take shape.

ROUND 8—QUANTITATIVE DEMAND TEST

The quantitative demand test is a consumer research survey in which the remaining concepts are exposed to consumers and a standard battery of questions are posed. The purpose of this round is to help us quantify the potential success the new product or service might have in the market.

This can be a relatively expensive market research effort, and as a result the number of concepts taken through the test will often be limited by budget constraints. Typically, I advocate taking about twenty concepts through this type of testing, but I have done so with as many as fifty.

Since the goal is to predict market potential, it is necessary to obtain a statistically reliable number of completed surveys per concept. Ideally, the number should be at least 300 as this offers a reasonably small 6 percent margin of error on survey response data (assuming a random sample is used and data integrity is strong).

The key question to ask in the survey is whether the respondent would personally be likely to purchase the new product or service. Additional questions are helpful to further understand the genuine appeal of the concept to the consumer and whether it solves a problem or makes it easier to achieve a desired outcome. And several diagnostic questions should also be added so that the data can be viewed by various segments of the population.

Results from the survey can be used to develop a simple business case for the concept. They can also validate key assumptions necessary to prove a market exists for a concept or that it can be profitably delivered to consumers.

The results of the quantitative consumer test become the most important information about the concept in defining the final concept rankings. And several concepts may be cut from the tournament if their performance is poor in this round.

Ideally, I like to end round 8 with ten to twenty concepts remaining in the tournament.

ROUND 9—STAKEHOLDER PRIORITIZATION OF TOP IDEAS

The final two rounds of the idea tournament involve the senior stakeholders. At large companies there are often several senior stakeholders, and thus it is important to first engage them individually before bringing them together in the last round for the decision on the "final few," or in other words, the winners of the idea tournament. To reiterate, by senior stakeholders I'm referring to the people within the company who are responsible for making final approval decisions regarding which concepts will be funded and move on to the back end of the innovation process.

Briefing the senior stakeholders individually and seeking their input on which concepts should be selected prior to a formal meeting with all of them together has several benefits. First, it provides an opportunity to immerse each stakeholder in the concepts and have them think about them. Second, by voting individually, the senior stakeholders are not swayed by any groupthink, and they have an opportunity to consider their position on each concept prior to the final meeting in round 10. Third and most important, it helps make the final meeting in round 10 more productive. Prior to inserting this step in the tournament process, I had found the final stakeholder review (round 10) to be a difficult meeting to manage. And often we could not get through an initial review and voting for all the concepts. By capturing the voting ahead of time, the final stakeholder review meeting becomes a much more manageable and efficient session.

The voting in this round is a simple thumbs-up or thumbs-down. Stakeholders can vote for as many concepts they wish to continue. Final budget constraints will determine which concepts are actually funded. I also ask each stakeholder to identify a concept they would champion. And no concept can win the idea tournament without having a champion. This is important because without an identified champion, a concept is unlikely to have downstream support in the back end of innovation when the concept is designed and developed.

ROUND 10—FINAL STAKEHOLDER REVIEW

The final round consists of a meeting with the senior stakeholders in which we facilitate a debate regarding which concepts should be selected as one of the final few winners of the idea tournament. Since all the senior stakeholders have reviewed and voted on the concepts in round 9, we can begin the meeting by sharing the voting results and seeking agreement on the winning ideas.

There is no need to have only one winner. Budget permitting, there can be multiple winners. The important point is that for each idea tournament winner we must have sufficient reason to believe that the concept will be successful in the market based on the entire evaluation up to this point. The senior stakeholders then collectively cast the final consensus vote for or against each concept. I also strongly encourage requiring that each winning idea have one senior stakeholder who agrees to sponsor the idea through the back end of innovation. This helps ensure that tournament winners will have the required resources for back end of innovation activities.

CREATING AN IDEA TOURNAMENT FOR YOUR ORGANIZATION

I constantly revisit all aspects of the idea tournament process, and I have never run an idea tournament more than once in the exact same manner. I customize the process to meet with time and budget constraints of the clients and stakeholders. And I continually think about and search for new methods to improve the process. I would advise anyone that is tasked with evaluating a large number of ideas to use the steps presented here as suggestions and to create an idea tournament as you think it will best fit the needs of your organization.

SUMMARY

Idea tournaments are a great way to take the tedious task of evaluating hundreds or thousands of ideas and turn it into an exciting and engaging experience for a large team of participants. At the same time, idea tournaments can vastly improve how ideas are presently selected for development. By implementing the suggested steps in the idea tournament process, you gain many benefits, including:

- A set of ideas that are unique solutions and fit with company strategy
- Consumers understand the ideas and see value in them

- Large cross-functional groups of employees support the ideas
- Stakeholders are committed to the implementation of the top ideas

I hope you have the opportunity to implement an idea tournament in your organization and experience the thrill of identifying and implementing the final few.

NOTES

1. Mitch Ditkoff, "50 Great Quotes on Ideas," *Innovation Excellence*, http://innovationexcellence.com/blog/2010/11/15/50-great-quotes-on-ideas/.

2. Christian Terwiesch and Karl T. Ulrich, *Innovation Tournaments: Creating and Selecting Exceptional Opportunities* (Boston, MA: Harvard Business Press, 2009).

3. Malcolm Gladwell, *Blink: The Power of Thinking without Thinking* (New York: Back Bay Books, 2007).

4. Eric Ries, *The Lean Startup: How Constant Innovation Creates Radically Successful Businesses* (New York: Crown, 2011).

READING 14: QUESTIONS FOR THOUGHT

- What do you think are the most important steps in evaluating ideas when a company or organization is making decisions on which items it should invest in for growth?
- In addition to the methods in the reading, how else might you consider evaluating ideas to ensure optimal selection for the organization?
- Thinking about an organization that you have been a part of, which of the methods for evaluating ideas do you think would be the most difficult to implement? Why?

SCREENING AND DEVELOPMENT TOOLS

The following reading is another short excerpt from the book *The Idea Agent: The Handbook on Creative Processes* by Jonas Michenak and Andréas Breiler. In the reading, two simple methods are prescribed for rating ideas against agreed-upon criteria. In this manner, all ideas can be objectively measured and thus enable organizations to make rational decisions on which ideas to move forward to the stages of design and development.

The advantages of these methods are that they can be conducted without taking up vast amounts of time and resources. In addition, they can be conducted either in groups or as an individual exercise and then shared with the larger cross-functional team. By enabling lots of employees from different parts of the organization to take part in idea evaluation, you gain some of the same desirable benefits derived from including diverse groups of employees in idea generation. These include incorporating a range of viewpoints and leveraging an array of internal expertise. In addition, when the opportunity to participate in the exercise is offered to a large number of employees, it fosters a feeling of inclusivity in the innovation process.

SCREENING AND DEVELOPMENT TOOLS

BY JONAS MICHANEK AND ANDRÉAS BREILER

THE FOUR-FIELD MATRIX

The Four-Field Matrix is a method used to rank the usability of ideas and is probably the most common of all the screening and evaluation methods. Nine- or 16-field matrices are also frequently used to achieve a greater differentiation and to increase opportunities to apply more values on the various axes. It is important to emphasize that this should not only be seen as a placement exercise, but one that enables you to transfer (and enrich) as many ideas as possible into the optimum fields.

STEP BY STEP

1. Carefully think through, or ask the project owner, which parameters to apply for evaluating your ideas using the Four-Field Matrix. Typical parameters are: risk, realizability, cost, or level of innovation (see p 77). Select two parameters and allocate two assessment levels to them—for example, high risk and low risk, or high innovation level and low.

2   Draw the matrix on a whiteboard or a large sheet of paper with four fields of equal size in a large square (see Figure 15.1). Write the parameters next to their respective fields.

3   Introduce the exercise and explain why you have chosen these particular parameters. What is your purpose for evaluating the ideas using these parameters?

4   Let team members place ideas in the matrix fields that they consider most appropriate. The best effect is achieved if this is done in groups by individual idea, but if time is short it can be done individually.

5   When all the ideas have been placed in the matrix, try to ensure that they've been accurately assessed. Does the team agree on the placement of ideas—in other words, the assessment of ideas—in the matrix? If results are acceptable, then it's time to advance the best ideas to the next stage of the process, but you usually need to apply two or three matrices to pick out the best ideas based on your criteria.

Our example is based on the focus area: "How could a 24-hour service for a county authority be organized?"

The authority's strategy was to rapidly realize a concept for 24-hour servicing of its citizens. The most important parameters for idea assessment were therefore: Will the service be accessible 24 hours a day? How long will it take for the authority to create it?

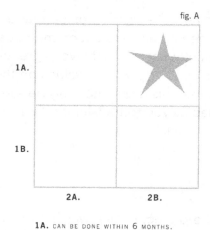

1A. CAN BE DONE WITHIN 6 MONTHS.   2A. CAN'T BE ACCESSED 24 HOURS A DAY.

1B. WILL TAKE MORE THAN 6 MONTHS TO DO.   2B. CAN BE ACCESSED 24 HOURS A DAY.

Figure 15.1

6   If results are unsatisfactory—in other words there are too few ideas placed in the optimum field in the matrix—then it's essential to examine the existing ideas and try to enrich and advance them on the basis of the selected criteria to enhance their quality (fig. B). This is done most effectively through discussions in small groups.

SITUATION

The Four-Field Matrix is a technique that is used to pick out the ideas that are most relevant to the focus area and the strategy of your organization. It's a common method for processing and developing a large number of ideas quickly and assessing them accurately.

RESULT

An idea map that provides a good overview and a relevant assessment of ideas and concepts. However, to do your ideas justice, you should apply several matrices with contrasting axes. The method also develops ideas from a "Post-it level" to a more tangible level.

PARTICIPANTS
1–8.

TIMEFRAME

5 minutes of introduction + a minimum 25 minutes in groups. Can last several hours depending on the number of ideas and how much focus is put on idea development.

ENVIRONMENT

A large wall space with a large sheet of paper or a whiteboard on which to draw the matrix.

MATERIALS

The Four-Field Matrix requires the use of Post-its or an abundant supply of scotch tape. Large numbers of pens and large sheets of paper should be made available to allow room for idea development.

KESSELRING

In product development contexts, a wide variety of screening tools have been used through the years. One of the most well known is Kesselring from 1951. It consists of a table with a number of defined selection criteria on one axis and ideas or concepts on the other. Kesselring has inspired a number of followers, among others Pugh's concept selection matrix from 1990 and Ulrich and Eppinger's model for concept selection from 2000.

To achieve success with such an advanced idea evaluation matrix requires investing time in discussing and defining the criteria that will form the basis of your proposed selection. If you choose the more advanced model (see model B on the next page), these criteria must also be weighted before the criteria selection process is complete.

STEP BY STEP

1 Begin by describing the ideas so that your team is fully aware of what they'll be assessing.

2 Define your criteria. Usually there'll be some criteria that you've applied previously in four- or nine-field matrices and these should obviously be applied here as well. This method often produces new, more detailed criteria that you, in collaboration with the project owner, have kept in reserve from start up or during the idea process.

3 If you choose model B, weight your criteria internally.

4 Assess your ideas in relation to the parameters and document the results in the table. A figure-based points system is most common, but you can also use pluses and minuses, or different color-coding systems.

5 Try to summarize or form an impression of the best ideas.

6 If the central issue or need is very important, or if the ideas are not of sufficiently high quality, try to develop their weak points.

MODEL A

	IDEAS AND CONCEPTS		
	Idea A Battery	**Idea B Combustion**	**Idea C Solar cell**
Selection criteria	Points	Points	Points
Development resources	3		
Market potential	4		
Safety	2		
Consumer convenience	5		
Ease of production	2		
Possible add-on products	1		
Quality assurance	4		
Total points	21		
Ranking	1		
Continue with idea? Y/N			

MODEL B

IDEAS AND CONCEPTS							
		Idea A Battery		Idea B Combustion		Idea C Solar cell	
Selection criteria	Weighting	Points	Weighted value	Points	Weighted value	Points	Weighted value
Development resources	15%	3	0.45				
Market potential	25%	4	1				
Safety	10%	2	0.2				
Consumer convenience	15%	5	0.75				
Ease of production	10%	2	0.2				
Possible add-on products	10%	1	0.1				
Quality assurance	15%	4	0.6				
Total points			3.3				
Ranking			1				
Continue with idea? Y/N							

READING 15: QUESTIONS FOR THOUGHT

- Think about an organization you are currently or have been a part of. What do you think would be some criteria that would make sense to use in evaluating ideas for that organization? Why?

- Why do you think these methods of evaluating ideas can help lead to optimal idea selection?

- The methods in the reading for evaluating ideas could be characterized as being highly analytical. What do you think are the advantages and disadvantages of using analytical methods for evaluating ideas?

DESIGNING NEW PRODUCTS & SERVICES

Once the evaluation of ideas is complete and ideas have been selected for funding, the next phase of the innovation process begins. This is often called the back end of innovation. In the earlier front end of innovation, we are working with insights, ideas, and concepts. Essentially, we are just working with words. Although investments are being made in conducting consumer research and perhaps some concept prototyping, relatively large amounts of money are not being spent in the front end of innovation. This all changes when we enter the back end of innovation. We now have our big ideas that we believe in, that we are placing our bets on, and we are ready to begin designing, crafting, and ultimately developing the ideas into products and services for commercial launch.

Designing new products and services is a critical part of innovation. Funds are being spent and the risks are high as new product and service success rates are notoriously low. But, companies that implement a rigorous and well-planned design phase can mitigate those risks. It is also important to have a culture in place that embraces innovation principles that are often the antithesis of how businesses tend to operate in America. The notions of business experimentation, rapid prototyping, and fast failure run counter to the just do it approach and short-term-results orientation that many businesses operate under.

The two readings in this chapter focus on the business philosophy known as design thinking. In the first reading, design thinking is introduced via a profile one of the world's leading design firms, IDEO. The second reading in the chapter shares insights on how design thinking can be more effectively implemented in businesses that do not presently exhibit a culture of innovation.

DESIGN THINKING AND INNOVATION AT IDEO

The term *design thinking* has become widely prevalent in the field of innovation. Accordingly, a book about business innovation must explain this concept, which carries a bit of mystique and intrigue. The term design thinking and the philosophy behind it was popularized in the last two decades by David Kelley of the iconic design firm IDEO. Kelley, his firm IDEO, and the concept of design thinking reached national prominence in profile segments that appeared on ABC's *Nightline* and CBS's *60 Minutes*.

In the next reading, the authors provide a fascinating history and behind-the-scenes look at the process and principles of design thinking. The article begins with a brief history of IDEO, often referred to as the most successful design firm in the world, before segueing into a description of design thinking. The article details the design thinking process at IDEO, which includes five steps:

- Observing product usage
- Ideating
- Developing prototypes
- Refining prototypes
- Implementing the design solution

The end of the article offers a description of the unique work environment at IDEO. The company shuns traditional hierarchy and organizes work in teams. The office space itself is open to facilitate maximum collaboration. All these characteristics are consistent with the design thinking frame of mind.

The authors Vivek Gupta and A. Harish have published dozens of business research articles for the IBS Center for Management Research.

DESIGN THINKING AND INNOVATION AT IDEO

BY **VIVEK GUPTA AND A. HARISH**

"Design thinking is an approach that uses the designer's sensibility and methods for problem solving to meet people's needs in a technologically feasible and commercially viable way. In other words, design thinking is human-centered innovation."[a]

—**Tim Brown, CEO, IDEO, in February 2010.**

"I haven't seen anything like them before. They're creative and strategic, eclectic, and passionate. They're cool but without attitude."[b]

—**Tom Wyatt, President, Intimate Apparel Group**[c]**, in May 2004.**

---

a www.ideo.com/thinking/approach, Accessed on February 21, 2010.

b "The Power of Design," www.businessweek.com, May 17, 2004.

c The Intimate Apparel Group is a subsidiary of the Warnaco Group. The Warnaco Group was founded in 1874 and was one of the leading apparel brands in the world as of 2009. Warnaco sold its products under several brands including Calvin Klein, Speedo, Chaps, Warner's, and Olga.

INTRODUCTION

In October 2009, IDEO Inc (IDEO), a California-based design consultancy company, announced that it had won four SparkAwards[d] for its designs. The awards IDEO won were for its innovative design solutions developed for a financial services firm, a healthcare firm, a social awareness program, and its own intranet application. Later, in November 2009, IDEO was selected by the US White House to provide design solutions to strengthen the American civil service. The company was also chosen by the Iceland government to help it come out of a financial crisis[e] and by WK Kellogg Foundation to improve elementary education[f]. According to industry experts, IDEO's capability and innovative approach to solving issues that ranged from product design to service design were the reasons for its being selected for these prestigious projects.

Founded in 1991, IDEO was considered as the most successful design consultancy firm in the world. According to *Business Week*, it had received more design awards than any other design consultancy till 2009. IDEO had received more than 300 awards at various design competitions and events since its inception. The company had over 1000 patents to its credit and had designed solutions for over 4000 clients. In March 2009, *Fast Company* placed IDEO 10th in the list of most innovative companies in the world. It also said that IDEO had served 24 of the top 25 companies on the list of most innovative companies in the world.

IDEO had been consistently providing innovative solutions to its clients from several industries like healthcare, FMCG, hospitality, financial services, automobiles, and even charitable institutions. The company believed in a human centered design[g] where it focused on designing solutions that provided the user with better experience and utility. IDEO's strength was its workforce, which came from diversified backgrounds,

---

d   Spark is a community of designers and creative people. It is driven by the principle that design can make significant, positive changes in the world. The Spark Awards competition was created in 2001 to promote designs and the work of designers and encourage people to explore their creativity. It is the world's first participatory design awards competition where designers from all the communities of the world, from design experts to amateurs, can participate.
e   Iceland faced a financial crisis in 2008–09 when the top three banks in the country collapsed because of their failure to refinance their short-term debt and the run on deposits by their customers. The crisis involved a fall in the Iceland's currency value, and stock markets losing over 90% of their market capitalization. Iceland's stock index OMX Iceland All-Share Index GI (OMXIGI) with a base value of 1000 as on base date of December 31, 1997, touched a peak of 3502.48 on July 18, 2007, and fell to a low of 165.95 on April 01, 2009. Several rating agencies downgraded Iceland's sovereign debt to below investment grade.
f   WK Kellogg Foundation partnered with IDEO to engage several stakeholders like parents, teachers, and schools that could impact children's elementary education in the US. The partnership between IDEO and WK Kellogg Foundation resulted in reports including Tangible Steps Toward Tomorrow; New Designs for Early Education, Ages 0–8; which helped the foundation in improving the elementary education and children development initiatives.
g   Human centered design is a design philosophy and a process in which the needs, wants, and limitations of the end users of a product or service are given extensive attention at each stage of the design process.

and its flat organizational structure. IDEO's years of experience in working for several industries helped it develop a strong knowledge base. Its friendly work culture helped it retain its employees and fostered innovation.

IDEO believed in open source innovation. Unlike other design firms, which kept their design processes and methodologies secret and used them as a competitive advantage, IDEO disclosed several of its business secrets. IDEO encouraged its clients to think innovatively and foster innovation in their organizations. It even conducted educative workshops for them. The company also helped its clients develop a culture that fostered innovation within their firms. Adam D. Nemer, Medical Operations Services Manager at Kaiser Permanente,[h] said, "Consulting firms usually come in, go away, and return with heavy binders that sit on the desk. With IDEO, we partner up and work side-by-side. We are internalizing their methodology to build our own culture of innovation."[i]

BACKGROUND NOTE

IDEO was formed in 1991 through the merger of four firms—David Kelley Design (DKD), ID Two, Moggridge Associates (Moggridge), and Matrix Product Design (MPD). DKD was a design firm founded by a Stanford Mechanical Engineering professor David Kelley (Kelley) in 1978. Kelley earned his electrical engineering degree from Carnegie-Mellon University in 1973. After working with National Cash Register and Boeing for three years after graduation, he pursued his Masters in the Joint Program for Design at Stanford University and graduated in 1978. DKD was the company that designed Apple Computer's first mouse in 1983.

Moggridge was a product design consultancy founded in 1969 in London by Bill Moggridge (Bill). ID Two was a design firm founded by Bill in 1979 in San Francisco and was known for designing the first Laptop Computer called GRiD Compass **(Refer to Exhibit 16.1 for Apple Computer's First mouse and Grid Compass).** Bill graduated from the Center School of Art and Design of London in 1966. He strongly followed the user-centered design process in product development.

MPD was founded in 1986 by Mike Nuttall (Nuttall), a former employee of Moggridge. Nuttall held a BA degree in Industrial Design from Leicester College of Art & Design and an MA degree from the Royal College of Art in London. Both Bill and Nuttall focused on designing hi-tech products and moved to San Francisco from London in the late 1970s as it offered more opportunities.

---

h   Kaiser Permanente is a California-based integrated managed care organization. It was founded in 1945 and had operations in more than nine states as of 2009. It was one of the largest health maintenance organizations in the US.
i   "The Power of Design," www.businessweek.com, May 17, 2004.

Prior to their merger to form IDEO, DKD, ID Two, and MPD collaborated with Microsoft to design the first dove-bar shaped mouse in 1987. DKD contributed engineering design expertise, ID Two brought in the human factor to the design, and MPD provided industrial design expertise to the dove-bar mouse design **(Refer to Exhibit 16.2 for IDEO's Case Study on dove-bar mouse).** The mouse turned out to be a highly successful product with sales crossing million units in the first two years. In 1990, DKD opened its offices in Boston and Chicago.

In mid-1991, IDEO Product Development Inc (IDEO) was formed with headquarters in Palo Alto. Tim Brown (Brown) was made Head of IDEO's San Francisco office. Through the 1990s, IDEO worked for several industries including FMCG, computer hardware, automobiles, healthcare, apparel, and real estate. Though Kelley was made the President and CEO of IDEO after it was formed, the organization followed an extremely flat organization structure.

In January 1996, Steelcase, which had been a client of IDEO since 1987, acquired a majority stake in IDEO. Steelcase allowed IDEO to operate as an independent unit. In 1999, IDEO designed a product called Leap Chair for Steelcase. This product was the result of four years of research involving 11 studies made by 27 scientists from four universities. The Leap Chair was designed to address the occurrence of back pain among the American workforce as well as to increase employee productivity.

In the year 2000, the Leap Chair received the Silver Industrial Design Excellence Award (IDEA)[j] from the Industrial Design Society of America (IDSA)[k]. In 2002, a research conducted on 200 employees found that their productivity increased by 17.8% after they started using the Leap Chair. IDEO got wide publicity in 1999 when ABC Nightline[l] challenged it to redesign a common shopping cart within four days. The company successfully redesigned the shopping cart with several user-friendly features and ABC Nightline dedicated a whole episode to broadcasting the design process that IDEO followed to design the cart.

Till the late 1990s, IDEO's projects were predominantly product based. In the late 1990s, the company entered the services design sector. In 2002, IDEO started the IDEO U (IDEO University), an initiative to teach its clients how to be innovative. IDEO U was an innovative initiative where the company provided its clients with an array of customized workshops that helped them enhance their own design process. In 2001, Brown was made the CEO and President of IDEO and Kelley became its Chairman.

---

j   IDEA is an international competition that honors design excellence in products, ecodesign, interaction design, packaging, strategy, research and concepts.

k   Established in 1938, IDSA is the world's largest, member-driven society for product design, industrial design, interaction design, human factors, ergonomics, design research, design management, universal design and related design fields as of 2009.

l   ABC Nightline is a late-night news program broadcast by the American Broadcasting Channel (ABC), a US-based television network owned by The Walt Disney Company.

In 2002, IDEO released Method Cards. Method Cards were a collection of 51 cards that explained the diverse ways by which design teams could understand the people for whom they were designing products. Method Cards provided different techniques designed using varied subjects like anthropology, psychology, biomechanics, and other disciplines that put the human being at the center of the design process. The cards were divided into four suits representing four methods of empathizing with people—Learn, Look, Ask, and Try. Each card represented a technique with a photo on one side and how IDEO had used that particular technique for a client on the other. Method Cards were made available to outsiders at a price of US$ 49. On revealing its design secrets to the outside world, Tom Kelley, General Manager at IDEO, said, "It takes a certain amount of organizational confidence to do this. You can only do it if you believe you're going to be doing even more sophisticated things."[m]

By the mid-2000s, some analysts started viewing IDEO as a rival for management consulting firms like McKinsey, Boston Consulting Group, and Bain as it was providing consumer focused solutions to its clients who based their strategies on these solutions. In many instances, IDEO even helped its clients to design their business models. In September 2007, Steelcase announced that it would be selling its stake in IDEO to its managers and that the transition of complete ownership to IDEO managers would be over within five years.

In December 2008, IDEO published the Human Centered Design (HCD) toolkit for helping NGOs and charitable institutions that were working to uplift people living below the poverty line in Africa, Asia, and Latin America. Using the HCD toolkit, these institutions could get to understand the needs of these people in new ways and find innovative and financially sustainable solutions for them. By the end of 2009, IDEO had over 550 employees working in eight offices spread across the US, the UK, and Asia.

IDEO adopted a new approach to design in the early 2000s known as design thinking. Design thinking refined IDEO's design methodology further and helped it to design a solution after taking a holistic view like how, when, where the user would use the designed solutions and what the value proposition for the user would be.

DESIGN THINKING

In 2003, IDEO decided to rename its approach as 'design thinking' as opposed to the earlier 'design'. The employees at IDEO referred to themselves as design thinkers. According to Kelley, "We moved from thinking of ourselves as designers to thinking of

---

m   Daniel H. Pink, "Out of the Box," www.fastcompany.com, October 01, 2003.

ourselves as design thinkers. We have a methodology that enables us to come up with a solution that nobody has before." Brown defined design thinking as an approach that used the designer's sensibility and methods for problem solving to meet people's needs in a technologically feasible and commercially viable way **(Refer to Figure 16.1 for Design Thinking Approach of IDEO).**

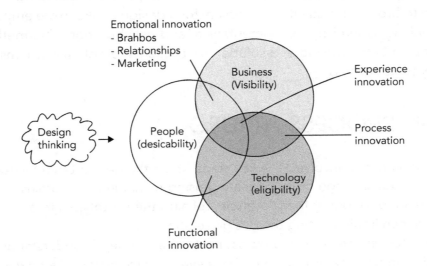

Figure 16.1. Design Thinking Approach of IDEO

Source: www.ideo.com.

The change from design to design thinking by IDEO was in line with the increased significance given to the role of design in the business world. Until the mid 20th century, the design process was mostly applied at a later stage of product development after the core job was done. The design process was used only to make the product, which had already been developed, aesthetically attractive. From the latter half of the 20th century, however, design began to play a major role from the earlier stages of product development in some industries like electronic appliances, automotive, and consumer packaged goods. The role of design till then had remained tactical and contributed little value to the product. However, from the early 2000s, companies started approaching design companies to create better ideas that met customer demands. The role of designers, which had been mostly related to physical products, changed at that time with the advent of the knowledge-based industry.

Kelley explained Design Thinking briefly in three steps—inspiration, ideation, and implementation. The Inspiration step involved getting insights from the real world by observing people; Ideation involved intensive brainstorming and prototyping that helped the designers arrive at probable solutions to a problem; and

Implementation was where the design that had been developed in the ideation phase was implemented. During the process of implementation, there were a lot of discussions held with the client organization to get the design approved and at times, the clients asked the designer to redo the work if they were not convinced about the proposed design. Hence, IDEO suggested involving the clients right from the beginning of the design process to avoid a delay in the implementation phase. According to Brown, the qualities necessary for a design thinker were empathy, integrative thinking, optimism, experimentalism, and collaboration. The methodology followed at IDEO for arriving at a solution to its clients' problem was considered to be the key to its success.

DESIGN PROCESS AT IDEO

IDEO's design process involved five key steps where the design team focused on observing the product usage history; ideating using techniques like brainstorming and body storming, developing the prototype, refining the prototypes to arrive at a final design, and then implementing the design solution.

The first step in the design process involved an in-depth understanding of the concerned product or service or sometimes even a place history like how a particular product, service, or place had been used till that particular point in time. The design team made efforts to understand how the customers had been using the product or service both by observation and customer interviews. The team conducted extensive research on the target customers to get to know both the stated and unstated expectations from the product or service.

The second step in the design process was brainstorming. In this phase, a team that was working on that particular project would meet in a specially designed brainstorming room in their IDEO office to put forward their ideas related to the project. IDEO had established a set of rules that needed to be followed in the brainstorming session. The participants in the brainstorming session used sticky notes to write their ideas and stick them on any surface in the brainstorming room for others to view them and, if possible, develop new ideas using them. A typical brainstorming session in IDEO lasted for 60 minutes and that session was considered productive if around 100 ideas were generated **(Refer to Table 16.1 for rules followed in brainstorming sessions at IDEO and Exhibit III for a visual on the brainstorming session at IDEO).**

The third phase was called prototyping. In this phase, the participants created prototypes of the product designs that came up at the brainstorming session using their choice of materials like foam, plastics, etc. Another type of prototyping used was 'body storming' where different types of customers were identified and their potential usage of the product or service was enacted. Storyboarding and scenarios were other techniques used for prototyping. Storyboards were visual depictions of a sequence of consumer uses of a particular product or service whereas scenarios were text-based stories of uses. According to IDEO, storyboarding and scenarios provided the designer with a concrete view of the design which helped in finding out issues in a product or service which otherwise would have remained hidden till the product was rolled out.

Table 16.1. Rules Followed in Brainstorming Sessions at IDEO

Defer Judgment:
Don't dismiss any ideas.
Any idea is a good idea, no matter how crazy.
Nothing can kill the spirit of a brainstorm quicker than judging ideas before they have a chance to gain legs.

Encourage Wild Ideas:
Embrace the most out-of-the-box notions because they can be the key to solutions. The whole point of brainstorming is coming up with new and creative ideas.

Build on the Ideas of Others:
No "buts", only "ands."
Sometimes people say crazy and bizarre things, like "make it on Mars", but there is some element of truth in it. When you build on the ideas of others, you might bring those crazy ideas back down to earth and make them real innovations.

Stay Focused on the Topic:
Always keep the discussion on target.
Otherwise you can diverge beyond the scope of what you're trying to design for.

One Conversation at a Time:
No interrupting, no dismissing, no disrespect, no rudeness. Let people have their say.

Be Visual:
Use yellow, red, and blue markers to write on big 30-inch by 25-inch Post-its that are put on a wall.
Nothing gets an idea across faster than drawing it. Doesn't matter how terrible of a sketcher you are.

Go for Quantity:
Aim for as many new ideas as possible. In a good session, up to 100 ideas are generated in 60 minutes.
Crank the ideas out quickly.

Source: www.greenbusinessinnovators.com.

The fourth phase was to shortlist the ideas that had been presented in the earlier phase. The design ideas were critically analyzed in this phase by the team members to find all their merits and demerits. After considering the feedback from all the team members, the best design idea would be chosen. Often, representatives of the client for whom IDEO was designing that particular design idea also participated in this phase. IDEO tried to involve its client in the design process right from the beginning so that they could also contribute their insights and experiences and also get trained on the solutions. Analysts said that involving clients in the process helped IDEO cut down on the time consuming process of client buy-in where the client had to be convinced to accept the design suggested by IDEO.

The last step in the design process was the implementation phase during which the design thinkers focused on aspects like cost, manufacturability, durability, quality control, and maintenance. Though these aspects had been dealt with in the previous phases, they were reviewed further after refinement of the prototypes in the fourth step so that the suggested design did not result in negative outcomes during its implementation by the client. If the design thinkers found any unanticipated outcomes from their design in this stage, they made the required changes to the design before delivering it to the client.

INNOVATION AT IDEO

Since its inception, IDEO had had significant expertise in designing solutions for clients from various industries. The company always focused on providing innovative solutions to its clients' problems rather than simply suggesting solutions that had been tried by other companies when faced with similar problems. Industry experts opined that IDEO did not use existing solutions as it believed that there could always be a better solution than an existing one. The company believed that each client was unique because of their business models and strategies though the problems they faced were similar to those that had already been solved by IDEO or any other consultancy firm.

IDEO had developed a four-point agenda for innovation. These included determining innovation bias, innovating experiences that made life better for people, recognizing the outcomes, and assessing the outcomes to manage innovation.

DETERMINE INNOVATION BIAS

According to IDEO, a company that tried to innovate should first determine its innovation bias. IDEO provided three types of innovation biases:

- **Human:** How might we become more relevant to people outside our existing markets?
- **Technology:** How might we leverage on this new technology in the market?
- **Business:** How might innovation allows us to grab market share from our competitors in this growing new market?

According to IDEO, the most successful innovations were those which met customer demand and hence having a human bias for innovation was critical. The technology and business factors were also important for innovation to be successful but these two factors had to be used to enhance the value proposition to the customer.

INNOVATE EXPERIENCES THAT MAKE LIFE BETTER FOR PEOPLE

After assessing the innovation bias, the next step was to find out why to innovate. IDEO opined that an ideal answer for this would be to create experiences that made life better for people. IDEO suggested that innovating companies create value; the rewards would follow. Even though it was important to be human-centered, innovations should have economic benefit. The outcome of innovation for a company was growth. Organic growth could come from creating new markets, differentiating itself in an established market, or by improving the fortunes of a declining industry using innovative products. Design thinkers had to choose one of the three options that fitted the company's growth intention. IDEO created a tool called 'Ways to Grow' to help design thinkers to identify, describe, and prioritize opportunities for growth **(Refer to Figure 16.2 for Ways to Grow).**

IDEO viewed and referred to customer segments as users rather than markets. It provided design thinkers with different cues on how to use the 'Ways to Grow' tool to innovate and grow. It suggested viewing a new product offering in different ways including how new the user was and how new one should make the offering **(Refer to Table 16.2 for IDEO's Way of Viewing New Product Offerings).**

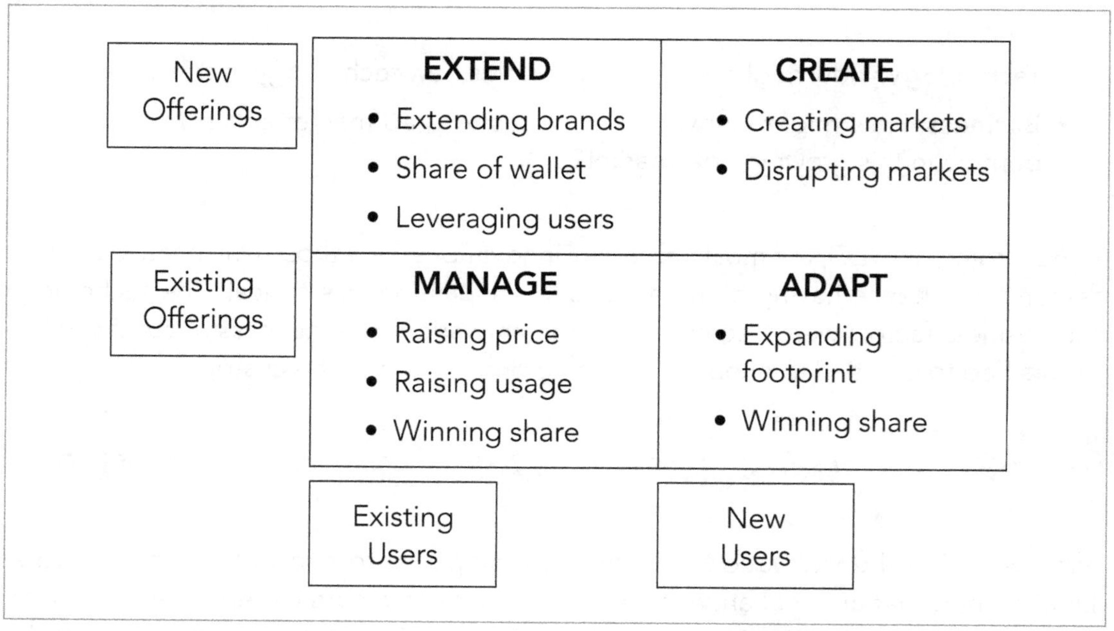

	EXTEND	CREATE
New Offerings	• Extending brands • Share of wallet • Leveraging users	• Creating markets • Disrupting markets
Existing Offerings	**MANAGE** • Raising price • Raising usage • Winning share	**ADAPT** • Expanding footprint • Winning share
	Existing Users	**New Users**

Figure 16.2. Ways to Grow

Source: www.ideo.com.

Table 16.2. IDEO—Viewing New Product Offering

How new is the user?

Contexts: Will a user experience the offering in a new context? Is the context new for the offering?

Occasions: Will a user experience the offering at a new time?

Jobs: What is a user trying to accomplish using the offering?

Mindsets: Are the user's emotions, hopes, and aspirations new to your company?

How new should you make the offering?

Value Proposition: Are there new visceral, reflective, and behavioral attributes and benefits that can be offered to the user?

Business Model: Are there new demand-side aspects of the business model like pricing, frequency of payment, or modes of ownership?

User Journey: When, where, why, and how might a user experience the offering? Which components of message, sample, trial, usage, disposal, re-use, maintenance are critical in shaping that experience?

Technology: In order to deliver on the value proposition, will we—or could we—use technologies that are new to our organization or to the people who will use them?

Source: Innovation, the IDEO Way, Point of Credit Union Research & Advice, February 01, 2008.

RECOGNIZE OUTCOMES

According to IDEO, design thinkers could use the 'Ways to Grow' tool to match the growth intention with the outcome of their innovation. Doing so would provide design thinkers with more clarity on how to proceed further in the process of innovation. IDEO recognized three basic standard outcomes of innovation—Incremental Innovation for existing users and existing offers, Evolutionary innovation for existing users and new offerings or existing offers and new users, and Revolutionary Innovation for new users and new offerings **(Refer to Figure 16.3 for Innovation Outcomes).**

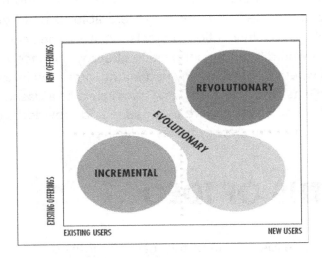

Figure 16.3. Innovation Outcomes

Source: www.ideo.com.

After identifying the innovation and growth goals, the design team discussed how best to match the resources and processes to achieve the desired innovation goal. They made efforts to allocate the right team to the right project. For instance, an incremental innovation project required execution focused people and processes whereas a revolutionary innovation project required exploration focused people and processes. IDEO's management opined that the mismatching of the growth intention and resources was one of the main reasons for the failure of innovation efforts.

ASSESS OUTCOMES TO MANAGE INNOVATION

The 'Ways to Grow' tool was used by the managers of the client company of IDEO to track, understand, and assess all the projects in the company's innovation portfolio. All the design thinkers mapped the innovation projects they were engaged to the respective quadrants in the

'Ways to Grow' tool from where the top management of the company measured the effectiveness of the company's innovation strategy. By tracking the progress of the innovation projects, they assessed the innovation strategies in different ways. They could identify several key issues like whether they were focusing more on incremental or revolutionary outcomes, whether they were able to build enough number of prototypes in evolutionary innovation projects, what the net present value of their innovation strategy would be, if the innovation strategy enhanced their brand image among users, and whether the company had learnt some new insights from its different innovation projects. The 'Ways to Grow' tool acted as a dashboard where all the innovation projects of a company were plugged in and provided a consolidated view of the company's innovation strategy to its leadership.

STRENGTHS OF IDEO

According to industry experts, one of the main strengths of IDEO was its human resources. When IDEO was formed in 1991, DKD brought in mechanical engineering expertise while MPD and ID Two brought in design expertise. Initially, the teams were a mix of mechanical engineers and designers. To them, IDEO added social scientists like psychologists and anthropologists who could understand the human related factors better. Instead of forming teams based on their expertise, IDEO followed a concept called hot teams. IDEO's hot teams were temporary teams formed for a particular project. After completion of the concerned project, the members of the corresponding hot team ungrouped and joined another team for a different project. Hot teams were usually led by a project leader. However, the project leader was not chosen based on hierarchy or seniority but according to the skill set and expertise required for executing that particular project.

IDEO's flat organization structure resulted in greater communication between the team members. IDEO had friendly employee policies and allowed its employees to choose the location and project they would like to participate in. The company encouraged its employees to work at different locations as that would provide them with ideas from the different cultures they come across.

Most of the employees at IDEO were loyal and had remained with the company ever since they had joined. IDEO's strength lay in the expertise it had developed over the years in various fields. The company used a technique called technology brokering in designing solutions where it tried to use designs developed for one industry while designing solutions for another industry.

IDEO's offices were designed to be as open as possible. Because of its open office design, teams could overhear the conversations of other teams. Often, designers working for one team helped out another team with probable solutions when they overheard the other team discussing a problem to which they themselves had developed a solution in their previous projects.

IDEO had a unique and innovative way of collecting and sharing knowledge among its design thinkers. The company observed that its design thinkers used to collect fancy and emerging tools, designs, and products and stored them in their desks. Design thinkers quite often tried to use their collections in creating prototypes for various projects. These objects varied from fabric that glowed in the dark to robots. All the offices of IDEO had tech boxes and a curator was appointed to manage them. All additions to tech boxes were updated by the respective curator on the IDEO's intranet website which could be accessed by its employees at any of the locations. Curators updated details of the products like price, manufacturer, size, weight, and a note (if available) from the design thinker and the project info where that particular product had been used. Some of the innovative products in the tech box not only provided IDEO's design thinkers with possible solutions but also inspired them with new designs. Often the tech box prevented design thinkers from wasting time reinventing something that was already available in the market **(Refer to Exhibit 16.4 for Tech Box at IDEO).**

Over the years, IDEO had developed 10 different roles an employee could play in the organization to foster innovation. The company divided these roles into three different personas—Learning Persona, Organizing Persona, and Building Personas **(Refer to Exhibit 16.5 for the details on the three personas).**

IDEO opined that different personas came in handy at different levels of a design process and often each team member would be able to play one of the different roles depending on the project, their experience, and expertise. IDEO believed that no company could remain complacent after succeeding in their innovation project and that they must continue gathering new information and learning from the changes happening in the external environment. The company said that encouraging employees with learning personas would help an organization stay abreast with the external environment.

Exhibit 16.1

Apple Computer's First Mouse and Grid Compass

Apple Computer's first mouse   **Grid Compass**

Source: http://mjspace.wordpress.com.

Exhibit 16.2

IDEO's Case Study on Dove-Bar Mouse

ID Two's human factors research suggested a small but significant change over previous versions of a mouse. It suggested moving the location of the mouse ball forward, from under the palm to under the fingertips. This enabled more precise control and resulted in measurable performance differences as compared with earlier models.

The MPD's industrial design effort examined and tested dozens of shapes in comfort and aesthetic studies that led to the famous Dove-Bar form, a significant advance over the boxy mice prevalent at that time. Extending the size of the two buttons all the way to the device's edges added to both the beauty and the functionality of the mouse. To signal its more frequent use, the left button was given a defining ridge and made slightly larger than the right. A glossy finish provided a durable and easily cleanable surface. DKD's mechanical engineers collaborated with Microsoft's Japanese partners to establish a set of component and manufacturing specifications to allow the mouse to be made to high quality standards.

The mouse also incorporated innovative manufacturing methods. The Microsoft logo was double-shot molded to avoid the inevitable fading that would occur with pad printing. Instead of the optical sensors used in previous models, mechanical sensors decreased power consumption to allow the mouse to be used with a number of computers—a separate adaptor box and multiple cables were also provided for universal connections.

Source: www.ideo.com.

Exhibit 16.3

Visual of a Brainstorming Session at IDEO

Source: http://lifetravelling.com.

Exhibit 16.4

Tech Box at IDEO

Source: http:// isoamu.exblog.jp/7216381.

Exhibit 16.5

IDEO—Three Personas

LEARNING PERSONAS

The Anthropologist is the one who observes human behavior and develops a deep understanding of how people interact physically and emotionally with products, places, and services.

The Experimenter is the one who prototypes continuously, often by employing trial and error methods. For the experimenter, processes are more important than tools and they test and retest prototypes to arrive at an efficient solution.

The Cross-Pollinator is the one who explores other industries and cultures and translates the findings to fit the unique needs of the company s/he works for. Cross-pollinators possess the skill of drawing associations between seemingly unrelated ideas.

ORGANIZING PERSONAS

The Hurdler is the one who has a knack of overcoming the hurdles and bottlenecks that come in the way of innovation. Hurdlers possess superior problem solving skills and an expertise in tackling something that has never been encountered before.

The Collaborator is the one who has the skill of bringing different groups together and helps in creating new combinations and multidisciplinary solutions. Collaborators value teams more than individuals.

The Director is the one who has a clear idea of the bigger picture and has a firm grasp on the pulse of the organization. Directors possess the ability to set the stage, target opportunities, bring out the best in the teams, and get things done.

BUILDING PERSONAS

The Experience Architect is the one focused on creating remarkable and compelling experiences to the users of a particular product. These people are experts at creating experiences that go beyond mere functionality and address the unexpressed or latent needs of the customers.

The Set Designer is the one who looks for a chance to liven up the workplace everyday. The set designers make intelligent changes to the physical work environment in the office space that helps in stimulating the creativity of innovation team members and maintain their energy levels. Set designers often make changes in the workspace to balance the private and collaborative work opportunities.

The Caregiver is the one who is an expert in delivering customer care in a manner that goes beyond mere service. The caregiver is the foundation of human-powered innovation. For instance, a nurse in a hospital who guides patients through various processes in the hospital to provide them with a comfortable experience is said to be playing the role of caregiver.

The Storyteller is the one who captures one's imagination through compelling narratives for an innovation. These people often use several modes of communications like videos, animations, and even comic strips that fit in with their skills and message.

Adapted from Ten Faces of Innovation by Tom Kelley and Jonathan Littman.

SUGGESTED READINGS AND REFERENCES

1. Andrew Hargadon, **The Best Practices of Technology Brokers**, *How Breakthroughs Happen*, April 08, 2003.

2. Daniel H. Pink, **Out of the Box**, www.fastcompany.com, October 01, 2003.

3. Brad Stone, **Reinventing Everyday Life**, *Newsweek*, October 27, 2003.

4. Bruce Nussbaum, **The Power of Design**, *Business Week*, May 17, 2004.

5. **IDEO's Collaborative Design Process**, www.businessweek.com, March 21, 2005.

6. Tim Brown, **Strategy by Design**, www.fastcompany.com, June 01, 2005.

7. Manuel Sosa and Ritesh Bhavani, **Fail Early, and Fail Often—IDEO Service Design**, www.managementtoday.co.uk, August 01, 2005.

8. By Nicole C. Wong, **The Brains behind IDEO**, www.mercurynews.com, November 07, 2005.

9. James M. Pethokoukis, **The Deans of Design**, *U.S. News & World Report*, February 10, 2006.

10. *The Ten Faces of Innovation: IDEO's Strategies for Beating the Devil's Advocate and Driving Creativity Throughout Your Organization*, January 2007.

11. Janet Wiscombe, **IDEO: The Innovation Factory**, www.workforce.com, January 2007.

12. **Innovation, The IDEO Way**, *Point for Credit Union Research & Advice*, February 2008.

13. Linda Tischler, **A Designer**, *Fast Company*, February 2009.

14. Julia Loffe, **Zen and The Art of Security**, *Fortune*, May 25, 2009.

15. Ben Hammersley, **Reinventing British Manners The Post-It way**, www.wired.co.uk , November 03, 2009.

16. Paul Solan, **Need to Supercharge Your Business? Think Like a Designer**, www.bnet.com.

17. www.ideo.com/thinking/approach, Accessed on February 21, 2010.

READING 16: QUESTIONS FOR THOUGHT

- How do you feel the design thinking approach could benefit companies or organizations that you have been a part of?

- What did you find most intriguing about the design thinking process? Why?

- What do you find most interesting about the design firm IDEO? Why?

WHY DESIGN THINKING IN BUSINESS NEEDS A RETHINK

In the previous reading we learned about the notion of design thinking. Most companies could benefit from the core principles of design thinking in which innovators start by gaining a deep understanding of and empathy for customer needs and then quickly build, test, and refine prototype solutions.

The next reading addresses a key issue in the implementation of design thinking. While the principles of design thinking make sense in theory, in practice they run into various barriers from current business methods. The authors outline these barriers and propose a set of solutions that will help enable companies to fully realize the benefits of design thinking. The root cause of the barriers is an age-old problem that innovators run up against, which is convincing people to change from the status quo. "Think different" was a mantra at Apple under Steve Jobs, but it is still not the prevailing philosophy in most parts of the business world.

Martin Kupp is on the faculty at the European School of Management and Technology based in Berlin. Jamie Anderson is a professor in strategic management at Antwerp Management School and the Lorange Institute, Switzerland. Jörg Rechenrich is an artist, a founder of Art-Thinking Consulting, and professor of innovation and creativity at the Lorange Institute, Switzerland.

WHY DESIGN THINKING IN BUSINESS NEEDS A RETHINK

BY MARTIN KUPP, JAMIE ANDERSON, AND JÖRG RECKHENRICH

To reach its full potential, the popular innovation methodology must be more closely aligned with the realities and social dynamics of established businesses.

In recent years, "design thinking" has become popular in many industries as established companies have tried to apply designers' problem-solving techniques to corporate innovation processes.[1] Key elements of the design thinking methodology include fast iterations; early and frequent interaction with customers; agile process design with less hierarchy; and a learning-by-doing approach that involves building prototypes and creating mock-ups of any kind as early as possible in the process.

Here's how design thinking initiatives are supposed to unfold in a corporate setting: A clearly defined innovation challenge is presented to a team trained in design thinking. The team conducts research to better understand the problem. Drawing on their insights, they propose a variety of solutions, start building prototypes, and in the end, identify a fresh, profitable business opportunity.

That's how the process is supposed to work—but it hardly ever does. Over the past seven years, we have helped more than 20 companies pursue

Martin Kupp, Jamie Anderson, and Jörg Reckhenrich, "Why Design Thinking in Business Needs a Rethink," *MIT Sloan Management Review*, vol. 59, no. 1, pp. 41-44. Copyright © 2017 by MIT Sloan Management Review. Reprinted with permission.

more than 50 design thinking initiatives and have found that such initiatives rarely proceed according to the textbook model. Innovation is an inherently messy process, made even messier because it conflicts in many ways with established processes, structures, and corporate cultures. Fortunately, once you understand the challenges, you can avoid the most common pitfalls.

The root of most of the problems is the disconnect between design thinking and conventional business processes. After all, most companies' successes are built on delivering predictable products by repeatable means. That means organizations almost instinctively resist bringing fuzzy, messy, and abstract vision into the equation. This antipathy toward design thinking runs deep, all the way from the C-suite to line workers. We find that employees often try to dodge design thinking assignments, shying away from the habits and mindsets the methodology requires.

The organization of the teams themselves leads to a second difficulty. The design thinking methodology calls for egalitarian, self-organized teams, but this isn't how most established large companies work. In fact, the design thinking teams we have studied tend to have clear process and project owners, usually senior managers. These managers not only supervise the design thinking project but also assign tasks to team members and are responsible for its outcome. To make things worse, these senior leaders often supervise 12 to 15 design thinking projects at a time. This maximizes the leader's time but reduces the teams' efficiency, hinders passion and commitment, and slows progress.

In many companies, four cultural factors tend to aggravate these structural limitations:

Specialization Specialization often leads to a tacit agreement that makes certain tasks the territory of certain departments. This has two effects on design thinking. First, participants from different departments often have difficulty communicating because of their very specific viewpoints. Second, many people who belong to departments that are traditionally considered less creative, such as accounting or internal audit, suffer from low levels of what management thinkers David and Tom Kelley call "creative confidence."[2] If you've never been encouraged to see innovation as part of your job and have been told that you're no good at it, you'll probably take people's word for it. This may reduce friction and make the organization function more comfortably, but it also reduces the chance of a creative spark.

Human Speed Bumps Managers in some departments (particularly legal, compliance, and regulatory affairs) tend to see their role as basically to stop things from happening. To get the most out of a design thinking exercise, people in these departments must embrace a can-do attitude and focus their creative energies on exploring how else things

THE LEADING QUESTION

What challenges do design thinking initiatives in big companies face?

FINDINGS

Organizations whose success is built on predictable operations instinctively resist fuzzy and messy innovation processes.

Many established companies punish failure, which discourages the risk-taking that design thinking requires.

Design thinking teams need a lot of autonomy to function well.

can be done. It takes a special kind of leadership to enable this supportive culture in traditionally conservative and risk-averse functional domains.

Focus on Monetary Results In projects with a high degree of novelty, the expectation should be around the amount of learning that takes place, not the result. Focusing too early on monetary results (or other metrics) can discourage creativity—and ironically, reduce the chances of a profitable long-term result.

Failure Phobia Many established companies punish failure, which discourages the risk-taking design thinking requires. In a workshop with a large consumer goods company, we asked participants to formulate hypotheses regarding consumers' buying behavior in one product category. Instead of formulating useful hypotheses, participants developed ones that were so broad and unspecific that they would be impossible to test. We soon realized that the workshop attendees were avoiding mistakes for which they could be held accountable. Unfortunately, reducing their personal risk of failure meant reducing their collective chance of success.

Our research suggests that companies need to take five steps to take full advantage of the potential of design thinking:

1. Encourage top managers to champion design thinking initiatives. We find that design thinking teams require two kinds of attention by top management: proactive and follow-up. Proactive attention comes in many forms, such as launching an initiative, taking part in the process, developing and submitting ideas, and removing obstacles. *Follow-up* attention is the energy the leader invests after the design thinking team does its work, such as pushing ideas through the organization and sometimes giving explicit feedback when ideas are not pursued. Such behaviors can help embed and sustain design thinking in established organizations.

However, the biggest limiting factor is that managers are spread far too thin. Rather than try to monitor the progress of 12 to 15 design thinking initiatives, managers are better off pursuing a single design thinking goal at a time.

2. Balance the teams. Balancing intuitive and analytical thinking is one of the biggest challenges when establishing an innovative culture. Such teams are very tricky for established organizations to manage, as it is difficult to allow people freedom while at the same time ensuring that they don't lose focus on other important business goals.

One key is for team members to recognize and appreciate the diversity of their experience and skills. For example, some members might focus more on workshop facilitation, whereas others may use their personal networks within the company to identify potential projects. The teams should include all pertinent functions, including marketing, sales, product management, and research and development.

3. Set ground rules. Design thinking teams need a lot of autonomy to function well. They should be empowered to act without getting permission for every tiny step. A good way to do this is to set minimal rules for the team, for example, by writing a list of five things they are not allowed to do, such as endanger brand perception or engage in illegal activities. Everything else, by default, they are allowed to do.

4. Integrate design thinking into product-development processes. Design thinking is often treated as yet another assignment from headquarters—just one more box to be checked. To change that perception, the teams responsible for design thinking should look more closely at their existing product-development processes. It can be helpful to integrate specific design thinking deliverables, such as early customer feedback in the problem-definition phase, larger-scale customer feedback in the market-solution phase, and prototypes and mock-ups throughout the process. Linking design thinking to innovation strategy should make it easier to measure the influence of design thinking on the quality and market fit of new products and services. More stakeholders will then see it as an integral part of product development, and not a parallel process.

5. Redefine the metrics. Because design thinking is about the early phase of the innovation process, teams should focus not on profit but on learning. By clearly defining learning outcomes through questions (such as "Why don't patients sign the consent form?"), you can then define precise hypotheses (such as "because the form is too long" or "because the language is incomprehensible"). Even if the overall project fails, the captured learning will lead you to a better question or another project.

SUPPORTING DESIGN THINKING

Too many enterprises have naively invested in training employees in design thinking methodologies, and then been disappointed when they don't see a tangible impact on innovation outcomes. Innovation is an inherently social process that involves not only inventing but also convincing people to do something in a new way. To be successful, a design thinking program must be closely linked with the organization's social dynamics. Without the right supporting mechanisms, you probably won't achieve the desired results.

Martin Kupp is an associate professor of entrepreneurship and strategy at the Paris campus of ESCP Europe. *Jamie Anderson* is an adjunct professor of strategic management at the Antwerp Management School in Antwerp, Belgium. *Jörg Reckhenrich* is an artist based in Berlin as well as a faculty member of CEIBS Zurich Institute of Business Education in Switzerland. Comment on this article at http://sloanreview.mit.edu/59113, or contact the authors at smrfeedback@mit.edu.

NOTES

1. Peter G. Rowe's book "Design Thinking," published in 1987, was the first publication to use the term. The book described a systematic approach to problem-solving used by architects and urban planners. The application of design thinking methodologies beyond architecture emerged in the 2000s; instrumental in this were works by Tim Brown and by Roger L. Martin. See P.G. Rowe, "Design Thinking" (Cambridge, Massachusetts: MIT Press, 1987); T. Brown, "Design Thinking," Harvard Business Review 86, no. 6 (June 2008): 84-92; T. Brown, "Change by Design: How Design Thinking Transforms Organizations and Inspires Innovation" (New York: HarperCollins, 2009); and R.L. Martin, "The Design of Business: Why Design Thinking Is the Next Competitive Advantage" (Boston, Massachusetts: Harvard Business Press, 2009).

2. T. Kelley and D. Kelley, "Creative Confidence: Unleashing the Creative Potential Within Us All" (New York: Crown Business, 2013).

READING 17: QUESTIONS FOR THOUGHT

- The reading mentions several corporate cultural issues that are prevalent in many organizations that inhibit or serve as barriers to design thinking processes. Which of these have you experienced in the companies or organizations you have been a part of?

- What additional cultural barriers have you experienced that might also inhibit design thinking? Why?

- Which of the suggested solutions in the reading do you think would work best in the companies or organizations that you have been a part of? Why?

- What other steps do you think companies could take that might better enable design thinking philosophies to thrive? Why?

7 IMPLEMENTING AN OVERALL PROCESS FOR INNOVATION

In the preceding four chapters we analyzed a series of individual steps that companies can take in their attempts to innovate. Now that we understand these various steps, this chapter seeks to tie them together into a coherent process for innovation. Companies can benefit immensely by having a clear and well-designed innovation process. This ensures the critical functions of identifying and implementing new products and services is managed appropriately.

We begin the chapter by introducing the most prominent innovation process, the Stage-Gate system. Variations of the Stage-Gate system have been in use by large companies around the world for several decades. Students of innovation therefore should have a grounding in this approach to managing innovation.

However, there is no single innovation process that can be labeled the right way to manage innovation. Innovation remains part art and part science. Accordingly, I have included several other readings in this chapter that suggest different processes for managing innovation. In the second reading in the chapter, we look at best practices that have been identified in managing innovation. And in the final two readings we look at methods specifically for managing breakthrough innovations as well as the mindset for how to achieve those breakthrough innovations.

THE STAGE-GATE IDEA-TO-LAUNCH SYSTEM

Robert Cooper developed the Stage-Gate system for managing new product development. His best-selling book, *Winning at New Products*, popularized the system and updated the process based on years of experience implementing Stage-Gate in many large companies. Most leading companies use some adaptation of the Stage-Gate process to manage innovation.

The following reading contains an excerpt from Cooper's book *Winning at New Products*. This reading provides a detailed overview of all the steps of the Stage-Gate system. It also provides examples of how Stage-Gate has been implemented in large companies. And it demonstrates the effectiveness of adopting an idea-to-launch system to manage innovation.

Part of the broad value of the Stage-Gate system is the clearly defined process that it brings to managing innovation. Innovation is often referred to as being "fuzzy," particularly in the early stages of the process. Since by definition innovations are new products, services, programs, or processes, they are not following the status quo for how things are managed within the company. As a result, the methods for managing innovation cannot simply leverage the existing ways of doing business. Every company, therefore, can benefit from having a process in place to manage innovation. Stage-Gate is one such process.

The basic framework of the Stage-Gate system is the notion of stages and gates, as the system's name suggests. Stages are the collection of activities that take place during a particular phase of the innovation process. Gates are setpoints in the process during which the results of the stage will be shared with a group of senior leaders who then make a go/no-go decision for the innovation to move to the next stage. This disciplined approach to managing innovation is helpful for many companies to ensure that there is proper management oversight and decision-making taking place. It also ensures that well-defined activities take place in the proper sequence.

Robert Cooper has published over one hundred academic journal articles. He is professor emeritus of marketing and technology management at the DeGroote School of Business at McMaster University and a Distinguished Fellow at the Institute for the Study of Business Markets at Penn State University.

THE STAGE-GATE®
IDEA-TO-LAUNCH
SYSTEM

BY ROBERT G. COOPER

A process is a methodology that is developed to replace the old ways and to guide corporate activity year after year. It is not a special guest. It is not temporary. It is not to be tolerated for a while and then abandoned.

—Thomas H. Berry, *Managing the Total Quality Transformation*[1]

WHAT IS STAGE-GATE?

Stage-Gate® is a *conceptual and operational map* for moving new-product projects from idea to launch and beyond—a blueprint for managing the new-product development process to improve effectiveness and efficiency. *Stage-Gate* is a system or process not unlike a playbook for a North American football team: It maps out what needs to be done, play by play, huddle by huddle—as well as how to do it—in order to win the game.

Stage-Gate is based on the premise that some projects and project teams really understand how to win—they get it![2] Indeed, *Stage-Gate* was originally developed *from research that modeled what the winning teams that undertake bold innovation projects do.*[3] But too many projects and teams miss the mark—they simply fail to perform. A closer inspection often reveals that these failed projects are plagued by missing steps and activities, poor organizational design and leadership, inadequate quality of execution, unreliable data, and missed time lines. So these teams and projects need help—help in the form of a *playbook* based on what winning teams do. *Stage-Gate* is simply that playbook.

STAGE-GATE NOW USED IN MOST LEADING FIRMS

A world-class process for product innovation, such as *Stage-Gate*, is one solution to what ails so many firms' new-product efforts.[4] Facing increased pressure to reduce the cycle time yet improve their new-product success rates, companies look to new-product processes, or *Stage-Gate* systems, to manage, direct, and accelerate their product innovation efforts. That is, they have developed a systematic process—a blueprint or playbook—for moving a new-product project through the various stages and steps from idea to launch. But most important, they have built into their playbook the many *critical success drivers* and *best practices* in order to heighten the effectiveness of their programs. Consider these examples:

> P&G's SIMPL new-product process is a *Stage-Gate* system implemented in the early 1990s—see Figure 18.1. Now in its third generation, SIMPL and related methods have been key to P&G's enormous successes in innovation in the last decade. The four-stage model was designed initially to handle internally-derived projects but has been extended to include "open innovation" projects as well.[5]
>
> 3M has traditionally had an enviable new-product track record. An innovative corporate culture and climate are often cited as 3M's secret to success. But for years 3M has also had in place various stage-and-gate systems in its businesses for managing the innovation process. Thus, creativity and discipline are blended to yield a successful new-product effort.

Corning Glass has always been a world-leading innovator, beginning generations ago with Pyrex glass and Corningware, and in more recent years, with fiber optics and glass for flat-panel displays. Corning's successes continue. What drives new products to market at Corning is the company's version of a *Stage-Gate* process, designed and installed in the early 1990s. The process has been refined and streamlined over the years, and also broadened in scope, so that today, virtually every resource-intensive project—from new or improved products through new manufacturing processes—is stage-gated.

Emerson Electric's NPD 2.0 is that firm's latest version of its stage-and-gate system, originally developed in the 1990s. "Since its introduction, Emerson New Product Development (NPD) teams have learned—quickly—that the Phase Gate process works.[6] The Phase Gate process is adapted from R.G. Cooper's *Stage-Gate®* approach which is based on large scale studies of product development practices of hundreds of international companies. The process provides a structured pathway of 'gates' to creation and product launch and beyond. 'The Phase Gate process plays to Emerson's traditional strengths of excellent execution and process,' says Randall Ledford, senior vice president and chief technology officer. 'So it's no surprise that we have learned so much from it so quickly.'"

DISCOVER	DESIGN	QUALIFY	READY	LAUNCH
Promising Consumer Proposition	Integrated Business Proposition	the Initiative	Prepare Market Launch	Execute Market Entry

Key Decision	Staff it?	Design complete? Start implementation?	Criteria met? Launch plan agreed?	Ready for launch?
Milestone	Project Establishment	Project Commitment	Launch Plan Agreement	Launch Authorization

Figure 18.1. P&G's SIMPL Stage-Gate Process Feature Five Stages and Four Gates and is Key to Driving the Firm's New Product to Market

Source: endnote 5.

Exxon Chemical began piloting a *Stage-Gate* process in its Polymers business unit in the late 1980s. So successful was the process that Exxon Chemical has rolled the method out throughout its entire chemical business, and around the world. According to the father of Exxon's Product Innovation Process, "The implementation of the PIP has probably had more impact on the way we do business than any other initiative at Exxon Chemical undertaken in the last decade." In recent years, the system has been modified and adapted to yield the company's new-generation *Stage-Gate* system.

Lego, the successful Danish toy manufacturer, replaces about one-third of its product line every year with new items—new castles, new towns, and so on. In order to accomplish this rapid introduction of new products consistently, successfully, and year after year, a process was needed. Today, Lego relies on a *Stage-Gate* new-product process to ensure that everything comes together for these many and rapid launches each year.

Stage-Gate methods work! We saw in the previous chapter the many testimonials in favor of adopting stage-and-gate idea-to-launch systems, as well as the quantitative results achieved. And the APQC best-practices study of product innovation found that having such a process was just a given. Here is an excerpt from that study:[7]

A new-product process—a "game plan" or playbook to guide NPD [new-product development] projects from idea to launch—is another much-heralded key to NPD success. By "new-product process," we mean more than just a flow-chart; the term includes all process elements—the stages, stage activities, gates, deliverables, and gate criteria that constitute a well-defined new-product process. For more than a decade, managements have been urged to design and implement such an NPD process, and they appeared to have heeded the experts. Indeed, having a well-defined new-product process is the *strongest practice* observed in the sample of businesses [in the APQC study]:

1. A clearly defined idea-to-launch new-product process: Businesses rate very high here, with 73.7 percent of businesses having such an NPD process, and only 7.6 percent lacking a process. This result is consistent with, albeit somewhat higher than, the PDMA's best-practice study, which reported 68 percent of firms claiming to have such an NPD process.

The report goes on: "Merely having a NPD process in place, however, does not separate the Best from the Worst Performers. Nonetheless, Best Performers *overwhelmingly do have a systematic new-product process*: Having such a process seems to be just a 'given' and thus a NPD process must be considered a best practice."

THE STAGES

Each stage is designed to gather information needed to move the project to the next gate or decision point. Different types of information—market, technical, operations—is important, and so the work within each stage is cross-functional: There is no "R&D stage" or "Marketing stage." And each stage is defined by the activities within it—a set of parallel and cross-functional tasks that incorporate

✓ best practices, for example, the nine vital market-related actions listed above (see p. 91),

✓ some of the success drivers, for example, quality of execution and sharp, early product definition,

✓ and the seven goals, for example, the quest for a superior, differentiated product, that we saw earlier in this and the last two chapters.

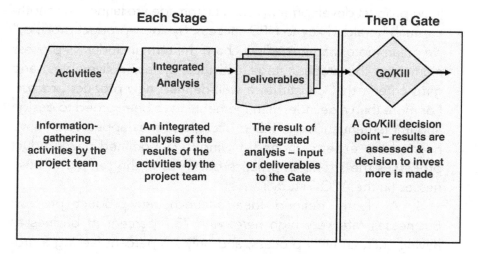

Figure 18.2. Stage-Gate Consists of a Set of Information-Gathering Stages Followed By Go/Kill Decision Gates

Source: Stage-Gate International Inc.

Some of these activities are mandatory; others are merely prescribed and highly recommended—*Stage-Gate* is a guide, not a rule book. These stage-activities are designed to gather information and drive uncertainties down. And each stage typically costs more than the preceding one: The process is an incremental commitment one.

The general flow of the typical *Stage-Gate* system is shown pictorially in Figure 18.3. The stages are:

Discovery: pre-work designed to discover and uncover opportunities and generate ideas

Scoping: a quick, preliminary investigation and scoping of the project—largely desk research

Build the Business Case: a much more detailed investigation involving primary research—both market and technical—leading to a Business Case, including product and project definition, project justification, and a project plan

Development: the actual detailed design and development of the new product, and the design of the operations or production process

Testing and Validation: tests or trials in the marketplace, lab, and plant to verify and validate the proposed new product, and its marketing and production/operations

Launch: commercialization—beginning of full operations or production, marketing, and selling

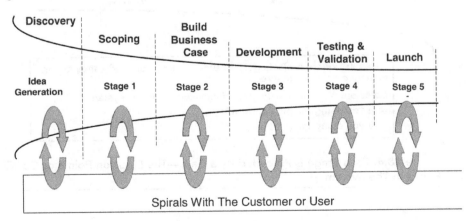

Figure 18.3. The Five Stages in The Typical Idea-To-Launch Stage-Gates System– From Discovery (Ideation) Through to Launch

Source: Adapted from Cooper, endnotes 2 & 4.

THE GATES

Preceding each stage is a gate or a Go/Kill decision point—see Figure 18.4.* The gates are the scrums or huddles on the rugby or football field. They are the points where the team converges and where all new information is reviewed. Gates serve as quality-control checkpoints, as Go/Kill and prioritization decision points, and as points where the path forward for the next play or stage of the process is agreed to.

The structure of each gate is similar (Figure 18.5). Gates consist of:

1 A set of required *deliverables*: what the project leader and team bring to the decision point (for example, the results of a set of completed activities). These deliverables are visible, are based on a standard menu for each gate, and are decided at the output of the previous gate. Management's expectations for project teams are thus made very clear.

2 *Criteria* against which the project is judged: These include readiness-check questions, must-meet or knock-out questions (a checklist designed to weed out misfit projects quickly), as well as should-meet criteria or desirable factors, which are scored and added (a point count) and used to prioritize projects.

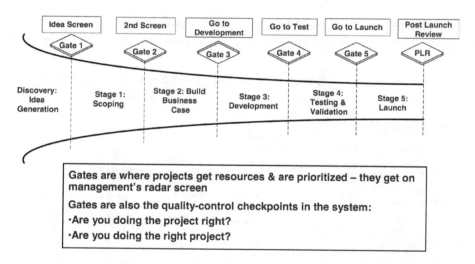

Figure 18.4. Each Stage is Preceded By a Gate—The Decision Points or Go/Kill Points in The System

---

* Strictly speaking, the gates follow the stages—gather information, then make a Go/Kill decision. But it's more practical to treat them as entrance gates—opening the door to the next stage.

3   Defined *outputs*: for example, a decision *(Go/Kill/Hold/Recycle)*, an approved action plan for the next stage (complete with people required, money and person-days committed, and an agreed time line), and a list of deliverables and a date for the next gate.

Gates are usually staffed by senior managers from different functions, who own the resources required by the project leader and team for the next stage: They are the gatekeepers.

AN OVERVIEW OF THE STAGE-GATE SYSTEM

Now for a bird's-eye look at the *Stage-Gate* system—an overview of what's involved at each stage and gate. In later chapters, we'll lower the microscope on the Discovery stage, or how to generate breakthrough ideas (Chapter 6). We then focus on the front-end or pre-development stages in Chapter 7. Chapters 8 and 9 take a close look at how to design and operate gates or decision points. And Chapter 10 focuses on the middle and back-end stages of the process. But for now, let's just have a quick walk-through of the model designed for larger new-product projects, which you can follow stage by stage in Figure 18.6.

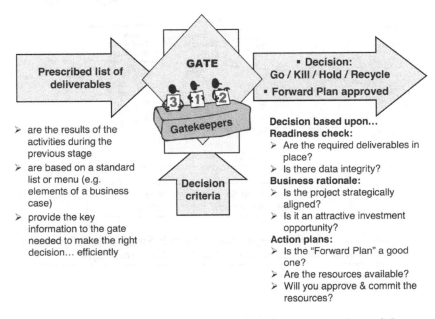

Figure 18.5. Gates Have a Common Format—Inputs, Criteria, and Output

DISCOVERY OR IDEATION

Ideas are the feedstock or trigger to the process, and they make or break the system. Don't expect a superb new-product process to overcome a deficiency in good new-product ideas. The need for great ideas coupled with the high attrition rate of ideas means that the idea-generation stage is pivotal: You need great ideas and lots of them.

Many companies consider ideation so important that they handle this as a formal stage in the process, the one we call Discovery—that is, they build in a *defined, proactive idea-generation and capture system.* Many activities can be part of the Discovery stage in order to stimulate the creation of great new-product ideas. Such activities include: undertaking fundamental but directed technical research, seeking new technological possibilities; working with lead or innovative users; utilizing VoC research to capture unarticulated needs and customer problems; competitive analysis and inverse brainstorming of competitive products; installing an idea-suggestion scheme to stimulate ideas from your own employees; scanning the outside world and employing "open innovation" to seek external ideas; and using your strategic planning exercise to uncover disruptions, gaps, and opportunities in the marketplace.

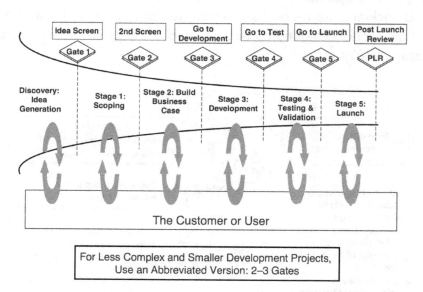

Figure 18.6. This Five-Stage Idea-To-Launch Stage-Gate® System is for Major and More Complex Product-Development Project

Source: Adapted from Cooper, endnotes 2 & 4.

GATE 1: IDEA SCREEN

The Idea Screen is the first decision to commit resources to the project: The project is born at this point. If the decision is Go, the project moves into the Scoping or preliminary investigation stage. Thus, Gate 1 signals a preliminary but tentative commitment to the project: a flickering green light.

Gate 1 is a "gentle screen" and amounts to subjecting the project to a handful of key must-meet and should-meet criteria. These criteria deal with strategic alignment, project feasibility, magnitude of opportunity and market attractiveness, product advantage, ability to leverage the firm's resources, and fit with company policies. Financial criteria are typically not part of this first screen, because so little is known, and besides, the resources to be committed are quite small at this phase. A checklist for the must-meet criteria and a scorecard (point-count rating scales) for the should-meet criteria can be used to help focus the discussion and rank projects in this early screen.

> *An example:* Exxon Chemical has implemented its PIP (Product Innovation Process), whose initial gate has a handful of key Yes/No criteria:
>
> | | |
> |---|---|
> | Strategic fit: | Does the proposal fit within a market or technology area defined by the business as an area of strategic focus? |
> | Market attractiveness: | Are the market size, growth, and opportunity attractive? |
> | Technical feasibility: | Is there a reasonable likelihood that the product can be developed and produced? |
> | Killer variables: | Do any known killer variables exist (e.g., obsolescence, environmental issues, legislative actions)? |

At this "Start Gate" meeting, project ideas are reviewed against these four criteria, using a paper-and-pencil approach: This list of must-meet criteria is scored (Yes/No), and the answers to all questions must be Yes; a single No kills the project. The gatekeepers include both technical and business (marketing) people.

STAGE 1: SCOPING

This first and inexpensive homework stage has the objective of determining the project's technical and marketplace merits. Stage 1 is a quick scoping of the project, involving desk research or detective work—little or no primary research is done here. This stage is usually done in less than one calendar month's elapsed time, and ten to twenty person-days' work effort.

A *preliminary market assessment is* one facet of Stage 1 and involves a variety of relatively inexpensive activities: an Internet search, a library search, contacts with key users, focus groups, and even a quick concept test with a handful of potential users. The purpose is to determine market size, market potential, and likely market acceptance, and also to begin to shape the product concept.

Concurrently, a *preliminary technical assessment* is carried out, involving a quick and preliminary in-house appraisal of the proposed product. The purpose is to assess development and operations (or source-of-supply) routes, technical and operations feasibility, possible times and costs to execute, and technical, legal, and regulatory risks and roadblocks.

Stage 1 thus provides for the gathering of both market and technical information—at low cost and in a short time—to enable a cursory and first-pass financial and business analysis as input to Gate 2. A preliminary Business Case is constructed here, but based on fairly uncertain or "guesstimates" data. Because of the limited effort, and depending on the size of the project, very often Stage 1 can be handled by a team of just several people—from Marketing and Technical. Consider this example of a preliminary technical and market assessment:

> *An example:* OMNOVA Solutions of Akron, Ohio, had the good fortune to uncover a new technology via fundamental research that has become the platform for a number of new-product projects. The new technology enables traditional polymers to have an extremely slippery surface, yet unlike other slippery materials, the resulting polymer retains its usual positive physical properties (e.g., abrasion resistance and toughness).
>
> The first product to be launched was vinyl wall-covering with a difference—it's a relatively low-cost, dry-erase whiteboard. Before embarking on extensive development work for this project, a preliminary assessment or scoping was undertaken. The company was already in the industrial wall-covering business, so ample in-house data on markets, sizes, and trends were available. Additionally, the project leader sought and found published

data—trade publications, reports, and so on—on the existing whiteboard market. Informal chats with some distributors revealed the pricing structure. Technical work was relatively limited at Stage 1, as fundamental research had already uncovered the technical possibility. Nonetheless a core group of scientists got together with Manufacturing people to discuss technical and manufacturing feasibility—note how early Manufacturing was involved in the project. Finally, a first-cut financial analysis was developed—based largely on guesstimates—but this sanity check revealed a huge opportunity.

GATE 2: SECOND SCREEN

The new-product project is now subjected to a second and somewhat more rigorous screen at Gate 2. This gate is similar to Gate 1, but here the project is reevaluated in the light of the new information obtained in Stage 1. If the decision is Go at this point, the project moves into a heavier spending stage.

At Gate 2, the project is subjected to a list of readiness-check questions, and also a set of must-meet and should-meet criteria similar to those used at Gate 1. Here, additional should-meet criteria may be considered, dealing with sales force and customer reaction to the proposed product, and potential legal, technical, and regulatory "killer variables," the result of new data gathered during Stage 1. Again, a checklist and scorecard facilitate this gate decision. The financial return is assessed at Gate 2, but only by a quick and simple financial calculation (for example, the Payback Period).

> *An example:* ITT Industries uses a well-crafted five-stage, five-gate product *Stage-Gate* system called VBPD.[9] The second gate, called the "Value Screen" follows the preliminary investigation, namely, the "Scoping Stage," and opens the door to a more detailed investigation, "Build the Business Case." The essence of this "Value Screen" gate is a reevaluation of the proposed project in light of the additional information gained from the Scoping Stage. The gate features a combination of must-meet and should-meet criteria. The must-meet items must yield Yes answers; the should-meet items are rated on scales—a point-count system on six questions:

1   Strategic (importance and fit)

2   Product and competitive advantage

3   Market attractiveness

4   Synergies (leverages our core competencies)

5   Technical feasibility

6   Financial reward

STAGE 2: BUILD THE BUSINESS CASE

The Business Case opens the door to product development, and Stage 2 is where the Business Case is constructed. This stage is a detailed investigation stage, which clearly defines the product and verifies the attractiveness of the project prior to heavy spending. It is also the *critical homework* stage—the one found to be so often weakly handled.

The definition of *the winning new product* is a major facet of Stage 2. The elements of this definition include target-market definition; delineation of the product concept; specification of a product-positioning strategy, the product benefits to be delivered, and the value proposition; and spelling out essential and desired product features, attributes, requirements, and specifications.

Stage 2 sees *market studies* undertaken to determine the customer's needs, wants, and preferences—that is, to help define the "winning" new product.

An example:[10] PumpSmart was an ill-fated project within the Goulds Industrial Pumps Division (U.S.) that was spawned by a single customer request. The customer had asked a Goulds' salesman: "Why don't you build an intelligent pump—one that can sense its own operating environment, and adjust its mode of operation to minimize wear and tear, minimize pump downtime, and maximize pump life?" A great idea, and it sailed through the Idea Gate and on into Development with little or no further customer research as the PumpSmart project. The final product consisted of an intelligent pump with multiple sensors located both upstream and downstream that measured pressure, flow, vibration, and temperature; these sensors were connected to a microprocessor (computer) that controlled a variable-speed motor. The pump could adjust its speed in response to different operating conditions and thereby reduce wear and maintenance.

PumpSmart was launched with great fanfare and proved to be a huge dud. The smart technology was brilliant, but the value proposition and product were weak. All was not lost, however. Sensing that the technology was indeed solid, Goulds' management had another try. By this time, however, Goulds' technical and marketing people had been through *extensive training on VoC*, and employed the technique on the new PumpSmart project. Teams of three people—from Technical, Sales, and Marketing—undertook in-depth interviews with key users, and also undertook walk-throughs at customer facilities where pumps were used.

Their conclusions: Although pump maintenance was an issue, it was not an overriding one. The customers' major point of pain was sky-rocketing electrical power costs. These pumps, often high horsepower, run flat out and consume lots of power. What the visit teams also observed was that beside each pump is a flow valve—often in the half-closed position. "That's how we control the volume or flow," explained users.

To the Goulds team, this was absurd: "It's like driving a car with your foot to the floor on the accelerator and using the handbrake to control the speed … very inefficient." The new PumpSmart was obvious: a much simpler version of the original PumpSmart, with a sensor downstream and upstream to measure flow demand and supply, a simple microprocessor, and a variable speed drive. When demand is low, the pump slows down, and significant electrical power is saved. In a new installation, there's not even a need for a valve—the pump is the flow controller. In a retrofit installation, PumpSmart pays for itself in less than a year in power savings.

The product has been a huge success, but it was only through VoC work, and in particular the observation and walkabout facet of the visits, that the insight leading to the breakthrough was discovered. Same technology as the ill-fated first PumpSmart project, but a very different product definition based on in-depth customer visits.

Competitive analysis is also a part of this stage. Another market activity is concept testing: A representation of the proposed new product is presented to potential customers, their reactions are gauged, and the likely customer acceptance of the new product is determined.

A detailed *technical appraisal* focuses on the "doability" of the project at Stage 2. That is, customer needs and "wish lists" are translated into a technically and economically feasible conceptual solution. This translation might even involve some preliminary design or laboratory work, but it should not be construed as a full-fledged development project. A manufacturing (or operations) appraisal is often a part of building the Business Case, where issues of manufacturability, source-of-supply, costs to manufacture, and investment required are investigated. If appropriate, detailed legal, patent, and regulatory assessment work is undertaken in order to remove risks and to map out the required actions.

Finally, a detailed *business and financial analysis* is conducted as part of the justification facet of the Business Case. The financial analysis typically involves a discounted cash flow approach, complete with sensitivity analysis to look at possible downside risks.

The result of Stage 2 is a *Business Case* for the project: The *integrated product definition*—a key to success—is agreed to; and a thorough *project justification* and *detailed project action plan* are developed.

Stage 2 involves considerably more effort than Stage 1 and requires inputs from a variety of sources. Stage 2 is best handled by a team consisting of cross-functional members—the core group of the eventual project team.

GATE 3: GO TO DEVELOPMENT

This is the final gate prior to the Development stage, the last point at which the project can be killed before entering heavy spending. Some firms call it the "money gate": Once past Gate 3, financial commitments are substantial. In effect, Gate 3 means "go to a heavy spend." And it's here that the shape of the funnel changes, as shown in Figure 4.10, taking on a gentler slope—that is, most of the Kill decisions are made in the early gates, at Gates 1, 2, and 3; relatively few projects are killed after Gate 3. Senior management at EXFO Engineering appropriately call this the "funnel leading to a tunnel."[11] Gate 3 also yields a sign-off of the product and project definition.

This Gate 3 evaluation involves a review of each of the activities in Stage 2, checking that the activities were undertaken, that their quality of execution is sound—the readiness-check questions. Next, Gate 3 subjects the project once again to the set of must-meet and should-meet criteria similar to those used at Gate 2. Finally, because a heavy spending commitment is the result of a Go decision at Gate 3, the results of the financial analysis and hurdles are an important part of this screen.

If the decision is Go, Gate 3 sees commitment to the product definition and agreement on the project plan that charts the path forward: the Development Plan and the Preliminary Operations and Marketing Plans are reviewed and approved at this gate. The full project team—an empowered, cross-functional team headed by a project leader with authority—is assigned; and resources—person-days and funds—are formally committed.

STAGE 3: DEVELOPMENT

Stage 3 begins the implementation of the Development Plan and the physical development of the product (or mapping out the details of the service and the IT work underlying the service). Lab tests, in-house tests, or alpha tests ensure that the product meets requirements under controlled conditions. For lengthy projects, numerous milestones and periodic project reviews are built into the Development Plan. These are not gates per se: Go/Kill decisions are not made here; rather, these milestone checkpoints provide for project control and management. However, missing a milestone or two usually signals that the project is off course and that calls for an immediate and emergency gate review. The deliverable at the end of Stage 3 is a partially tested prototype of the product.

The emphasis in Stage 3 is on technical work. But marketing and operations activities also proceed in parallel. For example, market analysis and customer feedback work continue concurrently with the technical development, with constant customer opinion sought on the product as it takes shape during Development. These are the "build-test-feedback-revise spirals" in Figure 18.6—the back-and-forth or iterative loops, with each development result, for example, rapid prototype, working model, first prototype, and so on, taken to the customer for assessment and feedback. Meanwhile, detailed test plans, market launch plans, and production or operations plans, including production facilities requirements, are developed. An updated financial analysis is prepared, while regulatory, legal, and patent issues are resolved.

GATE 4: GO TO TESTING

This post-development review is a check on the progress and the continued attractiveness of the product and project. Development work is reviewed and checked, ensuring that the work has been completed in a quality fashion and that the developed product is indeed consistent with the original definition specified at Gate 3.

This gate also revisits the economic questions via a revised financial analysis based on new and more accurate data. The Testing or Validation Plan for the next stage is approved for immediate implementation, and the detailed Marketing and Operations Plans are reviewed for probable future execution.

STAGE 4: TESTING AND VALIDATION

This stage tests and validates the entire viability of the project: the product itself, the production or operations process, customer acceptance, and the economics of the project. A number of activities are undertaken at Stage 4:

- *In-house product tests:* extended lab tests or alpha tests to check on product quality and product performance under controlled operating or lab conditions.
- *User, preference, or field trials of the product:* to verify that the product functions under actual use conditions and also to gauge potential customers' reactions to the product—to establish purchase intent.
- *Trial, limited, or pilot production/operations:* to test, debug, and prove the production or operations process and to determine more precise production costs and throughputs.
- *Simulated test market, test market, or trial sell:* to gauge customer reaction, measure the effectiveness of the launch plan, and determine expected market share and revenues.
- *Revised business and financial analysis:* to check on the continued business and economic viability of the project, based on new and more accurate revenue and cost data.

Sometimes Stage 4 yields negative results, and it's back to Stage 3:

An example: All was proceeding well for the OMNOVA dry-erase wall covering. A successful trial production run in Stage 4 yielded sufficient semi-commercial product to permit customer trials in several test office buildings. The product had been extensively tested in the lab on all known performance metrics—temperature, humidity, scuff resistance, and so on. But one small factor was overlooked—as so often happens. Some customers used a certain brand of dry-erase markers with a unique solvent. The result: When left on the whiteboard for several days, writing from this one brand of marker proved difficult to completely erase. And so "ghosts" appeared. This *ghosting problem* was never identified until real customers started using the product. But OMNOVA was alert and acted on the field-trial results. The problem was rectified, and now the commercial product meets all customer requirements.

GATE 5: GO TO LAUNCH

This final gate opens the door to full commercialization—market launch and full production or operations start up. It is the final point at which the project can still be killed. This gate focuses on the quality of the activities in the Testing and Validation stage and their results. Criteria for passing the gate focus largely on whether the Stage 4 test results are positive; the expected financial return; whether the launch and operations startup plans remain solid; and the readiness check—that all is commercial-ready for the launch. The Operations and Marketing Plans are reviewed and approved for implementation in Stage 5, and in some firms, so is the Product Life Cycle Plan (the plan that takes the product well beyond the launch phase, into maturity and even to product exit).

STAGE 5: LAUNCH

This final stage involves implementation of both the Market Launch Plan and the Operations Plan. Production equipment is acquired, installed, and commissioned (although sometimes this is done earlier in Stage 4, as part of the Stage 4 production trials); the logistics pipeline is filled; and selling begins. And barring any unforeseen events, it should be clear sailing for the new product ... another new-product winner!

POST-LAUNCH REVIEW

At some point following commercialization (often six to eighteen months later), the new-product project is terminated. The team is disbanded, and the product becomes a "regular product" in the firm's product line. This is also the point where the project and the product's performance are reviewed. The latest data on revenues, costs, expenditures, profits, and timing are compared to projections to gauge performance. Finally, a post-audit—a critical assessment of the project's strengths and weaknesses, what you can learn from this project, and how you can do the next one better—is carried out. This review marks the end of the project. Note that the project team and leader remain responsible for the success of the project through this post-launch period, right up to the point of the Post-Launch Review.

> *An example:*[12] Emerson Electric's NPD 2.0 stage-and-gate system builds in a rigorous post-launch follow-up as a way to ensure team accountability for achieving the project's sales and profit objectives.

"Post-Launch Review also sets up a systematic way to provide continuous learning and improvement of the NPD process through closed-loop feedback." These reviews occur one to two months after launch, and again twelve to twenty-four months after launch. "The initial follow-up would allow corrective action and a complete review of team performance. The latter review would provide accountability for results, and determine the next steps for the project or change the new NPD [new-product development] process."

Like Emerson Electric, many firms undertake two Post-Launch Reviews: one shortly after launch to make immediate course corrections and to undertake a retrospective analysis of the project while memories are still fresh; and the final review some twelve to eighteen months after launch to review actual versus promised results and terminate the project.

So there you have it—very simple in concept, yet remarkably robust as a way to drive new products to market. Before getting into the details of how the process works, and some of the added sophistication, flexibility, and new techniques that some companies have built in (outlined in the next few chapters), let's first make sure we're all on the same page regarding what *Stage-Gate* is and is not!

NOT THE SAME AS PROJECT MANAGEMENT

Stage-Gate is a *macro* process—an overarching process. By contrast, *project management* is a *micro* process. *Stage-Gate* is not a substitute for sound project management methods. Rather, *Stage-Gate* and project management are used together. Specifically, project management methods are applied *within the stages* of the *Stage-Gate* process. For example, during the larger, more complex stages (Stages 3, 4, and 5, Development, Testing, and Launch in Figure 18.6), project management methods must be applied, such as:

✓ A team initiation task to define the project—its mission and goals

✓ Team-building exercises

✓ Computer-generated time lines and critical path plans

✓ Parallel processing (undertaking activities concurrently rather than sequentially)

✓ Milestone review points (built into the action plans approved at each gate)

✓ Regular project reviews

Table 18.1. A Good Checklist—Characteristics of an Operational Stage-Gate System*

(Based on the APQC best practices in innovation study)

Clearly defined stages: An overwhelming majority of businesses use a series of defined stages—for example: Ideation, Scoping, Build Business Case, Development, Test, and Launch (72.4 percent of businesses [in the APQC study] have well-defined stages).

Activities defined for each stage: Some NPD processes lack specifics, for example, no clearly defined activities or expectations in each stage. Not so for our sample of firms: Activities and tasks are defined for each stage of their NPD (new-product development) process for 73.8 percent of businesses.

Defined Go/Kill gates: An important part of a well-constructed NPD process is gates or Go/No Go decision points. At gates, management meets with project teams to review the project, evaluate its merits, and make Go/No Go and resourcing decisions. Gates are a strong facet of most businesses' NPD processes, with 73.8 percent of businesses claiming proficiency here; only 13.3 percent of businesses lack gates.

Defined Go/No Go criteria at gates: Go/Kill criteria are considered important in order to better evaluate the merits of NPD projects and to assist management in making the Go/No Go decision. In spite of the logic of having such gate criteria, the lack of these criteria is fairly widespread (21.9 percent of businesses lack these criteria; only 46.7 percent claim to have well-defined gate criteria), and indeed this is a somewhat weaker facet of businesses' NPD processes.

Deliverables defined for each gate: A menu of what the project team is expected to deliver to each gate in the NPD—their "deliverables"—is a positive feature of best-in-class new-product processes and is also common among the sample of businesses. Overall, having well-defined deliverables is rated moderately strong, with 71.0 percent of businesses having such an explicit menu of deliverables to guide project teams.

Gatekeepers designated for each gate: Often it is unclear just who should undertake project reviews and whose signatures are needed for an NPD project to proceed. The locus of decision-making—the people who make the Go/No Go decisions at gates—is also an important feature of many firms' NPD processes. So it is with the sample of businesses: Most have the gatekeepers very well defined (71.9 percent of businesses), whereas 15.2 percent do not at all.

A visible, documented process: Some firms claim to have an NPD process; but on closer inspection, it's more a high-level and conceptual process—a few flow diagrams with boxes and diamonds and little more. To be operational, an effective new-product process should be well mapped-out, visible, and well-documented. Again, the sample of businesses does fairly well: 66.7 percent of businesses indicate that they have a well-documented and visible NPD process; only 14.3 percent do not.

Whether the NPD is really used: The true test of an NPD process is whether or not it is really used; or is it merely window-dressing in the business—a paper process? There is clear evidence that some businesses really are using their NPD process to drive new products to market, with the majority of projects operating within the process: More than half of businesses (52.4 percent) really make use of their NPD process. Somewhat disturbing is that although the great majority claim to have some type of NPD process in place (only 7.6 percent claimed not to have a process), 19 percent claim that their process is not really used.

An enabling process for project team: Another test of one's NPD process is whether or not it is a facilitating process, helping project teams get their products to market (rather than a bureaucratic process that stands in the way). This is one of the weakest elements of the NPD process, with 56.7 percent of businesses claiming that they have built too much bureaucracy into the process.

An adaptable and scalable process: Is the NPD process a flexible one, adapted to the needs, size, and risk of the project? Or is it a rigid one-size-fits-all process, failing to recognize the difference between major and minor projects? Two-thirds of the businesses in this study (65.2 percent) view their NPD process as flexible, adaptable, and scalable.

A process manager in place: A number of firms have designated a process manager—full- or part-time—to shepherd their NPD process, ensuring that it works. Duties often include: coaching project teams, facilitating gate meetings, ensuring project deliverables are ready and distributed to gatekeepers, training, keeping metrics, and so on. The lack of a process manager is fairly evident for a great many firms: 31.4 percent do not have this person in place; but 41 percent of businesses do.

* Taken from APQC study, endnote 7.

NOTES

1. A quotation describing the quality process, which has equal applicability to the new-product process. See T. H. Berry, *Managing the Total Quality Transformation* (New York: McGraw-Hill, 1991).

2. Section taken from R. G. Cooper, "The Stage-Gate Idea-to-Launch Process—Update, What's New and NexGen Systems," *JPIM* 25, no. 3 (May 2008): 213–232.

3. R. G. Cooper, "New Products: What Separates the Winners from the Losers," in *PDMA Handbook for New Product Development*, 2nd edition, ed. K. B. Kahn (New York: John Wiley & Sons, 2004), chap. 1, 3–28.

4. This chapter is taken from many sources. See endnote 1 in chap. 2; also Cooper, endnote 2 above; also R. G. Cooper, "Stage-Gate Idea-to-Launch System," *Wiley International Encyclopedia of Marketing: Product Innovation and Management,* vol. 5, ed. B. L. Bayus (West Sussex, U.K.: Wiley, December 2010).

5. M. Mills, "Implementing a Stage-Gate® Process at Procter & Gamble," Proceedings, First International Stage-Gate Conference, St. Petersburg Beach, FL, February 2007.

6. NPD 2.0 is described in R. D. Ledford, "NPD 2.0: Raising Emerson's NPD Process to the Next Level," *Innovations* (St. Louis, MO: Emerson Electric, 2006), 4–7.

7. R. G. Cooper, S. J. Edgett, and E. J. Kleinschmidt, *New Product Development Best Practices Study: What Distinguishes the Top Performers* (Houston, TX: American Productivity and Quality Center, 2002); and R. G. Cooper, S. J. Edgett, and E. J. Kleinschmidt, "Benchmarking Best NPD Practices—Part 3: The NPD Process and Decisive Idea-to-Launch Activities," *Research-Technology Management* 47, no. 6 (January–February 2005): 43–55.

9. D. Arra, "How ITT Drives Value-Creation with Value Based Product Development," Proceedings, Stage-Gate Summit 2010, Clearwater Beach, FL, 2010.

10. R. G. Cooper and A. Dreher, "Voice of Customer Methods Versus the Rest: What Is the Best Source of New-Product Ideas?" *Marketing Management Magazine,* Winter 2010, online extended version, http://www.marketingpower.com/ResourceLibrary/Publications/MarketingManagement/2010/4/38–48_Xtended version3.pdf.

11. EXFO Engineering is a medium-sized manufacturer of fiber-optic test equipment, with remarkably sound new-product methods; the firm has won the PDMA's "outstanding corporate innovator" award based on its portfolio management and stage-and-gate practices.

12. Ledford, endnote 6.

READING 18: QUESTIONS FOR THOUGHT

- Have you been part of an organization that had a formal innovation process such as the Stage-Gate system? If yes, how did you feel about that process? Did you think it was effective? Why?

- There have been many variations proposed to the Stage-Gate system, even by Robert Cooper himself. What would you do to modify the Stage-Gate system to ensure it was a good fit with a company that you have been a part of in the past or are familiar with? Why?

- Imagine you are responsible for managing an innovation project and must prepare for a presentation at one of the gates in the process. Pick one of the gates and visualize that you are presenting to an approver who will provide a go/no-go decision. What do you think would be the most important aspects in obtaining the "go" approval to move on to the next stage? Why?

INSTITUTIONALIZING INNOVATION

Successful innovation generally requires organizations to have a structure in place to manage and guide innovation. Companies that simply wait until the need arises to innovate will be unprepared for the complex tasks of creating and introducing new products or services. The most innovative companies approach innovation as a continuous process.

The following reading builds on this premise as the authors Scott Anthony, Mark Johnson, and Joseph Sinfield describe various considerations and alternative structures for developing and managing an innovation engine within a company. Their suggestions are based on extensive research with a wide range of businesses across many industries to understand best practices in managing the innovation process.

One important notion is that innovation for incremental ideas must be managed differently than innovation for breakthrough ideas, which require entirely new business models that may be disruptive to the core business. Incremental innovations by definition are building off of the existing core business; they can be managed within the framework of the existing business. But breakthrough innovations, which are disruptive to the core business, often require their own unique culture, processes, and evaluation parameters in order to be successfully nurtured. Initial success in such cases should be measured in terms of validation of key value and growth assumptions rather than hard financial measures.

The authors also note that there is no single "right" way to manage innovation. They propose four models for how companies can structure to manage innovation. These models cover a loose spectrum that at one end focuses on simply providing innovation training and at the other end advocates for a separate innovation group within the company.

Most important, however, is the simple point that senior company management must demonstrate a commitment to innovation in order for it to take root.

Scott Anthony is a leading consultant and author on business innovation. He holds an MBA from the Harvard Business School. In 2017, he won the Thinkers50 Innovation Award. Mark Johnson cofounded the innovation consulting firm Innosight with Harvard professor Clayton Christensen. He also holds an MBA from the Harvard Business School as well as a master's in engineering from Columbia University. Joseph Sinfield is an associate professor of civil engineering at Purdue University and earned his PhD from the Massachusetts Institute of Technology.

INSTITUTIONALIZING INNOVATION

BY SCOTT D. ANTHONY, MARK W. JOHNSON, AND JOSEPH V. SINFIELD

Building an engine that produces a steady stream of innovative growth businesses is difficult, but companies that are able to do it can differentiate themselves from competitors.

M any of the case studies describing how established companies have created new growth businesses focus on a single success. The companies that get it right—such as ING Groep NV, with its ING Direct online banking model, and the Procter & Gamble Co., with category-creating products such as Febreze and Swiffer—surely deserve respect and admiration. Big company managers know how hard it is for market leaders to create innovative growth businesses.

The punishing thing about innovation, however, is that the contest never ends. Create a new market, and other companies come flooding in. Parry one threat, and up pops another attacker, hungrily eyeing your core business. Success requires being able to go beyond isolated wins to develop deep capabilities that allow companies to disarm disruptive threats and seize new growth opportunities repeatedly. It requires the ability to churn out successful growth businesses year after year, over and over again.

In *The Innovator's Solution,* authors Clayton M. Christensen and Michael E. Raynor discuss how to institutionalize innovation. They argue that companies should begin planning for innovation well before they need to by appointing a senior manager to oversee the resource-allocation process, creating a team of "movers and shapers," and training employees to identify disruptive ideas.[1]

This article builds on those ideas and incorporates our field-based insights from working with companies on innovation issues over the past five years. (See "About the Research," p. 46.) Companies that create blueprints for growth, construct innovation engines and support the engines with the right systems and mind-sets can establish favorable conditions for substantial innovation. Although institutionalizing innovation is hard work, companies that build and maintain this capability can create substantial shareholder wealth and differentiate themselves from competitors.

CREATE A GROWTH BLUEPRINT

The first pillar of creating the capability to build new business involves articulating what the organization "wants to be" and allocating resources to achieve that vision. The senior management team must define strategic goals and boundaries and create a balanced portfolio of growth opportunities that reflects their strategy.

Business leaders are often skeptical about the notion of defining strategic goals and boundaries, believing that their strategy is already well defined and broadly known. Or they will argue that "removing boundaries" is the best way to allow managers to identify opportunities or create new growth. However, it is helpful for senior management to come to consensus around two topics: the strategic objectives and the specific options they will and will not consider to reach those objectives.

The first part of the discussion involves articulating the desired outcome of the company's innovation efforts and where it expects to find growth. Broadly speaking, growth comes from organic efforts or acquisitions that expand the core business, move into adjacent markets or create entirely new businesses. Companies should have a rough estimate of their financial targets and how much growth they expect to see from each of these categories.

Developing precise estimates is difficult, but even rough estimates can be useful. Consider the experience of a large consumer products company. Company executives estimated how much growth they expected from its core and from products in its development pipeline, and they were shocked at what they learned: Even under the most optimistic scenarios, it still needed to generate almost a billion dollars in new growth to meet its 10-year strategic objectives. Before the exercise, leaders had a vague sense that innovation was important. After the exercise, innovation became the No. 1 priority. The insight helped magnify the innovation challenge and rally key managers around the need to approach innovation differently.

The second part of the discussion determines which strategies the company will—and will not—consider following in order to reach its growth objectives. Companies need to have consensus around what is "desirable," "discussable" and "unthinkable" along a number of strategic dimensions. (See "Strategic Dimensions Affecting Innovation," p. 50.) Our fieldwork on this topic has taught us several lessons:

Misalignment reigns. Even organizations that go to great lengths to develop strategic plans, define a vision for the company and coin mission statements find significant internal misalignment. The classic question of "What business are you in?" can prompt very different and sometimes contradictory answers from members of the same management team.[2] Some leaders of a large chemical company, for example, saw the company as a "specialty business," while others thought of themselves as "raw materials suppliers for downstream value-adding industries." This dichotomy can lead to disjointed pursuits and disjointed strategy.

It helps to start at the center. Delegating goal and boundary definitions to business units without a strong corporate context can lead in too many directions and risk undermining corporate goals. Not enough communication between corporate and business units can compound the problem. Companies first should create goals and bounds at a corporate level. These conditions can then serve as guidelines for the somewhat narrower goals for subunits.

About the Research

The findings described in this article come from three streams of research. First, we conducted in-depth interviews at more than 40 organizations representing a range of industries, including retailing, chemicals, financial services, telecommunications, consumer packaged goods and high-tech. The purpose of the interviews was to understand how the organizations structured for and supported innovation. Second, we conducted a detailed survey of managers involved in innovation activities in conjunction with International Business Machines Corp. and the American Productivity & Quality Center Inc. Managers from close to 100 organizations in 14 countries provided information about innovation metrics and practices in their organizations. (The survey findings are reported in "Innovating on Your Own Terms," by George Pohle and Steve Wunker, available at www.innosight.com.) Finally, we synthesized our fieldwork from the past five years with more than 50 companies, including Aetna, Nokia, Procter & Gamble, Johnson & Johnson, Dow Corning, Wacker, Syngenta, Time Warner and E.W. Scripps.

Boundaries can be liberating. Managers frequently believe that letting chaos reign can unleash their company's innovative energy. Removing boundaries, the logic goes, helps managers spot or create innovative growth businesses. Yet companies often come to realize that having a blank slate can make it surprisingly hard for managers. As a senior manager at a leading consumer health company put it, "What are our odds of success if we trawl the ocean, hoping to catch a whale?" Even worse is having a team spend months digging into a strategy that the company won't embrace under any scenario. Somewhat paradoxically, setting constraints can be liberating. Innovators who know what a company wants to do (the goals) and what it won't do (the boundaries) can focus their creative efforts.

Managing the balance is critical. Setting boundaries in particular requires striking a delicate balance. If boundaries are defined too loosely, managers can lose their way. If boundaries are defined too tightly, they can run into the innovator's dilemma where they miss the new growth business that ultimately powers transformation in their industry. When the boundaries are set well, teams should be encouraged to push them when they come up and to revisit them on a regular basis in any case.

A Balanced Portfolio Good investors know the value of aligning their portfolio with their investment objectives. For example, an aggressive growth strategy might allocate 50% of the funds in small company stocks, 40% in large-company stocks and

---

A Simple View of the Innovation Process

Many companies have an innovation process where they generate ideas, validate the leading ideas and scale those ideas. Companies seeking to develop deep innovation capabilities need to augment that process with the ability to iterate and shape new growth ideas and conceive of different commercialization approaches.

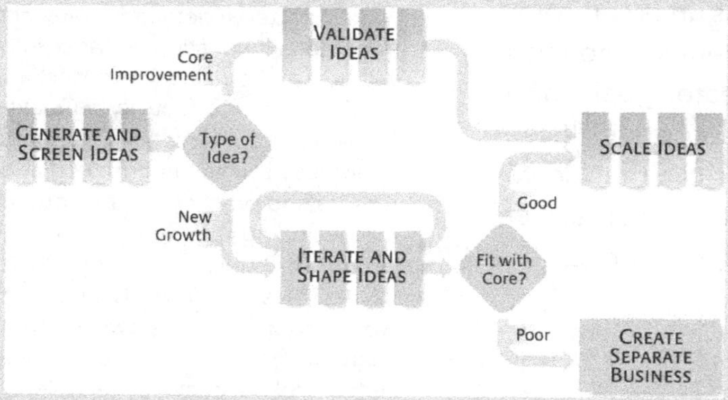

Figure 19.1

10% in bonds. In any given year, the portfolio could lose money, but in the long run it should produce strong growth. For less risk, the portfolio would have fewer stocks and more bonds. Although the upside might be lower, the odds of losing money in any given year will be lower, too.

Companies should approach growth in a similar way, with a mix of projects to satisfy their growth objectives. Ironically, organizations often find that their allocation of resources doesn't match their intended strategies. Often, the majority of their investments are in the category of incremental improvements, with few that qualify as new growth initiatives. While there's no "magic formula" for what the ideal portfolio should look like, a 50/30/20 split (targeting core improvements, logical extensions of the core business and new growth initiatives) can be a reasonable approach. This balance is not likely to be achievable in every unit in a large organization, however, and achieving the mix across the corporation may involve disproportionate investment in one unit of the organization over another.

It is important to remember that saying a portfolio is balanced is meaningless. Companies need to allocate resources appropriately toward the different types of innovation. Indeed, strategy doesn't determine how companies allocate resources; rather, how they allocate resources is what determines strategy.[3]

Therefore, companies need to make sure that they set aside resources—both people and dollars—for different types of innovation initiatives in a manner that is consistent with their strategic objectives.

Creating—and protecting—separate pools of resources is vital. Companies that put all of their innovation resources into a single pot often find that low-risk (and low-return) core initiatives end up crowding out the investments that might have higher risk and take longer to perform but offer greater growth potential.

In the early days, the most important investment that companies can make in a new venture is not dollars but time. In fact, it's dangerous to invest too much capital too early. Research suggests that startup ventures have less than a 10% chance of starting with the right strategy. The worst thing to do, then, is to be locked into a flawed strategy prematurely. The best approach is to "invest a little to learn a lot." As such, investing relatively small amounts in the early days can be sufficient—provided that there are managers specifically tasked with finding and nurturing new growth businesses.[4]

In contrast to 3M Co.'s famous "15% rule" encouraging scientists to spend up to 15% of their time on projects they find personally interesting, we believe that companies seeking to create innovative businesses will do better allocating a few people fully than many people partially. This is particularly true when the goal is to develop ideas that are significant departures from the core business. If creating new products is a background task, most managers are likely to default to approaches that have worked before instead of legitimately different approaches.

Of course, it takes discipline to maintain separate buckets of funding and people for different types of initiatives. If the core business runs into trouble, there is an overwhelming temptation to tap resources that the company has allocated to more speculative ventures in order to save the company. In the short run, this may make perfect sense; in the long run, it can be disastrous.

This temptation is one reason why it is important to keep the core business as healthy as possible. In fact, the best time to start investing in new growth businesses is when the company seemingly doesn't need it. When the core gets sick, companies are under the gun to grow new businesses quickly. The pressure can precipitate a complex set of decisions—targeting large markets already populated with strong competitors or forcing a technology into a market before it is ready—that can stunt new growth efforts.[5]

Consider the case of Delta Air Lines Inc. As its core business deteriorated in 2005, Delta decided to fold Song, its low-cost service, back into the core business and also sell its growing regional jet operation to raise cash. Unfortunately, the core wasn't healthy enough to provide "air cover" for new growth initiatives.

CONSTRUCT AN INNOVATION ENGINE

In our experience, the two most important components in the creation of any growth engine are a separate screening and development process that focuses on reducing the level of uncertainty and an innovation structure managed by a new growth board that helps oversee highly uncertain projects. Unless these elements are in place, new ideas tend to be modified to look like things the company has done in the past, undermining the company's ability to pursue highly differentiated new strategies.[6]

Screening and Development Companies have to treat different types of innovation opportunities differently. Although managers routinely approach different kinds of problems differently, companies tend to lump together things related to growth and manage them by a single set of metrics. This doesn't make much sense. An incremental improvement in an existing market just can't be measured, monitored and managed as if it were a bold new strategy in an emerging market. Pursuing fundamentally different opportunities the same way ensures that one of the opportunities will be underoptimized.

Generally speaking, new growth initiatives need to go through a more iterative development process, where the focus is on identifying and addressing the key assumptions and risks. The appropriate metrics that guide a new growth idea shouldn't be measures such as net present value or return on investment, which provide insights into the performance of the established core business; rather, companies need to use qualitative measures that relate to success in the target market.

Companies don't have to discard existing innovation processes. Rather, they can follow different paths for different types of innovations at each stage of the process—particularly where they test and shape ideas. (See "A Simple View of the Innovation Process," p. 47.) As the iterative development process eliminates risks from new opportunities, the new business can gradually transition to a company's core launch capability. This transition marks the formalization of a new business that someday may become part of the company's core. The exception is when the new venture is based on a business model that the core business sees as unattractive. The weight of historical evidence suggests that businesses that are disruptive to their core business need a great deal of organizational autonomy.

An oft-cited example is the retailing industry. In the early 1960s, there were hundreds of general merchandise retailers. Most of them failed to make the transition to discount retailing, but Minneapolis-based Dayton-Hudson Corp. was a notable exception: It launched a subsidiary called Target. Today, most people are familiar with the subsidiary, not the parent. Other industry leaders such as Hewlett-Packard and IBM have followed similar approaches to create winning disruptive businesses.[7]

When new ventures are internally disruptive, Vijay Govindarajan, professor of international business at the Tuck School of Business at Dartmouth, advises against mindlessly "borrowing" core assets. Those assets often carry the wrong kind of "DNA," which will limit the degree of freedom or take the team off their disruptive course.[8] For example, borrowing a core brand might reduce initial marketing expenditures but could force a new venture to hew too closely to the traditional standards of the parent. A salesperson trained in the ways of the core business might rely too heavily on customers he knows instead of the new customers he'll need to cultivate to make the business work.

Structuring for Success It is hard for new growth initiatives to succeed without structural support. For example, in early 2006, Scripps Newspapers' senior vice president Mark Contreras allocated more than $1 million to create a fund for proposals that wouldn't naturally fit the company's core newspaper properties. Contreras appointed Bob Benz, Scripps's general manager of interactive business, to oversee the fund. Benz, Contreras, two other Scripps representatives and three outsiders were chosen to govern the fund.

The group meets regularly to evaluate new ideas and review the progress of funded ideas. Managers who want to submit ideas complete "idea resumes" that provide a basic overview of the idea, the reason why the idea is worth funding and the critical assumptions that need to be addressed. Benz and his team regularly run innovation workshops at each of the company's 14 newspaper properties to help trigger the sorts of ideas the fund seeks. As of October 2007, the fund had evaluated close to 100 proposals, funded around 15 and had four businesses with real growth potential. As Benz describes it, "These investments aren't big bets. They're small disbursements designed to test key assumptions in the ideas that are being submitted. ... If we fail, we want to make sure everyone learns from our missteps. And when we succeed, we want to ensure that all of our papers can leverage that success. ... We don't think we have all the answers, not by a long shot. But we believe we're heading in the right direction."[9]

Scripps's approach of creating a fund is just one way to structure for innovation. (See "Innovation Structures.") Regardless of the approach, a small oversight board (often called a "ventures board" or "growth council") can be the glue connecting different innovation efforts in a company. It can oversee the identification and early-stage development of new growth opportunities. Such a board can be a powerful tool for building new growth businesses and pulling senior management into the early stages of the innovation process.

Innovation Structures

There is no one-size-fits-all way to structure for innovation. The following describes four different structures to consider

1. Training units to help stimulate innovation

Companies that pursue this typically believe that their organization has the right basic infrastructure to support innovation. However, they also recognize that managers and teams may need help solving practical innovation problems, developing new mindsets or gaining exposure to important external developments.

Innovation training units help to build disruption-specific skills and culture. They methodically build the skills and change the mindset of core personnel to fuel internal innovation. For example, the Learning & Development unit within agrichemical giant Syngenta AG designs and executes training courses that foster innovative and leadership qualities.

Training can come from outside the organization as well. Infineum, a joint venture between ExxonMobil and Shell, created a small advisory board in 2007 to help it tap into external trends. The board includes the CEO, leaders from the unit's technology, intellectual property, supply chain and human

STRUCTURE	GOAL	STRATEGIC GOAL		INTERACTION WITH CORE		REQUIRED RESOURCES	
		Support	Create	Low	High	Low	High
TRAINING UNIT	Help internal innovators in their efforts to create new growth businesses						
FUNDING/ OVERSIGHT MECHANISM	Provide funding and assistance to internally generated ideas						
INCUBATOR	Kick-start innovation by incubating businesses that ultimately "land" in the core organization						
AUTONOMOUS GROWTH GROUP	Nurture and launch new growth businesses that extend beyond the core						

Figure 19.2

resource functions and external advisors. The board has a semi-structured dialogue on a quarterly basis with leaders of Infineum's growth initiatives.

2. Funding/oversight mechanisms to help shepherd innovation

Companies that find that internal innovators get "stuck" can champion innovation efforts and remove obstacles that would otherwise limit the potential for innovative ideas to succeed. Internal groups like the Scripps fund help to nurture and safeguard innovative efforts but still rely on the rank and file to drive individual initiatives forward. At General Electric, CEO Jeff Immelt created the Commercial Council, a team of about 12 senior executives. It holds monthly conference calls and quarterly meetings to discuss innovation proposals and growth strategies put forward by its business leaders.

3. Incubators to help accelerate ideas

Sometimes funding mechanisms aren't enough. Dedicated incubator groups can take rough ideas and relatively quickly turn them into something bigger, better, cheaper and faster. Once ideas have received a focused push, they can be reabsorbed into the core organization.

Shell Oil Co. created a program called "GameChanger" to help it proactively foster or prioritize novel ideas. Launching the program, Shell said that it "recognizes that a rich vein of innovative ideas runs through Shell Chemicals, but that new ways are needed to surface these ideas, take account of external influences and provide appropriate, staged financing for their development." This unit strives to develop real businesses that are "outside and between" the company's existing lines of enterprise by following

a process "outside the constraints and priorities of Shell's day-to-day business."[i]

4. Autonomous growth groups to launch businesses

Finally, companies seeking to launch businesses that are markedly different from their core business can set up autonomous groups to identify and develop noncore business concepts. Growth groups typically have a secure budget and decision-making autonomy.

At Dow Chemical Co. a separate, autonomous group identifies and develops noncore business concepts and explores concepts outside the core's comfort zone. It has a small group of fully dedicated innovation generalists plus other high-potential leaders who rotate in from the core business for periods of a year or more. The group also relies upon partial allocation of functional experts from the main organization. A modest budget allows it to quickly iterate solutions toward success, passing ideas back to the core business or seeking additional resources from the CEO to launch new businesses.

Companies do not need to embrace a single structure. Procter & Gamble employs multiple structures simultaneously. At a corporate level, its autonomous growth group called FutureWorks is dedicated to "building tomorrow's brands."[ii] Within its business units, new business development groups incubate new ideas. In 2005 P&G set up a training unit with "guides" to assist project teams working on disruptive ideas. Its chief technology officer manages a "Corporate Innovation Fund" that helps fund ideas that don't fit the normal prioritization process. Many of its core brands also have external advisory committees to stay abreast of key scientific developments.

i. Shell Chemicals, "Delivering on Our Commitment to Sustainable Development," (London: Shell Chemicals, 2003).

ii. D. Laurie, Y. Doz and C. Scheer, "Creating New Growth Platforms," Harvard Business Review 84 (May 2006): 80–90.

SUPPORT THE NEW GROWTH ENGINE

It takes more than a clearly defined strategy, allocated resources and a new growth engine to drive innovation. Unless management creates a supportive climate and leads by example, the effort can fall short. Companies that succeed in this area have senior managers who are actively involved in idea screening and development; share a common language of innovation; draw on substantial external input and create policies and incentives that encourage people to take managed risks on the path to innovative growth.

Deep senior management involvement. A systematic ability to innovate and grow needs support from the company's very top managers. Senior managers must clearly communicate the strategic importance of innovation. Their commitment must go beyond words to include active participation in the activities that promote innovation within the organization. In addition, senior management needs to change the way it interacts with project teams. In many companies, the relationships between senior managers and project teams are adversarial. It's one thing for senior managers to act as "devil's advocate" and poke holes in a project team's plans. But when a company commits to a new direction, senior managers need to become problem solvers, not just problem finders.

A useful way to think of senior management's role in supporting growth initiatives is to think about the distinction between television watching and working on a computer: Watching television typically involves "leaning back" to watch, while using a computer involves "leaning forward" to interact. Senior managers can lean back and review core improvements, but they must lean forward and roll up their sleeves to work on growth initiatives. Procter & Gamble embodies this principle. CEO A.G. Lafley regularly visits consumers in their homes; senior managers take part in brainstorming sessions with consumers; top technologists spend time in the labs to interact with scientists. The goal is to develop wisdom and insight about where new growth opportunities will come from over the next decade and beyond.

A common language. Companies with a common language are able to avoid some of the mental traps that can make the innovation difficult. These traps include pursuing perfection when "good enough" is often sufficient, overestimating knowledge of new markets and making big bets when it's better to begin with small ones.

Both senior managers and middle managers need to overcome these mindsets. Middle managers make many of the day-to-day decisions in a company. Well-intentioned middle managers who do what they have always done can default to core behavior when fresh thinking is required. A senior manager who doesn't "get it" can destroy a highly innovative approach by asking the wrong questions at the wrong time. A common language of innovation can help companies avoid these pitfalls.

Strategic Dimensions Affecting Innovation

Companies seeking to boost their ability to create growth through innovation need to be clear about their goals (what they want) and boundaries (what they won't do). Companies should set goals and boundaries for a wide range of strategic factors. The following factors can be useful areas to consider:

Which customer group can it target? If the company is consumer-focused, can it consider business customers? If the company is business-focused, can it consider targeting consumers?

Which distribution channel can it use? If the company typically relies on a retail channel, can consider going direct? If it typically uses mass channels, can it consider using niche channels?

What revenues does an idea have to reach at steady state? $100 million? $50 million? When is steady state?

What kind of margins does it need to obtain at steady state? Above the current margins? On par with the current margins? Or below the current margins?

What is the offering it will provide? If the company typically sells products, can it sell services? If it typically sells services, can it sell products?

What geography will it target? If the company typically launches locally, could it launch globally? If it typically launches globally, could it launch locally?

Which brand will it use? Can the company consider creating a new brand?

How will it make revenues? Can the company consider new revenue streams? Which ones are on or off the table?

Which suppliers and partners will it use? Can the company consider using new suppliers? Can it outsource things it normally does itself? Can it do things inside it normally outsources?

What tactics will it use? Can the company consider acquisitions and partnerships?

What go-to-market approach will it use? Can the company consider test markets with preliminary prototypes that aren't perfect?

Of course, there are other dimensions that may be relevant to particular industries. Pharmaceutical companies, for example, might want to incorporate perspectives on medical efficacy claims, chemical companies will need to consider allowable environmental impact and media organizations will want to consider advertising reach.

Language played a major role in one of the best-known examples of market disruption: Intel Corp.'s response to competitive threats at the low end of the microprocessor business during the late 1990s. At the time, Clayton Christensen was running a series of training courses with the company. By his count, he made 20 trips to Intel during this period, educating hundreds of company managers on the principles and language of disruptive innovation. Intel subsequently launched what became known as the Celeron processor, a stripped-down, low-cost chip to compete in the least-demanding tiers in its industry. The Celeron processor slowed the advances of disruptive attackers such as AMD Inc. and Cyrix Corp, and it became a substantial business for Intel.[10]

Christensen believes that education played a critical role in helping Intel formulate and execute its response to the competitive threat. "At the end of it all, I was talking with [then Intel CEO] Andy Grove," Christensen says. "He said, 'You know, the model didn't give us any answers to any of the problems, but it gave us a common language and a common way to frame the problem so that we could reach consensus around counterintuitive courses of action.'

"Without that," Christensen continues, "the only way you can reach consensus is when the numbers make the course of action absolutely clear, [but] the data is only available about the past."[11]

Extensive external input. In the last five years, companies have begun to realize the power of what Henry W. Chesbrough of the University of California at Berkeley's Haas School of Business calls "open innovation." P&G is an instructive example. Historically, the company had a reputation for being extremely insular, yet several years ago CEO Lafley put forward a challenge: by 2010, 50% of the company's innovations had to involve some form of outside connection. Since then, P&G has augmented its research and development capability with a new ability to "connect and develop." P&G's goal is to shift its internal mindset from "not invented here" to "proudly found elsewhere."[12]

Generally speaking, companies need to find ways to bring external perspectives into the innovation process. This involves having well-defined ways to interact routinely and repeatedly with their core customers, learn from noncustomers, monitor ongoing industry experiments, scan for emerging technologies and import ideas from other industries. Setting up regular ways to draw on external stimuli (including having unaffiliated experts on new ventures boards) can expose previously invisible opportunities for innovation.

Supportive human resources policies. Companies need to redesign their policies, incentives and development paths to be consistent with their appetite for innovation. Instead of looking for "right-stuff" managers who have succeeded in core assignments, they need to look for managers who have attended the right "schools of experience" so they can spot and nurture new growth businesses. For many companies, finding the right managers might require hiring people from the outside, because even the most capable internal managers may never have wrestled with challenges related to creating new growth businesses.[13]

Getting incentives for innovation right is clearly a large hurdle for established companies. Startup companies can issue equity that allows managers to share in a venture's upside potential. Providing meaningful incentives at an established company requires creativity. Companies need to find a way to link managed risk taking with pay structures, bonuses and/or career progression. Typically, "intrapreneurs" will not have the same upside as entrepreneurs, but they also will have significantly lower downside risk. Most new ventures fail; if an internal venture fails, managers tend to land on their feet without having to search for an entirely new job.

Companies need to design development paths that encourage high-potential employees to spend time working for growth initiatives. Working on risky ventures can be a great training ground for emerging leaders: Many of the challenges new ventures face are general management issues.

As companies develop HR structures to help them reach their innovation goals, they need to consider how they can offer promising employees the broadest possible exposure to new ways of problem solving and decision making. One way to do this is to rotate people through a variety of different jobs. Ideally, the training will enable them to become effective leaders for the next new core business.

CREATING THE CAPABILITY TO GENERATE a stream of innovative growth businesses doesn't happen overnight. Companies seeking to institutionalize innovation can start by conducting an audit of their innovation capabilities and developing a plan for addressing identified weaknesses. Changing an organization's culture and building new structures and systems can seem daunting. However, companies that are able to develop a shared viewpoint about the ultimate destination, take modest first steps and stand ready to make adjustments as they determine what works and what doesn't work have been able to make significant strides.

NOTES

1. C.M. Christensen and M.E. Raynor, "The Innovator's Solution" (Boston: Harvard Business School Press, 2003), 278–283.

2. See T. Levitt, "Marketing Myopia," Harvard Business Review 38 (July-August 1960): 24–47. Levitt cited many examples of how companies misunderstanding what business they were in caused them to miss opportunities for growth; for example, companies that thought they were in the railroad business missed opportunities to expand into aviation, shipping and logistics.

3. J.L. Bower and Clark G. Gilbert, "From Resource Allocation to Strategy" (New York: Oxford University Press, 2005). This book is an outstanding compendium of research on the resource-allocation process.

4. A. Bhide, "The Origin and Evolution of New Businesses" (New York: Oxford University Press, 2000); and J. Clayton, B. Gambill and D. Harned, "The Curse of Too Much Capital: Building New Businesses in Large Corporations," McKinsey Quarterly 3 (1999): 48–59.

5. This pathology is described in eloquent detail in Ettenson, "Innovator's Solution," chap. 9.

6. Consider, for example, Wal-Mart's ill-fated effort to create a social network; airlines-within-airlines like Delta's Song or United Airlines' Ted; Kodak's original $30,000 digital camera; newspaper Web sites that were carbon copies of the print publication; and Nokia's N-Gage phone. All of these approaches seem to suffer from insufficient separation from the core business and core processes, leading to compromised solutions.

7. Christensen, "Innovator's Dilemma"; see particularly Chapter 5, "Give Responsibility for Disruptive Technologies to Organizations Whose Customers Need Them."

8. V. Govindarajan and C. Trimble, "Ten Rules for Strategic Innovators: From Idea to Execution" (Boston: Harvard Business School Press, 2005).

9. "Voices of Disruption: Bob Benz," Strategy & Innovation 4, no. 4 (July-August 2006).

10. Intel's chairman of the board, Andrew S. Grove recounted some of his reflections on the insight he gleaned from his interactions with Christensen in A. S. Grove, Keynote Speech (presented at Academy of Management Annual Meeting, San Diego, California, Aug. 9, 1998), and T. Mack, "Danger, Stealth Attack," Forbes, Jan. 25, 1999.

11. C.M. Christensen, "Disrupting and Avoiding Commoditization" (presentation at the New Market Growth Innovation Workshop, Chatham, Massachusetts, Nov. 12–13, 2003).

12. L. Huston and N. Sakkab, "Connect and Develop: Inside Procter & Gamble's New Model for Innovation," Harvard Business Review 84 (March 2006): 58–66.

13. M. McCall, "High Flyers: Developing the Next Generation of Leaders" (Boston: Harvard Business School Press, 1998).

READING 19: QUESTIONS FOR THOUGHT

- The authors of the reading promote the notion that innovation managers should seek a balanced portfolio. What is meant by a balanced portfolio? Why do you think the analogy to investing is appropriate when thinking about innovation at a large company?

- The reading describes four different ways to organizationally structure to manage innovation. Thinking about companies or organizations that you have been a part of, which structure do you think would have worked best? Why?

- The authors advocate different innovation processes for incremental versus breakthrough innovations. Why do they indicate this is necessary?

INTRODUCTION TO LEAPFROGGING: HARNESS THE POWER OF SURPRISE FOR BUSINESS BREAKTHROUGHS AND LEAPFROGGING TO BREAKTHROUGHS

I often hear companies lament that their innovation processes are only yielding incremental innovations and not big breakthroughs. This is most likely because their innovation processes are not structured to deliver breakthrough-type innovations. Many companies find it easy and natural to generate incremental innovations. These innovations are often simple improvements to existing products and services. Breakthroughs, however, often require both a different process as well as a different mindset.

The next two readings provide some insights around what it takes to produce breakthrough innovations. Both readings are short excerpts from the book *Leapfrogging: Harness the Power of Surprise for Business Breakthroughs* by Soren Kaplan. The first of the two readings introduces the notion that breakthrough innovations require companies to look for "surprises" and adopt thinking that challenges the status quo.

The second reading suggests a specific process that enables companies to generate breakthrough innovations. The steps are revealed from the point of view of the thoughts and feelings the innovator is likely to experience at each point. Feelings of doubt, for example, are common throughout the process due to the uncertainty inherent in this type of work. Thus, it is not just a process that is required to achieve breakthrough innovation but also a proper mindset that must be adopted by the innovator as well.

Soren Kaplan is a best-selling author, a speaker, and a professor at the University of Southern California Marshall School of Business.

INTRODUCTION TO LEAPFROGGING

HARNESS THE POWER OF SURPRISE FOR BUSINESS BREAKTHROUGHS

BY SOREN KAPLAN

IT'S ULTIMATELY ABOUT LEAPFROGGING

One of the goals of this book is to uncover and share the deeper leadership experiences and dynamics that are success factors during the often "messy" process of creating business breakthroughs. I define *leapfrogging* as *the process of overcoming limiting mindsets and barriers to create business breakthroughs*. I named this book *Leapfrogging* because when it comes down to it, that's exactly what achieving business breakthroughs is all about. It's about leapfrogging our mindsets so we can overcome the hidden assumptions and barriers that constrain us. It's about leapfrogging the expectations of customers, partners, employees, and the rest of the world so we can surprise them with a dramatic increase in value over what they're getting today. It's about leapfrogging the competition so that we can create a remarkable difference between ourselves and what others are doing. This transformation in value—whether through a product, service, business model, or process—is what I refer to as a *business breakthrough* throughout the book. Admittedly, the word *business* is a relative term. As I'll show through a variety of examples beginning in the first chapter, these types of breakthroughs are equally applicable to nonbusiness organizations.

My messages are simple:

Business breakthroughs deliver surprise. Our brains are wired to appreciate positive surprise. Great ideas surprise us with a strong dose of remarkable newness in ways that add value to our lives and challenge our assumptions about what we thought possible.

Surprises are strategic tools that drive breakthroughs. By proactively seeking out and using surprises as "guideposts" when they occur, we can gain new insights, generate ideas, and discover new directions for ourselves and our organizations.

Business breakthroughs transform people and organizations. Breakthrough business success doesn't simply result from a great idea. It involves a challenging and transformative journey through deep ambiguity, unforeseen events, and inevitable failures in order to come out on the other side to achieve business breakthroughs.

Leapfrogging isn't easy. When we're in the process of challenging the status quo, people take notice. At first they can be critical, telling us that what we're doing is impossible, unimportant, or even wrong. But if we persist and start to succeed, eventually criticism can give way to recognition and praise. Leapfrogging is about the journey of traversing ambiguity to find clarity. It's about finding direction in ourselves as leaders, which in turn creates new opportunities for our organizations. It's about revealing new possibilities to customers, clients, business partners, or others so they see themselves in our own hopes and aspirations, and then jump on board to join us on our journeys.

This book is the result of hard research and soft insight. It draws upon my twenty years of hands-on experience, research studies from universities around the world, and case examples from diverse organizations including global companies, start-ups, and nonprofits. I spoke to many people while writing this book. Some were clients and colleagues. Others were referred to me because they had achieved an undeniable breakthrough, or were currently involved in the process of doing so. Some were running multi-billiondollar businesses with tens of thousands of employees. Others were in much smaller organizations with only several people.

Most of the book's examples come directly from my work or discussions with these leaders who possess track records and stories of breakthrough success from organizations including Gatorade, OpenTable, Intuit, Four Seasons, Philips, Colgate-Palmolive, Kimberly-Clark, and numerous others. And I don't focus only on organizations that have created breakthrough products. I intentionally include examples from outside of the traditional mold, since today's world is much more about services, business models, processes, brands, and global collaboration. A number of examples also demonstrate how breakthroughs can relate to specific business functions, like finance, information technology, and marketing.

Many leaders have confidentially admitted to me that they have questioned themselves, their strategies, and the abilities of their teams and organizations during their journeys to their breakthroughs. On the exterior they portray themselves as confident, self-assured, and ready to take the world by storm. In the privacy of their corner offices, however, they acknowledge feelings of doubt, fear, and surprise, but they adamantly believe that they need to keep these experiences hidden away like skeletons in a closet. Massimo d'Amore, President of PepsiCo's Global Beverages Group, shed light on this dynamic when he said to me, "If anyone who's led a breakthrough says they didn't have a single doubt, you know they are lying. The challenge is to deal with ambiguity and doubt while balancing it with the determination leaders must show to their own teams. When we were reinventing Gatorade, I had many doubts during the difficult days but I always managed to keep them away from the team so they wouldn't be distracted from their journey. Deep-down I always knew it was the right journey to take, but when everyone's telling you what you're doing is crazy, it's hard not to have doubts." Discussions like this one reveal that some of the most important underlying leadership dynamics and secrets to breakthrough success are systematically hidden, since the very nature of creating business breakthroughs involves experiences that are pervasively considered to reveal weakness—including admitting to being surprised.

LEAPFROGGING TO BREAKTHROUGHS

BY **SOREN KAPLAN**

THE JOURNEY TO BREAKTHROUGHS INVOLVES DISTINCT PHASES

The leapfrogging life cycle traces the path to breakthroughs by describing the leadership and organizational dynamics involved at various phases over time. The truth is that achieving breakthrough business success is a dynamic process that can't be "managed" in the traditional sense. A lot of trial and error goes into it. Success often depends on how well we address the "soft stuff"—how we deal with uncertainty and ambiguity, how engaged and invested we are personally, how we deal with both small setbacks and large failures, and how we respond to surprises.

The leapfrogging life cycle quite literally depicts the ups and downs involved in creating breakthroughs. In the coming chapters, I'll present a number of real-life examples and supporting research studies to bring each of these phases to life. For now, here's a brief overview of what occurs in each:

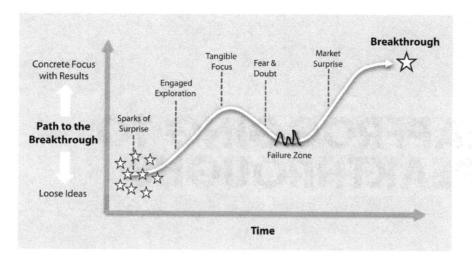

Figure 21.1. The Leapfrogging Life Cycle

Sparks of Surprise   Breakthroughs often start with "Sparks of Surprise"—initial insights into a need, problem, or opportunity area that deeply resonate with our interests, values, and motivations. This leads us to question our long-held assumptions or realize that there might just be a better way to do things. At this early stage we usually don't yet have a specific idea or solution; we just sense that "something big is out there" that we're compelled to better understand and define.

Engaged Exploration   With a new conviction of purpose, we go out into the world with excitement. Our curiosity engages us in a way that compels us to explore new areas beyond our day-to-day routine. Through this "Engaged Exploration," we learn everything we can about the problems, needs, challenges, requirements, and gaps pertaining to our area of interest. When we put ourselves into situations that push us beyond our comfort zone, we often experience surprises that challenge our existing mental models. When this happens, our eyes open up to a whole host of possible new directions.

Tangible Focus   Our exploration teaches us new things, which helps us to arrive at a new level of insight. With a sense of the true nature of our breakthrough, now it's time to put some solid stakes into the ground to make it real. As we move forward, the steps we take to bring our breakthroughs to life can result in further surprises. These surprises continue to challenge our assumptions and help us hone in on what, exactly, we need to create and how best to do it. I call this new level of insight "Tangible Focus."

How can "focus" be "tangible"? After all, at this early stage we're still desperately trying to "sculpt fog." I don't mean that the focus can be touched in the physical sense. I simply mean that we've achieved a firmer grasp of our subject area. Our focus may be in the form of a hard conclusion or just hunches and hypotheses. It's during this phase that all of our excitement and learning coalesce into a solid sense of direction that's grounded in real action.

Fear and Doubt (and the Failure Zone)   Now that we've put a mental stake into the ground, so to speak, we see things differently. We look at problems, needs, challenges, requirements, or gaps through a new lens. But as we move forward, outline solutions, and test our ideas, we realize that many of our initial thoughts and assumptions were only partly correct and need to be revised. As it becomes clear that a lot of hard work lies ahead, and that the answers we're looking for are far from clear-cut, we question what we're doing. Our initial enthusiasm starts to wane. Fear and doubt set in. We enter what I call the "Failure Zone," the graveyard of a million potential breakthroughs.

The reason many people fail at this point isn't a matter of ability, but mindset. It's not that we can't overcome the challenges or get the work done. It's because we simply give up. We aren't prepared to let go of the status quo and embrace the realm of ambiguity and uncertainty. I've seen it play out this way time and time again. But I've also seen plenty of people persist to push through the failure zone. And that's when the really good stuff starts to happen.

Market Surprise   Those who forge on don't always achieve instant success, but they do start to experience wins that provide rewards in the form of additional learning, positive feedback, and results. They adapt and modify their approaches. And, as they do so, they gain greater motivation to persevere. Others begin to recognize the value of the new solution or approach. The wins begin to snowball and the market starts to experience the positive surprise associated with the breakthrough first hand. This generates broader interest and buzz, which build momentum and accelerate the journey to the breakthrough.

LEAPS		STRATEGY
L	Listen	Start with yourself, not the market
E	Explore	Go outside to stretch the inside
A	Act	Take small simple steps, again and again and again
P	Persist	Take the surprise out of failure
S	Seize	Make the journey part of the (surprising) destination

Figure 21.2. The LEAPS Model

I want to emphasize again that the leapfrogging life cycle is admittedly a gross simplification of what can be an incredibly complex process. In reality, there are fits, starts, highs, lows, successes, and failures in each phase of the life cycle. Some of these phases overlap and can even repeat themselves, which creates cycles within the life cycle. But I'm a strong believer that simplicity is the antidote to complexity. To this end, I've created the acronym LEAPS that highlights specific things leaders can do to find insight, direction, and the strength to successfully navigate each phase of the leapfrogging life cycle themselves, and with their teams and organizations.

The LEAPS model maps to the leapfrogging life cycle by providing guidance and tools to successfully address the dynamics within each life cycle phase. [...]

SURPRISES OFTEN JOIN US ON OUR JOURNEYS

First and foremost, the leapfrogging life cycle is intended to outline the overall process of leading business breakthroughs. While by now it should be pretty evident that the power of surprise is a key theme in this book, I want to emphasize that not every phase of the leapfrogging life cycle is necessarily laden with surprises. But, uncertainty and ambiguity are ever-present throughout the process of creating breakthroughs, and because of this, surprises can show up anywhere and at any time—and it's helpful to be ready for them.

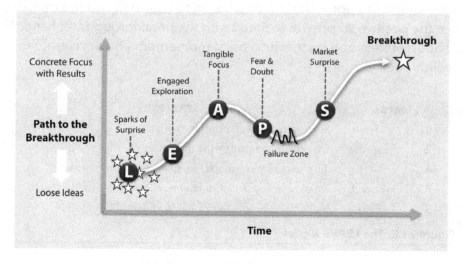

Figure 21.3. LEAPS Model Mapped to the Leapfrogging Life Cycle

In the following chapters I'll review each phase of the leapfrogging life cycle in detail. I'll bring the leapfrogging process to life through a variety of examples, some from organizations you'll recognize and others that will likely be new to you. I'll show you how to use the power of surprise to let go of things, uncover things, and create things—and I'll show you how to challenge assumptions and overcome the barriers that create artificial boundaries and limit possibilities. I'll also provide questions and exercises that you can use to jump-start the leapfrogging process for yourself and in your own organization.

READINGS 20-21: QUESTIONS FOR THOUGHT

- The author suggests that breakthrough innovations often start with "sparks of surprise." What is meant by this?

- Think about a recent breakthrough innovation in the current marketplace. Now think back to what might have been a surprise insight that led the innovators to begin the path to developing the breakthrough innovation. What do you think the surprise insight might have been?

- The model proposed for achieving breakthrough innovation is very different from the approach suggested in the earlier readings in this chapter for managing innovation. Why do you suppose such a vastly different way of thinking is needed when focusing solely on breakthrough innovation?

- The model for achieving breakthrough innovations in the reading emphasizes the need to be persistent as "fear and doubt" set in. Can you think of a time when you were working on a project and you reached a point similar to what the reading refers to as "the failure zone"? How do you think innovators can best "persist and push through the failure zone," as the reading suggests is necessary to achieve breakthrough innovation.

8

INNOVATION PROFILES

Learning is best conducted in an active mode by "doing" in addition to reading and listening. When you can practice something you have learned, the quality of your learning increases dramatically. That's why in my college class I have students take part in a semester-long group project in which they fictitiously innovate for a well-known company. I encourage students to submit their top innovation concepts at the end of the semester to those companies that have open innovation programs. These programs, run by several companies, accept ideas from consumers and offer compensation for accepted ideas.

The next best thing to practicing innovation is to study how innovation leaders conduct innovation. In this chapter we will look at four companies that are well known as some of the leading innovators in the world. The first reading in the chapter focuses on Apple. Apple's stunning series of innovations, starting with the iPod, enabled them to leap from the middle of the pack in the Fortune 500 to become the world's largest-ever publicly traded company. The fascinating story of how they achieved this innovation success is both interesting and instructive.

The second reading in the chapter is a short article that highlights the unique culture at 3M. 3M is an unheralded innovator as they are not an iconic Silicon Valley brand. But their long track record of innovative success extends far beyond Scotch Tape and Post-it Notes.

The third reading shares insights from Amazon, a company that has transformed or disrupted several industries. Amazon has successfully leveraged key customer insights to generate breakthrough innovations.

The fourth and final reading of the book is an award-winning case study on Google, which includes detail around the unique and innovative culture that has been credited with Google's rise to become one of the most important companies in the world.

INNOVATION AT APPLE

One of the best ways to learn about any subject is to observe the leaders in the field. Just watching a professional golfer or basketball player can help you pick up little tips on how to improve your game. Unfortunately, it is not as easy to watch companies innovate. We can see the results of their innovations when they launch new products or services, but we can't get a front seat to how the innovation process takes place. That's why case studies, such as the one in the following reading, can be extremely valuable and captivating reading.

The next reading, "Innovation at Apple," is a case study originally published in 2011 that provides both a brief history of Apple and insights regarding how innovation takes place at the company. Apple's tremendous successes in the twenty-first century with the iPod, iTunes, iPhone, and iPad have fueled the rise in its stock price to the point where the company is now the largest in the world in total market capitalization.

Under the visionary leadership of Steve Jobs, Apple's mantra was "Think Different." And many of their practices are vastly different than the typical Fortune 500 company. Jobs was never the typical CEO. He was the unofficial chief innovator in an age before most companies had a role of chief innovation officer (and many still do not today).

Following the untimely death of Steve Jobs, questions surrounded Apple's ability to achieve the same level of innovation going forward. The case study closes with a discussion on this topic. Although Apple has introduced the Apple Watch and the Apple Home Pod—both of which may ultimately turn out to be breakthrough innovations—the magical run from the iPod to the iPad may be a tall order for anyone to match.

This reading was published by the IBS Center for Management Research. The editor, Debapratim Purkayastha, heads the case research center at IBS. The case writer, Maseeha Syeda Qumer, has authored dozens of case studies for the IBS Center for Management Research and is the winner of the 2018 Case Centre Outstanding Case Writer award.

INNOVATION AT APPLE

BY **DEBAPRATIM PURKAYASTHA AND MASEEHA SYEDA QUMER**

"Apple is a very disciplined company, and we have great processes. But that's not what it's about. Process makes you more efficient. But innovation comes from people meeting up in the hallways or calling each other at 10:30 at night with a new idea, or because they realized something that shoots holes in how we've been thinking about a problem.[…] And it comes from saying no to 1,000 things to make sure we don't get on the wrong track or try to do too much. We're always thinking about new markets we could enter, but it's only by saying no that you can concentrate on the things that are really important."[1]

—Steve Jobs, founder of Apple Inc.

"Apple is Steve Jobs, Steve Jobs is Apple, and Steve Jobs is innovation. You can teach people how to be operationally efficient, you can hire consultants to tell you how to do that, but God creates innovation. ... Apple without Steve Jobs is nothing."[2]
—Trip Chowdhry, an analyst with Global Equities Research LLC[a], in 2011.

---

a Global Equities Research LLC is a US based equity research firm specializing in fundamental research on global equities in the technology sector.

The iconic founder of technology major Apple Inc. (Apple), Steve Jobs (Jobs), passed away on October 5, 2011, aged 56. Jobs's demise led to speculations about the consequences for Apple and its ability to continue to innovate without him. Jobs was succeeded by Timothy Cook as CEO, but some analysts raised concerns about whether the company would thrive without Jobs's vision and flair for innovation. They were apprehensive whether Apple which was synonymous with innovation would continue to break new ground without Jobs. According to Jason O. Gilbert, a technology reporter for *The Huffington Post*, "The biggest challenge for Apple is the one whose answer is difficult precisely because it is hard to define: How do you replace someone whose talents seemed to go beyond design and imagination to almost-ethereal, zeitgeist-y qualities? How do you hand over responsibility for maintaining an aura? For Apple, as for any company, that's a high bar, one it will likely fail to reach. Apple's coolest days are probably behind it."[3]

BACKGROUND NOTE

Apple was founded by Steve Jobs, Stephen Gary Wozniak (Wozniak), and Ronald Gerald Wayne (Wayne) on April 1, 1976. Working at Jobs's garage they designed a personal computer (PC) that was sold as Apple I. The company was incorporated as Apple Computer, Inc. on January 3, 1977. Thereafter, the company grew by introducing many innovative and commercially successful products such as Apple II (1977) and Apple III (1980).

Right from its inception, Apple had been a company committed to building great products using the latest technologies. The strong R&D focus that Jobs and Wozniak insisted on helped Apple to differentiate itself from its competitors. Apple products enjoyed wide recognition among end-users both for their attractive designs and their powerful applications in high-end computing in the education, multimedia, and entertainment industries. A large portion of this credit went to Jobs who had always seen himself as a product architect rather than as a businessman.

Apple brought out a number of innovative products and innovative features in the early 1980s. In its early days, Apple's product development strategy focused on replacing existing products with new ones at regular intervals. For instance, Apple I was replaced by Apple II and then Apple II by Apple III. When Apple III failed in the market and there was an onslaught of competition, Jobs was compelled to create products that would differentiate them from the traditional low-end computing products. In 1981, Apple's competitor International Business Machines Corporation[b] (IBM) introduced the IBM PC which was powered by the MS-DOS operating system and Intel's micro-processors. It became a common standard for PCs and as a result, Apple's market share began to decline.

In 1983, following his visit to Xerox's Palo Alto Research Center, Jobs along with other engineers developed the Lisa, which had a Graphical User Interface (GUI) and a Windows-based operating system that allowed several programs to run simultaneously. It was priced at US$ 9,995. But the Lisa proved to be a commercial failure because of its high price and limited software capabilities. After the failure of the Lisa, Jobs concentrated on developing a cheaper machine with a different operating system. The result was the Apple Macintosh (Mac) released in 1984 with a new Mac OS.

Apple's Board of Directors was unhappy with Jobs for spending a huge amount of the company's time and resources on developing the Macs. In 1984, the actual sales of the Mac were only 20,000 units as against the projected sales of 80,000 units. Analysts attributed the poor sales to the Mac's limited applications and support of software programs. Moreover, the company was troubled by internal problems such as arguments between divisions and poor inventory tracking which led to overproduction. Between 1983 and 1984, Apple's net income fell by 17%. In May 1985, Jobs was dismissed from the post of Vice President of Apple and Head of the Mac division by John Sculley (Sculley) whom he had himself brought in as CEO in 1983. Later in September 1985, Jobs resigned as chairman of Apple and with some former Apple executives, founded a new company called NeXT Computers Inc.[c] (NeXT).

After Jobs's exit, Apple prospered for some time under Sculley's leadership. In 1987, Apple introduced the Mac II which recorded good sales. The company also introduced new products such as the laser printer, laser writer, and page maker. In 1988, Apple's income grew to US$ 400 million compared to US$ 217 million in 1986. In 1990, Apple experimented with a number of other products including digital cameras, portable CD audio players, speakers, video consoles, and TV appliances. The most notable was the introduction of the PowerBook 100 in 1991, a portable PC considered the prototype of the modern laptop. In 1993, Apple launched a Personal Digital Assistant (PDA) called Newton which failed commercially. This was followed by a series of major product flops which affected Apple's reputation and the company started losing market share. The board then decided that it was time for a leadership change and in June 1993, Michael Spindler (Spindler) was appointed CEO in place of Sculley.

---

b   Headquartered in Armonk, New York, IBM is a multinational computer technology and IT consulting corporation. For the year ended 2010, the company reported revenues of US$ 99.870 billion. IBM exited the PC business in 2004.
c   NeXT was a computer manufacturing company which built computers for students that ran on a UNIX derived NeXT step operating system.

With Apple slipping further into trouble, Spindler was replaced by Gil Amelio (Amelio) in February 1996. In December 1996, Apple acquired NeXT for US$ 377 million in order to develop Apple's next-generation OS, Rhapsody. This marked the re-entry of Jobs into Apple. Because of his inability to revive Apple's fortunes, Amelio was eased out in July 1997. The board replaced Amelio with Jobs, who assumed the role of Interim CEO in September 1997.

Jobs began restructuring the Apple product line. He immediately discontinued the licensing agreement that promoted clones of Apple's products. He dropped 15 of the company's 19 products, withdrawing Apple's involvement in making printers, scanners, portable digital assistants, and other peripherals. Jobs closed down some plants, laid off thousands of workers, and sold stock to rival Microsoft Corporation[d] (Microsoft) for US$ 150 million in exchange. From 1997, Apple began to focus exclusively on desktop and portable Macs for professional and consumer customers. In August 1998, Apple unveiled the iMAC, a sleek and colorful computer that personified Apple's skill in design and functionality. Priced at US$ 1,299, the product was a big success and sold over 278,000 units in the first six weeks. In 1999, Apple's sales grew by 3.2% and net income registered a 94% gain. Stock climbed up by 140% to US$ 99 per share. By the end of the decade, Jobs was appointed as the CEO of Apple permanently. Realizing that the company's culture had changed under successive CEOs, Jobs emphasized that Apple should move back to the culture existing when he was at the helm and that the energy and flair of Apple's past should be recreated.[4]

On November 10, 1997, Apple launched a website (www.apple.com/store) to sell directly to customers online. In January 1999, Jobs announced a fifth consecutive profitable quarter and released the new PowerMac G3, a professional desktop machine. In July 1999, Jobs introduced the iBook for the low-end portable market. In 2001, Apple opened a number of retail stores across America which sold not only Apple computers, but other digital products, such as MP3 players, digital cameras, and PDAs. In January 2001, Apple launched the iTunes[e] software wherein users could copy tracks from CDs onto their computers or could download MP3 music files from the Internet and sort and play them. On October 23, 2001, Apple launched the iPod, a portable music player that could store up to 1000 songs. Later in 2002, Apple released the Windows compatible iPod. On January 11, 2005, Apple introduced the iPod Shuffle, a digital audio player which used flash memory. Between 2003 and 2008, Apple sales

---

d   Microsoft Corporation is a US-based computer technology corporation that develops, manufactures, licenses, and supports a wide range of software products for computing devices. For the year ended 2011, the revenues of the company were US$ 69.94 billion.

e   iTunes is a digital media player application for playing, downloading, and organizing digital music and video files. Users can connect to the iTunes Store to find, purchase, and download third-party digital music, audio books, music videos, movies, and iPod games.

tripled to over US$24 billion and profits increased significantly from US$42 million to US$3.5 billion.[5]

Addressing the Macworld Conference & Expo[f] on January 9, 2007, Jobs announced that from that point, Apple would be called Apple Inc., with the word 'Computer' being dropped from its name. The event also saw the announcement of the iPhone, the first mobile phone from the company. With Jobs at the helm, Apple staked out new ground by launching innovative products in the music (iPod) and mobile phone (iPhone) markets. Experts said that while Microsoft, the leading player in the market at that time, maintained status quo, Apple concentrated on developing stylish and cool products targeted at youth. As a result, Apple raced ahead in the competition and took the lead. In May 2010, Apple overtook Microsoft to become the world's most valuable technology company in terms of market capitalization.

On January 27, 2010, the company introduced the iPad, a tablet PC. This was followed by the launch of the iPad2, an improved version of the iPad, in March 2011. On August 24, 2011, Jobs stepped down as CEO of Apple citing health reasons.[g] Tim Cook[h] (Cook), the company's COO, was appointed as the new CEO. In October 2011, Cook unveiled the new iPhone 4S, an advanced version of the iPhone. (Refer to Exhibit I for a timeline of Apple's products).

APPLE'S APPROACH TO INNOVATION

At Apple, innovation was a way of life and a part of its corporate DNA. Apple's success was attributed to its ability to develop innovative products. Over the years, the company launched some great products in the market which became the benchmark for customer experience. For five consecutive years (2006-2011), Apple was ranked number one on the world's most innovative companies list compiled by BusinessWeek (Refer to Exhibit II for the top 10 most innovative companies list).

Since its inception, Apple had focused on innovation and had ventured into those markets where it could make a significant contribution. According to analysts, one of the main goals of the company was to make technology seamless for the customer. With its motto, "Think Different," Apple followed a self-contained operating style

---

f   Macworld Conference & Expo is an annual trade show held in the US dedicated to the Apple Macintosh platform.
g   Jobs was diagnosed with a rare form of pancreatic cancer in August 2004. The tumor was removed from his pancreas later that year. Jobs took six months' medical leave for a liver transplant in 2009. In January 2011, Jobs took his third medical leave of absence citing health reasons and returned in March 2011.
h   Before being named CEO, Tim Cook was Apple's Chief Operating Officer (COO) and was responsible for all of the company's worldwide sales and operations. He also headed Apple's Macintosh division.

that kept it ahead of its competitors, experts added. In the process of trying to out-do itself, Apple seldom acknowledged competition. The company manufactured those products which were meaningful and profitable. For creating such products, it employed people who were hard working and committed. Jobs was seen as the source of Apple's innovation as it was he who was credited with inspiring Apple employees to come out with path-breaking products. He wanted Apple's products to be perfect in every way (Refer to Box I for Key Elements in Apple's Approach to Innovation).

According to some employees, the work culture at Apple was driven by a passion for products and attention to the minutest details. Most of the decisions related to product development came from Jobs. Employees were given clear-cut directives and were closely supervised. "We hire people who want to make the best things in the world. You'd be surprised how hard people work around here. They work nights and weekends, sometimes not seeing their families for a while. Sometimes people work through Christmas to make sure the tooling is just right at some factory in some corner of the world so our product comes out the best it can be. People care so much, and it shows,"[6] said Jobs.

Experts said that Apple carried out disruptive innovation[i] wherein it launched new technologies and products that dominated and broke the market standard. The company took risks and entered new markets. A case in point was the launch of the iPod and iTunes which redefined the nascent MP3 player market and created new business models. The company regularly upgraded its products through supportive innovation. For instance, Apple launched different versions of the iPod such as Shuffle, Nano, Classic, and Touch. At Apple, innovation came not only from within but also from outside. Apart from in-house thoughts, Apple sourced ideas for new product development from start-ups and academic researchers. For instance, the idea for the development of the iPod came from a consultant whom Apple had hired to work on one of its projects.

Apple's approach to innovation was not to spread itself thin with an array of products but to focus on developing a select group of products in each category. "One traditional management philosophy that's taught in many business schools is diversification. Well, that's not us. We are the anti-business school,"[7] said Cook. Once a new product was launched, the company cut off development support for the earlier product. For instance, Apple dropped its most popular iPod Mini the day it introduced the iPod Nano.

---

i Disruptive Innovation is a process by which a product or service takes root initially in simple applications at the bottom of a market and then insistently moves up the market, eventually displacing established players.

As Apple was mainly involved with innovation, the company's policy was to keep things confidential. Apple believed that a company did not have to open up its innovation processes in order to build great products and services. Jobs created and fostered a culture of secrecy at Apple. The company had created this mystique by being very secretive about its activities. It did not share information about product innovations with employees fearing leaks. Apple attempted to restrict information in a bid to maintain the surprise factor associated with the launch of Apple products. Apple kept its employees in the dark about new product launches unless they were involved in the making of the product. This created a lot of buzz around new product launches. The company was known for splashy product launches shrouded in secrecy and rehearsed to perfection. The media and Apple fans speculated about what products the company would launch in the future. Gene Munster, an analyst from Piper Jaffray & Co.,[j] said, "They don't communicate. It's a total black box."[8]

Box 22.1
Key Elements in Apple's Approach to Innovation

- Think differently
- Enable a product-oriented culture instead of one driven by technology or money
- Always make a profit to keep making good products
- Hire people who want to make the best things in the world
- Innovation comes from passionate, dedicated people
- Focus on where you think you can make a significant contribution
- Own and control the primary technology in your products

Source: http://www.bia.ca/articles/BenchmarkingInnovationinaTimeoftransition.htm

PRODUCT INNOVATION

Apple became the leading technology company in the world by creating cutting edge products. The company constantly innovated with its business model to respond to market needs and challenges and to deliver quality products and services. The

---

j   Based in Minneapolis, Minnesota, Piper Jaffray & Co is a middle-market investment banking firm which offers financial advice and investment products to targeted sectors of the financial services marketplace.

technology behemoth combined new technology with simplicity to come out with cool and simple products, experts said.

Jobs was the chief innovator at Apple who was involved in the sourcing of the initial idea for a new product. He was not only involved in product design and development but also in how new products were launched and marketed. He did not believe in the concept of a target market and focus groups as he felt that consumers were not aware of what they really wanted in a new product and that it was his responsibility to show them what they needed. According to Jobs, "It's not about pop culture, and it's not about fooling people, and it's not about convincing people that they want something they don't. We figure out what we want. And I think we're pretty good at having the right discipline to think through whether a lot of other people are going to want it, too. That's what we get paid to do. So you can't go out and ask people, you know, what's the next big [thing].There's a great quote by Henry Ford, right? He said, 'If I'd have asked my customers what they wanted, they would have told me "A faster horse."'"[9]

While designing a new product, Apple followed the 10 to 3 to 1 approach wherein Apple designers came up with 10 entirely different pixel perfect mock ups of any new product. Later the number was culled to three and engineers worked upon the selected designs for some more months before zeroing in on the final design. At times, Jobs discarded finished concepts at the very last minute. At Apple, a group called Top 100 met annually for an intense three-day strategy session led by Jobs at an undisclosed location. Attendees were not allowed to drive themselves; instead they rode in buses from Apple's headquarters. They were not allowed to discuss their participation in the meeting. At the meeting site, rooms were checked for electronic listening devices to prevent leaks. Some observers said Apple mapped its product's innovation cycle 5 to 10 years into the future to avoid competition. The product development team at Apple was a tight-knit group comprising world-class designers and engineers who worked on crucial projects. During the development of any application, the teams of engineers and designers gathered for two complementary meetings every week, one to brainstorm and the other for production details. Engineers worked for 90 hours a week to reach deadlines.

Product development at Apple was veiled in secrecy. Secrecy was built into the corporate culture and the company always maintained tight control over information. Employees were fired for leaking news to outsiders. Employees who worked on important projects had to pass through multiple check points which included multiple badge-triggered security doors and number pads for offices. Work spaces were typically monitored by security cameras. In product testing rooms, employees had to cover up devices with black cloaks when they were working on them, and turn on a red light as a warning whenever the cloaks were removed so that other employees would be careful about the product. Generally, employees were not informed about new product development except for those working on the product and many of them were usually as surprised about the new product announcements as outsiders. Employees involved in product development were not allowed to disclose details of the product to other employees. "While secrecy is beneficial during development, and helps make a big splash on introduction of a product—the paranoia still runs deep after the product has shipped. The default answer to any question is "say nothing publicly", and this philosophy is driven out of fear, even for purely technical discussions,"[10] said a Lead Software Engineer at Apple.

Some of Apple's game-changing innovations were the Mac, the iPod, the iPhone, and the iPad (Refer to Exhibit III for a brief note on these products) Apple's winning streak began with the Mac which was launched in 1977. In the third quarter ended June 2011, Apple sold 3.95 million Macs, a 14% increase over the same quarter of the previous year.[11] The iPod launched in 2001 pushed Apple to the top position in the technology industry. In 2005, the combined sales of the iPod and iTunes accounted for 39% of the company's total revenue. This was followed by the launch of the iPhone in 2007. Within a year of its launch, Apple iPhone sales grew to over 5% of Apple's revenue. The iPhone was named the 'Invention of the Year' by *Time* in 2007. By April 2010, Apple had sold more than 51 million iPhones and more than four billion applications were downloaded from the AppStore[k]. In the third quarter ended June 2011, Apple sold 20.34 million iPhones a 142% growth compared to the corresponding quarter of the previous year. The iPad launched in January 2010 redefined the Tablet industry. Apple sold over 15 million iPads in just nine months in 2010, generating revenues of over US$9.5 billion.[12] During the third quarter ended June 2011, Apple sold 9.25 million iPads, a 183% unit increase over the previous quarter. Experts said though Apple delivered some flop products like the Apple TV and the Mac Cube[l], the company continued to innovate and had strengthened the technology on its existing products.

INNOVATION IN CUSTOMER EXPERIENCE

Apple's innovation strategy was customer centric. The company designed new products around the needs of the user, not the demands of the technology. It came out with such products which created value for both the company and its customers. Apple products were such that consumers never really realized they needed just these until

---

k   Launched in July 2008, the App Store is an online digital application distribution platform for the iPad, the iPhone, and the iPod. In July 2011, the App Store surpassed 15 billion app downloads.
l   Launched in 2000, Mac Cube was a small cube-shaped Macintosh PC. It was discontinued in 2001 due to poor sales.

they were launched in the market. These products empowered customers through their high quality user experience. According to industry observers, Apples products were desired by the market as customers eagerly awaited a new product launch and were even willing to pay a price premium for the product.

Apple believed in leading its customers and not following them. Apple adopted user-centric innovation wherein it took feedback from customers for new product designs. Occasionally, the otherwise secretive company leaked new product ideas to the market to see what kind of response the product would generate. By making customer experience a top priority, Apple created products that were not only easy to use but also provided a strong visual and emotional attraction. According to Jonathan W. Seybold, founder of Seybold Seminars[m], "Apple has been so successful because its product conception and development are NOT customer-driven in the sense that you advocate. They are driven by an uncanny ability to look at where technology is going, to form a vision of what might be possible, and to relentlessly execute that vision. This has always involved pushing the technology a step or two further and faster than anyone else had thought possible. And it has always involved Steve demanding a product that is finished and polished and refined in a way that no other company would have done. "[13]

To develop an emotional connection with its customers, Apple launched the Apple Store, a chain of retail stores which sold Apple products in 2008. Experts called it an innovative retail experience as it offered interactive product, service, and support information to Apple customers. In September 2011, for the eighth consecutive year, Apple topped the US consumer satisfaction survey in the personal computer industry released by the American Customer Satisfaction Index (ASCI)[n] (Refer to Exhibit IV for ASCI scores by Industry (Personal Computer)). With 87 points, Apple maintained its dominance in the PC industry in terms of customer satisfaction. "In the eight years that Apple has led the PC industry in customer satisfaction, its stock price has increased by 2,300%. Apple's winning combination of innovation and product diversification—including spinning off technologies into entirely new directions—has kept the company consistently at the leading edge,"[14] said Claes Fornell, founder of ACSI.

---

m   Seybold Seminars was a leading seminar and the premier trade show for the desktop publishing and pre-press industry.

n   The American Customer Satisfaction Index is a national economic indicator of customer evaluations of the quality of products and services available to household consumers in the US. Data from interviews with approximately 70,000 customers annually are used as inputs to measure satisfaction. Results are released on a monthly basis with all measures reported using a 0 to 100 scale.

INNOVATIVE LEADERSHIP

Jobs was the chief innovator at Apple. Since rejoining Apple in 1996, he had focused heavily on innovation and he played an important role in the product development process. He ensured that new ideas were aligned with the company's vision. He emerged as the one of the most innovative business leaders in the world. Talking about Apple's struggle to innovate in the initial years, Jobs said, "You need a very product-oriented culture, even in a technology company. Lots of companies have tons of great engineers and smart people. But ultimately, there needs to be some gravitational force that pulls it all together. Otherwise, you can get great pieces of technology all floating around the universe. But it doesn't add up to much. That's what was missing at Apple for a while. There were bits and pieces of interesting things floating around, but not that gravitational pull."[15]

According to experts, Jobs's dedication to excel made Apple an icon of innovation. He had a strong influence on the culture at Apple, they said. Jobs inspired employees at Apple to come out with unconventional products by thinking differently. He created an environment in which employees were encouraged to believe that they were better than the rest. It was Jobs's vision to make the best possible products that encouraged engineers and developers to develop the best possible products, said industry observers (Refer to Box II for seven principles of innovation inspired by Steve Jobs).

Jobs believed that Apple's advantage came from its ability to make unique, or what he called 'insanely great' products which drove profits and enhanced shareholder value. Employees also believed that Apple was in business for more than just making money.[16] Moreover, the employees at Apple were looked upon as a bunch of mutinous arrogant kids who were seen as rebelling against the old order. Yet, according to Jobs, they came out with products that were 'insanely great'. At least in the initial years, the employees shared a deep distaste for IBM, according to some analysts. While IBM focused on building huge machines, Apple worked toward developing inexpensive computers for "every man, woman, child, and chimpanzee on earth."[17]

Jobs generally spent time sharing new ideas with the product development team. He keenly monitored every aspect of product development process right from conception to execution and would not accept anything less than perfection from his employees According to tech veteran Scott Jordan, "Most legendary entrepreneurs satisfy themselves with creating or revolutionizing one industry. A very few impact more than one. Only the rare Edison comes along, maybe once a generation, to yank the steering wheel of history multiple times with light bulbs and electric generation and gramophones and moving pictures. Steve Jobs is one of those. Like Edison, many of his innovations leveraged others' work. Like Edison, he has an instinctive ability to reach across fields to bring ingredients together. Edison didn't invent the light bulb, but he made it a success in business by building the necessary workgroups with the necessary diversity, assembling the necessary ecosystem with the necessary breadth, and finding the necessary message with the necessary appeal."[18]

Box 22.2
Seven Principles of Innovation Inspired by Steve Jobs

1 Do What You Love (Think differently about your career).

2 Put a Dent in the Universe (Think differently about your vision).

3 Kick Start Your Brain (Think differently about how you think).

4 Sell Dreams, Not Products (Think differently about your customers).

5 Say No to 1,000 Things (Think differently about design).

6 Create Insanely Great Experiences (Think differently about your brand experience).

7 Master the Message (Think differently about your story).

Source: Carmine Gallo, "The Innovation Secrets of Steve Jobs: Insanely Different Principles for Breakthrough Success," McGraw-Hill, 2010.

Jobs fostered a culture of secrecy at Apple. He created a mystique surrounding the company and its products. While some analysts called him a corporate dictator who made every critical decision at Apple, others opined that as an inventor Jobs was unparalleled as he created products that took the market by storm. "Jobs is a magnetic pitchman who sells his ideas with a flair that turns prospects into customers and customers into evangelists,"[19] said Carmine Gallo, a columnist and communication skills coach.

WHERE'S APPLE HEADED?

For the third quarter ended June 2011, Apple generated quarterly revenues of US $28.57 billion compared to US $15.70 billion in the corresponding period of the previous year. The company recorded a net profit of US $7.31 billion. International sales accounted for 62% of the quarter's revenue (Refer to Exhibit V for Apple's selected financial data and Exhibit VI for net sales by operating segment and by product).

On August 9, 2011, Apple briefly surpassed oil group Exxon Mobil Corporation° to become the most valuable company in the world in terms of market capitalization (Refer to Exhibit VII for stock price chart of Apple). It planned to expand its presence in China, one of the biggest mobile markets in the world, and in other countries where Apple products were not popular.

On August 24, 2011, Jobs resigned as CEO of Apple citing health reasons and handed over the reins to Cook. He said that the company must be able to continue without him. He passed away on October 5, 2011. Experts opined that Jobs's demise left a big leadership gap and that the company would struggle to stay ahead of its competitors as Jobs had been a visionary leader with extraordinary management skills. "I think Apple would be more of an ordinary company without him—it would be much less audacious, daring, and artistic,"[20] said Andy Hertzfeld, a former employee.

The biggest concern for all the stakeholders was how the company would perform without Jobs. They were apprehensive that the company's dependence on Jobs would limit its future growth. Some experts were of the view that some of Apple's employees might consider leaving the company because Jobs was no longer at the helm. Sales would be impacted as it was observed that customers generally bought Apple products because they were inspired by Jobs's brilliance and magical aura. "For loyal Apple users, the cult of Steve Jobs is intertwined with the success of the company and he is the brand. So how Apple goes about maintaining that will need to be addressed. It will be interesting to see to what extent Apple will codify the things Steve Jobs believed in,"[21] said Faisal Siddiqui, a consultant at Figtree[p].

There were some other concerns among investors about whether Cook shared a vision similar to that of Jobs and whether he would be able to retain Apple's top position in the technology market. The lukewarm response to Cook's first big product launch of iPhone 4S could be taken as a warning sign, they said. According to industry observers, the challenge before Apple's new CEO would be to continue Jobs's strategy of constant innovation, secrecy, and product development. Some analysts wondered whether Apple would continue to impress consumers with its products and whether Jobs's successor would be able to maintain the company's culture of innovation. "[W]hat people wonder about is what happens years from now, or maybe sooner. Can Apple keep its mojo as the tech company that made an incredible comeback and affected change in nearly every industry it got into during the past decade? Can Cook carve out his own place in the company's history, going beyond the role of changing how Apple puts together its products, into a role that defines what they are and how

---

o   Exxon Mobil Corporation is an American multinational oil and gas corporation. It is the world's largest company in terms of market capitalization (US$348 billion as of August 2011).
p   Figtree is an independent creative consultancy with offices in London, Paris, and Hong Kong.

they're perceived?"[22] asked Josh Lowensohn , a reporter for CNET News[q], perhaps echoing a question on many minds.

On the other hand, some experts said Apple was well positioned for the future as the company had the best executive group in the world that could focus on sound product development and gain investor confidence. Cook would lead the company successfully with his operational brilliance, they said. According to them, Jobs and Cook had already established a long-term roadmap for Apple which included strategies to create innovative new products. In the words of Lou Mazzucchelli, a tech analyst: "Even if everyone fell asleep, this is a $70 billion company. Apple knows its product road map the next few years. The execution may be a little different, and it will be interesting to see how its decision-making process changes. He (Jobs) was the final arbiter of taste within the company. How is that going to evolve? One person? By committee?"[23]

Exhibit 22.1

Apple-Product Timeline

YEAR OF RELEASE	PRODUCT
1976	Apple I
1977	Apple II
1978	Disc II
1979	Apple II+
1980	Apple III
1983	Lisa, Apple IIe
1984	Mac 128k, Apple IIc, Graphical User Interface (GUI)
1986	Mac Plus
1987	Mac II, Mac SE
1989	Mac Portable
1990	Mac LC, Mac Classic
1991	PowerBook 100
1992	Mac IIvx
1993	Newton Message Pad, Mac TV
1994	Power Mac 6100/60, QuickTake camera

q   Launched in 1996, CNET is an online media website that publishes news articles, blogs, and podcasts on technology and consumer electronics industries.

YEAR OF RELEASE	PRODUCT
1995	Quadra 610 (DOS compatible)
1996	Power Mac 6300/120
1997	Power Mac G3, eMate 300
1998	iMac/233
1999	iBook
2000	PowerMac Cube
2001	iPod, OS X
2002	iMac G4
2003	Power Mac G5
2004	iPod mini
2005	iPod shuffle, iPod nano
2006	iMac Core Duo
2007	iPhone, iPod classic, iPod touch
2008	iPhone 3G
2009	iPod nano (5th generation)
2010	iPad
2011	iPhone 4S, iPad2

*the list is not exhaustive
Source: www.apple-history.com

Exhibit 22.2

The Top 10 Most Innovative Companies: 2006–2010

RANK	2010	2009	2008	2007	2006
1	Apple	Apple	Apple	Apple	Apple
2	Google	Google	Google	Google	Google
3	Microsoft	Toyota Motor	Toyota Motor	Toyota Motor	3M
4	IBM	Microsoft	General Electric	General Electric	Toyota Motors
5	Toyota Motor	Nintendo	Microsoft	Microsoft	Microsoft
6	Amazon.com	IBM	Tata Group	Procter & Gamble	General Electric
7	LG Electronics	Hewlett-Packard	Nintendo	3M	Procter & Gamble
8	BYD	Research In Motion	Procter & Gamble	Walt Disney Co	Nokia
9	General Electric	Nokia	Sony	IBM	Starbucks
10	Sony	Wal-Mart Stores	Nokia	Sony	IBM

Source: http://bwnt.businessweek.com

Exhibit 22.3

Apple's Game Changing Products

The Mac

Apple redefined the PC industry with the launch of the Mac in 1984. Earlier in 1983, Apple developed the Lisa, a computer with a GUI. Though the Lisa never caught on, Apple was confident about the concept and developed a cheaper machine with a different operating system called the Mac. It was the first affordable computer and was faster than other PCs. The initial sales of Mac were not very strong. Jobs realized that the Mac lacked certain features like the ability to multi-task and adequate memory. He asked the developers at Apple to create new software for the Mac which would be more user-friendly than that of most other PCs, which were still using MS-DOS[r]. In 1985, the Mac computer line received a big sales boost with the introduction of the Laser Writer printer. Upon his return to Apple in 1998, Jobs revamped the Mac line and launched the iMac in 1998. Targeted at the low-end consumer market and designed with the internet in mind, iMac generated good sales. The Mac product line evolved over the years to include the MacBook Air, the MacBook Pro, the Mac mini, the iMac, and the Mac Pro.

The iPod

Apple spearheaded the digital music revolution by launching a portable music player, the iPod, in 2001. Prior to the launch of the iPod, music fans had to be content with cassette players or CD players. Moreover, the digital music market was fighting music piracy. All that changed with the launch of the iPod. Instead of developing an mp3 player from scratch, Apple developed the iPod through open innovation wherein the company sourced the idea from Tony Fadell, a former employee of General Magic, Inc[s]. Apple hired Fadell in 2001 as an independent contractor to develop the iPod. The product focused on the mp3 technology to load music and changed the way people listened to their music. The iPod was a hard disk based digital music player that was smaller than other hard disk mp3 players. Experts said that the iPod had an impressive industrial design, which was lacking in other hard disk players in the market.

The iPod revolutionized the mp3 player market and since its release evolved into a line of products that included the iPod Shuffle, the iPod Nano, the iPod Classic, and the iPod Touch. Apple's position as the world's number one innovative company (2006) was attributed to the exponential growth of the iPod. Experts said that the iPod had transformed Apple from a niche PC maker into a consumer electronics major. It was reported that since its introduction, Apple had sold over 330 million units of the iPod worldwide. Of these, 45 million were sold between July 2010 and June 2011.

The iPhone

After revolutionizing the mp3 market, Apple entered the competitive mobile phone market. Launched in January 2007, the iPhone marked Apple's entry into the mobile phone market. The iPhone was a combination of three products—a mobile phone, an iPod with touch

---

r   Released in 1981, MS-DOS (Microsoft Disk Operating System) is an operating system that uses a command line interface.

s   General Magic, Inc. developed a suite of voice infrastructure software products that enabled the creation of personality-rich voice access to new and existing Web-based enterprise applications. On April 1, 2004, the company went out of business as it filed for Chapter 11 bankruptcy

Continued

controls, and an Internet communications device—into a small handheld device. It was Apple's first consumer device to run on OS X with a touch-based user interface. According to industry observers, the iPhone dominated the Smartphone market and overtook established players such as Research In Motion Limited[t] and Nokia Corp[u].

The iPad

The iPad was the first hugely popular tablet PC. Apple had been toying with the idea of developing a tablet as it had observed that most tablets which were available in the market were either very bulky with low battery life or were not optimized for touch and offered no real benefit to users over a laptop. It was rumored that Jobs had killed several internal Apple tablet projects over the years and had ultimately launched the iPad in 2010. Based around a multi-touch display, the iPad was an enlarged version of an iPhone. It included specially redesigned versions of the standard suite of iPhone applications. Most significant among the iPad applications was iBooks, an eBook reader application.

---

t   Headquartered in Waterloo, Canada, Research In Motion Limited (RIM) designs, manufactures, and markets wireless solutions for the worldwide mobile communications market. Its products and services include the BlackBerry wireless platform, the RIM Wireless Handheld product line, and software development tools.

u   Nokia Corporation manufactures and sells mobile devices, and offers Internet and digital mapping and navigation services worldwide. It is based in Espoo, Finland.

Compiled from various sources

Exhibit 22.4

ASCI Scores by Industry (Personal Computer)

	BASELINE*	2007	2008	2009	2010	2011
Apple	77	79	85	84	86	87
Personal Computers	78	75	74	75	78	78
HP (Hewlett Packard)	78	76	73	74	77	78
Dell	NM	74	75	75	77	77
All Others	NM	75	72	74	77	77
Acer (includes Gateway)	NM	NM	72	74	77	77
Compaq (Hewlett Packard)	78	73	70	74	74	75

*All measures reported using a 0 to 100 scale.
Source: www.theacsi.org

Exhibit 22.5

Apple Selected Financial Data

(Amount in millions of US $, except share amounts which are reflected in thousands and per share amounts)

	2010	2009	2008	2007	2006
Net Sales	65,225	42,905	37,491	24,578	19,315
Net Income	14,013	8,235	6,119	3,495	1,989
Earnings per common share:					
Basic	15.41	9.22	6.94	4.04	2.36
Diluted	15.15	9.08	6.78	3.93	2.27
Cash dividends declared per common share	0	0	0	0	0
Shares used in computing earnings per share:					
Basic	909,461	893,016	881,592	864,595	844,058
Diluted	924,712	907,005	902,139	889,292	877,526
Total cash, cash equivalents and marketable securities	51,011	33,992	24,490	15,386	10,110
Total assets	75,183	47,501	36,171	24,878	17,205
Total long term obligations*	5,531	3,502	1,745	687	395
Total Liabilities	27,392	15,861	13,874	10,347	7,221
Total shareholder's equity	47,791	31,640	22,297	14,531	9,984

* The Company did not have any long-term debt during the five years ended September 25, 2010. Long-term obligations excludes noncurrent deferred revenue.

Source: http://files.shareholder.com/downloads/AAPL/1437009153x0xS1193125-10-238044/320193/filing.pdf

Exhibit 22.6

Apple Net Sales by Operating Segment and by Product

(Amount in millions of US Dollars except unit sales in thousands and per unit amounts)

	2010	2009	2008	2007	2006
Net Sales by Operating Segment:					
Americas	24,498	18,981	16,552	11,596	9,415
Europe	18,692	11,810	9,233	5,460	4,096
Japan	3,981	2,279	1,728	1,082	1,211
Asia-Pacific	8,256	3,179	2,686	-	-
Other segments net sales	-	-	-	1,753	1,347
Retail net sales	9,798	6,656	7,292	4,115	3,246
Total net sales	65,225	42,905	37,491	24,006	19,315
Net Sales by Product:					
Desktops	6,201	4,324	5,622	4,020	3,319
Portables	11,278	9,535	8,732	6,294	4,056
Total Mac net sales	17,479	13,859	14,354	10,314	7,375
iPod	8,274	8,091	9,153	8,305	7,676
Other music related products and services	4,948	4,036	3,340	2,496	1,885
iPhone and related products and services	25,179	13,033	6,742	123	-
iPad and related products and services	4,958	-	-	-	-
Peripherals and other hardware	1,814	1,475	1,694	1,260	1,100
Software, service and other sales	2,573	2,411	2,208	1,508	1,279
Total net sales	65,225	42,905	37,491	24,006	19,315
Unit Sales by Product:					
Desktops	4,627	3,182	3,712	2,714	2,434
Portables	9.035	7,214	6,003	4,337	2,869
Total Mac Unit sales	13,662	10,396	9,715	7,051	5,303
Net sales per Mac unit sold	1,279	1,333	1,478	1,463	1,391
iPod unit sales	50,312	54,132	54,128	51,630	39,409
Net sales per iPod unit sold	164	149	167	161	195
iPhone units sold	39,989	20.731	11,627	1,389	-
iPad units sold	7,458	-	-	-	-

Source: http://files.shareholder.com/downloads/AAPL/1437009153x0xS1193125-10-238044/320193/filing.pdf

Exhibit 22.7

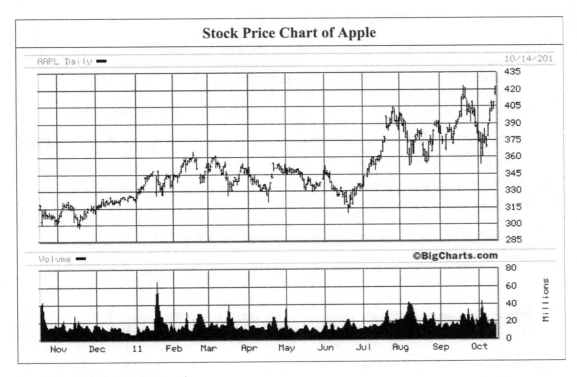

Source: http//bigcharts.marketwatch.com

NOTES

1. "The Seed of Apple's Innovation," www.businessweek.com, October 12, 2004.

2. Jason O. Gilbert, "Without Steve Jobs, Is Apple Still Cool?" www.huffingtonpost.com, August 25, 2011.

3. Ibid.

4. Eric Abrahamson, *Change Without Pain: How Managers Can Overcome Initiative Overload, Organizational Chaos, and Employee Burnout*, (Harvard Business School Press, December 4, 2003).

5. Opal Tribble, "Fortune: Apple Ranks Number One in Innovation and the Most Admired Company in USA," http://mac.blorge.com, March 7, 2008.

6. "The Seed of Apple's Innovation," www.businessweek.com, October 12, 2004.

7. Betsy Morris, "What Makes Apple Golden," http://money.cnn.com, March 3, 2008.

8. Brad Stone and Ashlee Vance, "Apple's Obsession with Secrecy Grows Stronger," www.nytimes.com, June 22, 2009.

9. "Steve Jobs Speaks Out," http://money.cnn.com, March 7, 2008.

10. "Apple, A Fortress of Secrecy?" www.glassdoor.com, October 5, 2008.

11. "Apple Reports Third Quarter Results," www.apple.com, July 19, 2011.

12. Marco Tabini, "Jobs Updates Apple Sales Figures," www.macworld.com.au, March 3, 2011.

13. Patricia Seybold, Scott Jordan, and Jonathan Seybold "Apple's Amazing Comeback," http://outsideinnovation.blogs.com, October 2, 2010.

14. "Customer Satisfaction with Personal Computers, Appliances and Electronics Hits a Wall," www.theacsi.org, September 20, 2011.

15. "The Seed of Apple's Innovation," www.businessweek.com, October 12, 2004.

16. Edgar H. Schein, *Organizational Culture and Leadership* (Third edition, Jossey-Bass Publishers, September 21, 2004).

17. Jean Lipman-Blumen and Harold J. Leavitt, *Hot Groups: Seeding Them, Feeding Them, and Using Them to Ignite Your Organization*, (Oxford University Press, USA, May 20, 1999).

18. Patricia Seybold, "Apple's Amazing Comeback," www.customerthink.com, October 2, 2010.

19. John H. Ostdick, "Steve Jobs: Master of Innovation," www.successmagazine.com, May 4, 2010.

20. Ina Fried, "Celebrating Three Decades of Apple," www.cnet.com, March 28, 2006.

21. Sarah Shearman, "Industry Analysis: Will Apple Survive without Steve Jobs?" www.marketingmagazine.co.uk, August 25, 2011.

22. "An Apple without Steve Jobs," www.zdnetasia.com, October 7, 2011.

23. "What's Next for Apple After Jobs' Death?" www.azcentral.com, October 7, 2011.

READING 22: QUESTIONS FOR THOUGHT

- Apple presents an interesting case for innovation study. Its path to developing great innovations did not necessarily follow the processes laid out in earlier chapters of this book. What did you find most interesting about Apple's approach to innovation? Why?

- Unlike most companies, Apple benefitted from a CEO who was a visionary and innovator himself in Steve Jobs. Jobs was also notorious as a hard-driving leader who demanded perfection and often got involved in the smallest details of product development. Imagine you were an employee at Apple in the first decade of the twenty-first century. What do you see as the benefits and drawbacks of having a CEO like Steve Jobs? Why?

- The reading was written in 2011, shortly after Jobs passing. As a result, the authors posed the question regarding whether Apple could sustain its ability to innovate under its new CEO, Tim Cook. How do you feel Apple has fared under Tim Cook's leadership?

INNOVATION MINDSET

The next reading provides some key principles of what it takes for companies to be innovative. For each key point, the article provides specific examples of how innovation is managed at 3M. Most people are familiar with at least some of 3M's products including Scotch Tape and Post-it Notes. But few people think of 3M as being one of the most innovative companies in the world. With headquarters in the Twin Cities of Minnesota, far from Silicon Valley, 3M doesn't receive the recognition it deserves. 3M is a company committed to continuous innovation and has expertise in dozens of industries. It serves all types of customers (consumers, businesses, and governments) around the globe with thousands of diverse products.

A few years ago, I had the opportunity to visit the Innovation Center at 3M in Saint Paul, Minnesota. I was able to experience firsthand the unique culture of this great company. I was most impressed with the importance placed on sharing, openness, and collaboration. These are important traits for innovation as they create the conditions necessary for the cross-pollination of ideas.

This brief article was coauthored by Vijay Govindarajan and Srikanth Srinivas. Govindarajan is a best-selling author and the Coxe Distinguished Professor at Dartmouth's Tuck School of Business. Srikanth Srinivas is a cofounder of Visualize ROI. He is also the author of *Shocking Velocity*.

INNOVATION MINDSET

WE CAN SEE IT IN ACTION AT 3M

BY **VIJAY GOVINDARAJAN**
AND SRIKANTH SRINIVAS

G reat innovators share a common quality—the *innovation mindset*—a robust framework that can be applied at micro (individual) and macro (organizational) levels: they see and act on opportunities, use *and-thinking* to resolve tough dilemmas and break through compromises, and employ their resourcefulness to power through obstacles.

Innovators maintain a laser focus on outcomes, avoid getting caught in the activity trap, and proactively *expand the pie* to make an impact. Regardless of where they start, innovators and innovative companies persist till they successfully change the game.

Take, for example, 3M, awarded the National Medal of Technology. 3M is consistently ranked in the top 20 of *America's Most Admired Corporations*. Over a 20-year period, 3M's gross margin averaged 51% and return on assets averaged 29%.

Innovative companies achieve excellence in five ways:

1. They provide forums for employees to pursue opportunities. One of 3M's strengths is how it treats promising employees: give them opportunities, support them, and watch them learn and thrive. 3M provides a rich variety of centers and forums to create a pool of practical ideas that are then nurtured into opportunities and provided the necessary resources for success. Scientists go out into the field to observe customers to understand their pain points. Customers also visit *Innovation Centers* set up to explore possibilities, solve problems, and generate product ideas. Scientists share knowledge and build relationships at the Technical Council, which meets periodically to discuss progress on technology projects, and the Technical Forum, an internal professional society where 3M scientists present papers—just two of 3M's fruitful forums.

Arthur Fry, a 3M employee, attended a Technical Council where Spencer Silver spoke about trying to develop a super-strong adhesive for use in building planes; instead, Silver accidentally created a weak adhesive that was a "solution without a problem." Fry, who sang in a church choir, had been losing the bookmark in his hymnbook. He noticed two key features of Silver's adhesive that made it suitable for bookmarks: the note was reusable, and it peeled away without leaving residue. Fry applied for and received funding to develop a product—the Post-it note.

2. They create an environment that fosters the right tension with "and thinking." One critical balance at 3M is between present and future concerns. Quarterly results are important but should not be the sole focus; staying relevant is also important but can't come at the cost of current performance. 3M has several ways to sustain this *and thinking*. Employing the *Thirty Percent Rule*, 30% of each division's revenues must come from products introduced in the last four years. This is tracked rigorously, and employee bonuses are based on achieving this goal. 3M also uses *and thinking* in their three research areas. Each area has a unique focus: Business Unit Labs focus on specific markets, with near-term products; Sector Labs, on applications with 3-to-10 year time horizons; and Corporate Labs, on basic research with a time horizon as long as 20 years.

3. They create systems, structures, and work environments to encourage resourcefulness and initiative. Reporter Paul Lukas noted: "A 3M customer identifies a problem, and a 3M engineer expresses confidence in being able to solve it. He bangs his head against the wall for years, facing repeated setbacks, until management finally tells him to stop wasting time and money. Undeterred, the engineer stumbles onto a solution and turns a dead end into a ringing success."

Richard Drew is one such an engineer. Running some Wetordry sandpaper tests at an auto-body shop to improve paint removal, he noticed that the painter couldn't mask one section of a two-tone car while painting the other. The tapes available at the time, back in the 1920s, either left a residue or reacted with the paint. Drew assured the painter that 3M could solve the problem and worked on it for two years, eventually receiving a memo from senior management instructing him to get back to work on the waterproof Wetordry sandpaper. Drew did, but he continued working on the tape project on his own time. The result: Scotch tape.

Figure 23.1.

3M has a rich set of structures and systems to encourage resourcefulness:

- *Seed Capital*: Inventors can request seed capital from their business unit managers; if their request is denied, they can seek funding from other business units. Inventors can also apply for corporate funding (Genesis Grant).

- *New Venture Formation*: Product inventors must recruit their own teams, reaping the benefit of 3M's many networking forums as they seek the right people for the job at hand. The recruits have a chance to evaluate the inventor's track record before signing up. However, if the product fails, everyone is guaranteed their previous jobs.

- *Dual-career ladder:* Scientists can continue to move up the ladder without becoming managers. They have the same prestige, compensation, and perks as corporate management. As a result, 3M doesn't lose good scientists and engineers only to gain poor managers (a common problem).

4. They focus on the right set of outcomes. They tailor what is measured, monitored, and controlled to suit their focus, and strike the right balance between performance and innovation. 3M has created measurement and reward systems that tolerate mistakes and encourage success. 3M rewards successful innovators in various ways: the Carlton Society, named after former company president Richard P. Carlton, honors top 3M scientists who develop innovative new products and contribute to the culture of innovation, and the Golden Step is a cash award. 3M also tells the stories of famous failures that later created breakthrough products to ensure a culture that stays innovative and risks failure for unexpected rewards

5. They ensure a continuing focus on expanding the pie by effectively converting non-consumers into consumers, and providing richer solutions to current consumers. In the process they transform their industry, community, country.

3M uses a R&D focus and a unique "15% rule" to expand the pie. 3M spends about 6% of sales on R&D (far more than competitors) This results not only in new products but also new industries. David Powell, 3M's VP of marketing, affirms: "Annual investment in R&D in good years—and bad—is a cornerstone of the company. The consistency in the bad years is particularly important."

William McKnight, who rose from his bookkeeping position to become chairman of 3M's board, explains: Encourage experimental doodling. When you put fences around people, you get sheep. Give people the room they need." 3M engineers and scientists can spend up to 15% of their time pursuing projects of their choice, free to seek unexpected, unscripted opportunities, for breakthrough innovations that cam expand the pie.

The innovation mindset is a *game-changing asset* for companies and individuals. Innovative companies like 3M use creative *and-thinking* and resourcefulness to pursue promising opportunities and strategically meet outcomes, while *expanding the pie*. They create the structure, systems, and culture to enable their people to think and do things differently to achieve extraordinary success.

Vijay Govindarajan is the Earl C. Daum Professor of International Business at the Tuck School of Business at Dartmouth and coauthor of *Reverse Innovation* (HBR Press, 2012). **Srikanth Srinivas** is an innovation catalyst and author of *Shocking Velocity.*
Visit **Vijay.Govindarajan@Tuck.Dartmouth.edu**.

READING 23: QUESTIONS FOR THOUGHT

- 3M has a long history of innovation and has exhibited many innovation best practices for decades. Which of the innovation practices mentioned in the reading would most appeal to you if you were an employee at 3M? Why?

- 3M is one of a few large companies that allows many of their employees to spend 15 percent of their time working on their own ideas for the company. How would you like this? How do you think this benefits the company?

- Sharing is a basic tenet at 3M. As the reading mentions, forums are available to share research and learn from other employees. How do you feel this environment of sharing helps innovation at 3M?

FAST LANE INNOVATION

Students in my class often hear me talk about the importance of focusing on the customer to drive innovation decisions. This doesn't mean always listening to exactly what customers say they want. It means ensuring you have a deep understanding of customer's problems, desires, and expected outcomes. This data then needs to be analyzed and turned into insights about the market, which in turn become the fuel for idea generation.

Amazon has grown quickly, moving from start-up to one of the world's largest companies in stock market value in just twenty years. One reason for their innovation success has been a brilliant focus on a few key customer insights. The next reading provides a brief overview of some of the factors that have contributed to Amazon's incredible ability to continuously innovate, including these customer insights. The reading goes on to describe five steps that all companies can take to increase the pace and success of their innovation efforts.

The reading is another excerpt from the book *First and Fast: Outpace Your Competitors, Lead Your Markets, and Accelerate Growth* by Stuart Cross.

FAST LANE INNOVATION

BY **STUART CROSS**

BUILDING UP SPEED: FOCUSING INNOVATION ON WHAT WON'T CHANGE

Amazon has led a transformation of the retail sector. From a standing start at the turn of the century, it is currently the most important retailer on the planet, even though it doesn't own a single physical store. By any definition you care to use, Amazon is an innovative business. But there is a secret to Amazon's ability to innovate and grow faster than its rivals.

Amazon's approach to innovation has been different. Rather than primarily focusing on the constant changes in the desires and needs of its various customer segments, the company has pinned its innovation activities on what won't change. For Amazon, the company has centered on three customer needs that Bezos and his leadership team have identified: range, price, and delivery speed. They took the decision that these factors will remain important to their customers over years and decades, not simply months and quarters. In many ways, these areas of focus look simple, even a little boring. But they have been critical to the company's success (see Figure 24.1).

The company's ability to focus on these factors has led to three key benefits:

1 **Bigger, Bolder, and More Disruptive Initiatives.** While its more traditional rivals have hedged their bets with investments across various channels, Amazon has been able to single-mindedly invest in its online business. The company's incessant focus on the needs and wants of its customers has also led it to make some big, bold decisions that have not only disrupted the market, but also the existing Amazon business model. Take the *Marketplace* concept, for instance. Most retailers look to control price and margins by buying and offering their products themselves, with no internal competition. The *Marketplace* has turned that thinking on its head. Amazon's own product buyers now face competition on Amazon's own real estate from third-party sellers who can offer both new and used versions of the product, and who can also offer ranges to shoppers that are not offered by Amazon. The downside of this decision is the risk that it lowers Amazon's revenues and profits. It is also likely to create more than a little angst across the buying teams! The upside is that the *Marketplace* elegantly meets Amazon's stated commitment to focus on customers' need for greater choice and lower prices. The concept may create some tactical difficulties for Amazon, but, strategically, it hits the bull's eye, particularly as it gives eBay competition for small independent retailers looking for a wide, national or global market. And if the decision has affected revenues and returns, it is hard to spot any downside within Amazon's reported results over the past few years.

2 **Organizational Alignment and Pace.** Amazon's consistent innovation focus on just three strategic priorities has also enabled the company to move more quickly. Focus builds understanding, and understanding builds engagement, alignment, and pace. Amazon's strategy and focus on three innovation platforms is far simpler, clearer, and easier to communicate than most corporation's strategies and enables the business to move at pace in a style that is similar to Southwest. Figure 5.2 highlights the launch of Amazon's major innovations between its launch in 1996 and 2014 and how they impact on the company's three customer priorities of greater choice, delivery speed, and lower prices. Most successful businesses would be happy with delivering just one or two of these game-changing innovations, but Amazon's focus and consistency have enabled the company to create a torrent, not a stream of innovation into its markets.

AMAZON'S
INNOVATION
DRIVEN GROWTH

2014 $89.0 billion
Amazon Prime Now launched in
Manhattan, offering one-hour
delivery service

$74.5 billion 2013
India site launched
AutoRip digital music service
Kindle MatchBook launched offering
free e-book for every physical book bought
Amazon Prime Air tested, using drones for delivery

2012 $61.1 billion
Kindle Fire HD

$48.1 billion 2011
Kindle Direct publishing launched
Free Instant Video and Kindle Lending
Library included in Amazon Prime offer

2010 $34.2 billion
Amazon Studios launched

$24.5 billion 2009
Acquired Zappos

2008 $19.2 billion
Acquired Audible

$14.8 billion 2007
Kindle launched
Digital music
AmazonFresh grocery delivery service tested

2006 $10.7 billion
Groceries first tested

2004 $6.9 billion

$8.5 billion 2005
Amazon Prime launched
(12 months free shipping for $75)

2002 $3.9 billion
Amazon Web Services
Clothing and accessories ranges

$5.3 billion 2003
Amazon e-commerce platform
available for third parties

2000 $2.8 billion
Amazon available in Japan and France
Marketplace launched
Kitchen and homeware ranges

$3.1 billion 2001
Free shipping on orders > £99
Look Inside the Book

1998 $610 million
Amazon available in UK and Germany
Music and video ranges

$1.6 billion 1999
Consumer electronics,
toys and games ranges

1996 $16 million
On-line book sales to the USA

$148 million 1997
Personal recommendations
1-Click shopping

Figure 24.1. Amazon's innovation landmarks

3   **Market Leadership.** Ultimately, Amazon's interconnected elements of consistent strategic focus, organizational alignment, and innovation pace have led to its position as one of retail's global market leaders in little more than a decade. In little more than 10 years, Amazon has become a Top 20 Global Retailer in terms of revenues and the retail leader in terms of thought leadership. If the company had followed most of its rivals' approaches, its strategy would have been more diverse and more responsive to changes in the competitive landscape of its markets. As a result, its portfolio of projects would have been less aligned and more cluttered and the company's managers would have been less clear about what was truly important. In turn, this would have created a sluggish, slow, and incremental business that followed, rather than led its markets. Strategic success happens when you are the first to profit from opportunities that are created by the dynamics of technological, social, and economic developments. Amazon's multichannel, traditional rivals have struggled to keep up because they do not have the purity of Amazon's strategic focus. Their lack of true strategic and innovation commitment reduces the pace of these organizations and diminishes their ability to become a market leader.

SHIFTING GEAR: ACCELERATION THROUGH ACTION

Convenience has always been important to grocery shoppers. For most of us, the weekly grocery shop is not a source of pleasure and delight, but is a chore that must be done—as quickly and as easily as possible. Back in the 1990s—or, as I tell my children, in the dim and distant days before the iPhone was a twinkle in Steve Jobs' eye—two U.K. grocery giants were battling for supremacy. The traditional market leader, Sainsbury's, was being overtaken by Tesco, a focused and aggressive business that had a clear customer strategy of ease and convenience for the United Kingdom's time-starved shoppers, under the tagline of "Every Little Helps." Both retailers had been working on reducing customer queuing time at the checkout. Customer research will tell you that queuing to pay ranks just above having your fingernails removed with pliers in shoppers' list of dislikes, so finding a cost-effective solution to this issue was a big opportunity for both rivals.

   Tesco's team had been struggling to make the financials work for its new service model, and was still refining its approach when management received word that Sainsbury's were ready to go live with their solution. Management had a decision to make. Should they let Sainsbury's be first to market with a better and faster queuing system, in the hope that once they had refined their own model customers would see that it was superior, or should they just launch their approach immediately and be seen as the queuing and convenience innovator in the market? The team decided to press the button and launch their solution ahead of Sainsbury's. Tesco's "One In Front" policy, where the retailer promised to open up the next available till if there was more than one person in the queue ahead of you, was an immediate success. Even though Sainsbury's launched its own solution a matter of days later, all the kudos and brand benefit was bestowed on Tesco. If Sainsbury's policy had a name, I have no idea what it was. Their solution was irrelevant as Tesco's flag was already firmly placed on that queue-busting summit. By being first to market—even with a solution that was not perhaps fully market-ready—Tesco was able to further tighten its grip on the U.K. grocery market. Being first had trumped being best.

In some markets—commercial jet engines, for example—every factor should be fully tested in all conditions before going into production. I would certainly prefer, for instance, that all the side effects of any prescribed drug I was asked to take had been fully understood and addressed before they were dispatched to my local pharmacy. But most of you aren't in the jet engine, pharmaceutical, or other life-threatening industries. Rapid, timely action, rather than further planning, is the key to success for most innovations. Here are five steps you can take to move your innovation into your market's fast lane:

1   **Clarify the Concept.** All innovation starts with an idea. The critical task at the idea stage is to be clear about the concept, and how the new product, service, or organizational approach will both work and improve performance. Often, a simple chart or visual helps to develop the required clarity. Southwest Airlines founder, Herb Kelleher, for instance, famously drew a triangle on a cocktail bar napkin to demonstrate how a new airline serving Houston, Dallas, and San Antonio in Texas could operate.

2   **Build a Series of Rapid Prototypes.** Version #1 is rarely completely success-ful. Neither are versions #2, 3, 4, or 10. You will fail with your initial prototypes. The idea is not to avoid failure, but to learn, adapt, and improve as quickly and as cheaply as you can. A critical element is to make sure that you don't "gold plate" your prototype; just make it good enough to allow you to learn quickly. We're not talking about months and months here, we're talking about days and weeks. Have a go, see what works, fix what doesn't and try again.

3   **Get Early, Objective Feedback.** Toward the end of the idea generation workshops that I lead, I ask the team to present their emerging ideas to a

panel of real customers. This stage in the process has two big advantages. First, it ensures that the team involved in the workshop develops real ideas that they can articulate and explain to "normal" people. There is no room for buzzwords or theoretical concepts; the ideas must be clear and practical. Second, the customers can provide immediate feedback on the ideas, enabling the development teams to more clearly focus on the next stage of their work. I believe that early customer feedback is vital to the innovation process, but don't expect to receive 100 percent approval. The more innovative your concept, the more likely it is that there will be resistance and distrust of it as people take time to come round to more radical ideas. Your aim is to gain evidence that your target customers believe that the idea has the potential to deliver genuine customer benefits.

4   **Confirm the Business Model Potential.** This is the step that might take time, but which is crucial to longer-term success. It marks the difference between pace and haste. Google founders Larry Page and Sergey Brin, for instance, spent two years or more searching for a profitable business model for their search engine before they settled on an advertising-driven model that enabled them to fully expand the service and drive its subsequent relentless growth. Two years may seem a long time, but sometimes you need to balance pace with patience. Brin and Page could have gone with their first business model concept, but that may have led to the company's early demise. Instead, they waited until they had an "80 percent solution," which has been fundamental to the company's amazing success.

5   **Launch Phase 1—*and* Develop Phases 2, 3, and 4.** The launch of an innovation is not the end of the process; it is the beginning. You should see the delivery of a new innovation to your organization or your market as an ongoing process not a one-off event. Even before Version 1 of your innovation is in use, your teams should be developing the next one or two versions so that you build up both pace and momentum. Apple's management of the iPod product development process has been a great example of this approach. In just a few years from its initial launch, Apple delivered a series of updates to the iPod range that offered both greater storage capacity and functionality at lower prices. The iPod didn't succeed so spectacularly because of the initial version, but because of the stream of constantly improving, market leading, and increasingly value-for-money products that customers absolutely loved. The combination of bigger storage capacity, improved functionality, better design and lower prices, and the pace at which Apple managed its product innovation pipeline also made it exceptionally difficult for potential rivals such as Sony or Microsoft to mount an effective competitive strategy, enabling Apple to dominate this niche until and beyond the launch of the iPhone.

These five steps rely on higher levels of management judgment, commitment and prudent risk-taking than more conservative, risk-averse, and planning-led innovation approaches. That said, I am not advocating a kamikaze approach where you simply close your eyes and hope for the best, but neither am I suggesting that you should have total confidence in your solution before moving. If you are to accelerate innovation through action, you must be open to new ideas and approaches, to trust your judgment, to seek out and learn from objective, customer-centered feedback, and to give your teams the confidence to commit to implementation, showing them that they can refine and improve any problems along the way.

READING 24: QUESTIONS FOR THOUGHT

- The reading indicates that Amazon has three key strategic priorities, which are based on a set of key customer insights that relate to core customer needs and which change little over time. These priorities have served as the guide to innovation at Amazon. What are the three priorities? Why do you feel this approach has worked for Amazon?

- How have the three strategic priorities led directly to Amazon developing industry-changing, disruptive new business models?

- The reading closes with five steps that companies can take to accelerate their innovation efforts. Why do you think these five steps are effective?

CORPORATE ENTREPRENEURSHIP AND INNOVATION AT GOOGLE, INC.

Alphabet (Google's parent company) has become legendary not only for its meteoric rise to become one of the world's largest and most influential companies but also because of it's unique, innovative culture. At Google, employees operate differently than in most other global corporations. Steps are taken to maintain a start-up atmosphere. Employees have reportedly been granted time to work on their own ideas, company programs have been instituted to engage all employees in problem solving, and open communication of ideas is strongly encouraged. This culture stands in stark contrast to the often-stifling work environment that exists in many large companies today where employees do not feel connected to innovation activities.

The next reading features an award-winning case study titled "Corporate Entrepreneurship and Innovation at Google, Inc." Originally published in 2013, the case study offers an interesting overview of Google's rise to the top of the corporate world as well as fascinating details about Google's innovation practices.

This is another reading published by the IBS Center for Management Research and edited by Debapratim Purkayastha. The case writer is Adapa Srinivasa Rao. The case study won both the 2014 AESE Case Writing Competition and the Human Resource Management/Organizational Behavior category at The Case Centre Awards and Competitions in 2015.

CORPORATE ENTREPRENEURSHIP AND INNOVATION AT GOOGLE INC.

BY DEBAPRATIM PURKAYASTHA AND ADAPA SRINIVASA RAO

"One of the primary goals I have is to get Google to be a big company that has the nimbleness and soul and passion and speed of a start-up."[1]

—Larry Page, CEO of Google, in 2011

"Google proved that you could systematize innovation. This meant you could create an environment where are asking why things are the way they are, and wondering if they can be done in a different way—where you look outside your own field for an idea."[2]

—Eric Schmidt, Executive Chairman of Google, in 2011

By August 2013, Google, Inc., known more for its dominance in the area of internet search till then, began to overtake its major rivals in innovation. The firm started working on a lot of other projects and increased its spending on research and development, thus gaining an edge over its competitors *(See Exhibit I for revenue, profits and R&D expenses).* Some analysts predicted that Google had started outpacing Apple, Inc.[a]

---

a   Apple Inc., headquartered in Cupertino, California, US is one of the biggest technology companies in the world. It mainly focuses on designing and selling consumer electronics products.

Debapratim Purkayastha and Adapa Srinivasa Rao, "Corporate Entrepreneurship and Innovation at Google, Inc.," *IBS Center for Management Research*, pp. 1-17. Copyright © 2014 by IBS Center for Management Research. Reprinted with permission by The Case Centre.

(Apple) in design, an area traditionally dominated by Apple. Google achieved this feat by making innovation an everyday process rather than as a necessity during times of crisis. It followed a unique 'launch and iterate' process to innovation where the new products developed were initially made available to the public as beta versions. Google improved these new products after getting feedback from the early users. It also practiced the system of using lead users to find new and innovative applications for its products. In addition to this, its CEO and co-founder, Larry Page (Page), continuously pushed the employees to go in for 'moon shots', i.e., create products and services that were 10 times better than the competition. According to Page, "How exciting is it to come to work if the best you can do is trounce some other company that does roughly the same thing? That's why most companies decay slowly over time. They tend to do approximately what they did before, with a few minor changes. It's natural for people to want to work on things that they know aren't going to fail. But incremental improvement is guaranteed to be obsolete over time. Especially in technology, where you know there's going to be non-incremental change."[3]

Google heavily leveraged on its employees to improve the innovative spirit in the company. It made it easy for employees to express their ideas through various initiatives like TGIF, Googlegeist, FixIts, Google Moderator, etc. These channels facilitated open communication within the organization and gave Google the agility of a startup in innovation. An HR policy called 'Innovation Time Off' introduced in the year 2010, allowed Google's employees to work on any company related work of their choice other than their regular job tasks for 20 percent of their total working time. This HR policy proved pretty successful, leading to the innovation of many products like Gmail, Google Talk, and Google News. To keep its innovation engine chugging, Google started to develop a number of new products and services like Google Glass, the Google Driveless Car project, and Project Loon.

Google's management tried its best to make sure that its growing size did not stifle its innovative spirit. It continued looking for new and promising ideas everywhere and ensuring the voice of every employee was heard. Many of the ambitious projects which failed in the market were quickly jettisoned so that the company could swiftly move on to developing new products. For example, the lessons learnt from its initial failures in social networking helped it to develop its successful 'Google+'. Despite these successes, some industry experts as well as Google's own investors were skeptical about the commercial viability of many of the new products that the company was developing. "It's not easy coming up with moon shots. And we're not teaching people how to identify those difficult projects. Where would I go to school to learn what kind of technological programs I should work on? You'd probably need a pretty broad technical education and some knowledge about organization and entrepreneurship. There's no degree for that. Our system trains people in specialized ways, but not to pick the right projects to make a broad technological impact,"[4] said Page. To come up with such projects that could also be commercialized was an even bigger challenge. Moreover, as Google grew to scary proportions in terms of product-market diversity as well as employee strength, the challenge before Page, co-founder Sergey Brin, Executive Chairman, Eric Schmidt, and other members of the top management team was how to keep the entrepreneurial spirit alive in the company (*See Exhibit II for profiles of Google's top management team*).

BACKGROUND NOTE

Google's roots lay in a research project on search engines taken up by two PhD students at Stanford University, Larry Page (Page) and Sergey Brin (Brin) in 1996. Google pioneered a new technology called 'PageRank', which determined the importance of the website by the number of other pages linked to it and their importance that linked back to the original site. This new technology was a shift from the earlier method followed by other search engines which ranked the results by the number of times the search terms appeared on the page. The search engine was initially called 'BackRub' as it determined a website's relevance by checking its back links. The name was finally changed to Google, based on the word 'Googol'—the number one followed by a hundred zeroes.

Google's primary domain 'www.google.com' was registered in September 1997 and the company was incorporated in September 1998 in a friend's garage in California, USA. In 1999, Google moved its headquarters to Palo Alto, California, home to several other technology companies. Google's mission was "to organize the world's information and make it universally accessible and useful."[5] In addition to its mission, the company wrote "10 things" in Google's initial years and the founders made it a point to revisit these from time to time to see if they still held true (*See Exhibit III for the '10 things'*).

Google started to sell advertisements associated with search keywords. This advertising model was successful and Google started getting a major part of its revenues from search related advertising. From 2001, the company based its growth strategies on acquiring many small companies with innovative products. It added many other products to its product portfolio like Google Earth[b] and YouTube[c] in this way. Apart from acquiring other companies, Google also launched its own products like the free

---

b   Google Earth is a virtual globe, map, and geographic information application owned by Google.
c   YouTube is a video sharing website owned by Google. Users can upload, share, and view videos on the website.

webmail, called 'Gmail' in April 2004. Gmail was also well received by the web community due to the massive increase in storage space provided by Google (initially one GB). The success of Gmail and YouTube made Google the undisputed leader on the internet, with the company overtaking many other established internet companies like Yahoo! Inc.[d] (Yahoo).

Google's promoters were hesitant to go in for an Initial Public Offering (IPO) as they were apprehensive that public scrutiny and financial regulations would make the company less agile.[6] But due to the demands of venture capitalists who wanted to cash out, Google filed for an IPO in April 2004.[7] In the IPO prospectus, Google's founders attached a letter subtly warning potential subscribers that Google was not a conventional company and did not aim to be one.[8] The dual class equity structure proposed by Google's founders proved controversial. Google's IPO comprised only the issue of Class A shares, each of which was entitled to a single vote. Google's founders, venture capitalists, and other insiders held Class B shares which were entitled to 10 votes per share.[9] Critics lambasted this share structure as they felt that it gave the founders significant management control and could lead to potential management abuse. But Page and Brin defended the structure on the grounds that it would help them fulfill their long-term vision for the company without getting bogged down by short-term financial demands.[10]

By the mid-2000's, Google faced a new challenge in the form of the ever-expanding high-end mobile phones dubbed as smartphones. Developing applications for the variety of platforms on which these smartphones were available proved to be cumbersome for Google. The company therefore decided to launch its own open source platform for mobile phones, which would give application developers the freedom to develop applications for various mobile phones without depending on any handset manufacturer or service provider.[11] Hence, Google acquired an open-source mobile platform called Android from Android, Inc. and released its first version in the market in 2009. Android proved to be an instant hit in the market and soon emerged as the dominant mobile platform in the world. Other than acquiring other smaller companies for launching new products, Google also focused on innovation and spent huge sums of money on developing new services. Over a period of time, Google nurtured the culture of innovation, coming out with disruptive technologies from time to time. The company had fanned out into hosting services like video and mapping, enterprise services, e-mail and chat, social networking space, payment gateway services, mobile operating software, and wireless device sales (See Exhibit IV for Google's market share in key products). Its revenues for the year 2013 were

---

d   Yahoo! Inc., headquartered in Sunnyvale, California, USA, is an internet company which provides services like search engine, webmail, online mapping, etc.

US$ 50.18 billion *(See Exhibit V for Google's Financials)*. The company had more than 44,000 employees worldwide.

GOOGLE AND INNOVATION

Google had made innovation an everyday process rather than looking at it as a necessity during times of crisis. By the year 2013, it had started to overtake its rivals in areas where it had been lagging traditionally. It started to catch up in social search and social networking with companies like Microsoft Corporation[e] (Microsoft) and Facebook, Inc.[f] (Facebook). Some analysts were of the view that Google had overtaken Apple in design—an area that had long been dominated by Apple *(See Exhibit VI for a comparison between Google and Apple)*. Google typically supported more than 100 new business concepts in various stages of development at any given time. The information about these projects was maintained in a central, searchable database. Of this, nearly, 70 percent of the projects supported the company's core business in some way, 20 percent represented emerging business ideas, and 10 percent were speculative experiments.[12]

PROJECT KENNEDY

Soon after Page took over as CEO of Google in 2011, he initiated Project Kennedy, which focused on the redesigning of the company's most important products under a single design language.[13] As most of Google's products evolved independently, they had a single unifying design standard. Google's initial search page was designed by its co-founder Brin himself as the company did not have the money to recruit a graphic expert.[14] The main goal of design at Google initially was to meet the needs of its users efficiently. Google followed a similar design philosophy for its later products like Gmail, Google Earth, Chrome, etc. The result was a not so remarkable design for its products which was comparable with its competitors like Apple. Project Kennedy focused on giving a consistent look and feel to several of Google's products and focused on design elements like refinement, elasticity, simplicity, and usefulness.[15]

---

e   Microsoft Corporation, headquartered in Redmond, Washington, US, is leading multinational software corporation.

f   Facebook, Inc., headquartered in Menlo Park, California, US, is a leading social networking service in the world.

'LAUNCH AND ITERATE'

In its bid to emerge as the leading technology company, Google started to lay a lot of emphasis on innovation. It followed a very unique process of innovation when compared with other technology companies. It evolved a 'launch and iterate' approach to innovation[16], which was quite different from other technology companies. Ever since it was founded, Google did not release the final version to consumers at the time of the initial release of a product. Almost all the products developed by Google were first developed as test versions (known as beta versions) at the time of their launch. The products remained in the beta stage for a long period, sometimes ran into multiple years.[17] In the beta stage, Google tried to obtain feedback on the performance of the products from consumers and kept on improving them by modifying some features or adding new ones. A final market version was released only after all the modifications had been made. From this stage, the product continued to expand at its own pace. This 'launch and iterate' model of innovation was in contrast to the 'perfect it before you sell it' approach followed by other technology companies like Apple. Some analysts opined that it was Google's approach to innovation that helped it to win the long-term innovation war with its rivals.[18]

Over a period of time, Google made its consumers and shareholders believe that all the initial versions of its products were experimental. After the initial period of testing, products which failed during the test phase were quietly withdrawn from the market. Google's strategy of using beta also made people believe that they would see significant improvements in the products in the future. Page said that the beta label on its products also had to do with "messaging and branding" rather than being a reflection of technical development.[19] Another advantage of this policy was that a product failure like the Google's much hyped up Google Wave would not affect Google's brand image and share value.

LEAD USERS

Google also followed a strategy of lead users to check its products before they were released into the market. A lead user was a person who faced needs that would be seen in the general market place months or years later.[20] Lead users extended the utility of products/services into new ways that had not been considered or approved by the firm that was producing the product.[21] For its more recent wearable gadget Google Glass, Google organized a social media contest. People who wanted to be its lead users had to enter into the contest called 'If I had a Glass' and explain to the company the uses to which they would put the Glass, which would make them a good lead user.[22]

Google got feedback on the product from these lead users to make further improvements to it. The lead users also helped Google to find new uses for products yet to be released into the market. For instance, Pedro Guillen, a Spanish surgeon. performed a knee surgery and telecast it live on the Internet with the help of Google Glass. In return, he obtained real-time suggestions on the surgery from surgeons all over the world.[23] This collaborative approach to innovation gave Google an edge over its competitors.

Though Google had been considered a laggard in innovation for quite a few years, its unique approach toward innovation helped it emerge as one of the most innovative companies in the world. Some analysts opined that Google was even overtaking Apple, considered as the most innovative technology company in the world under its ex-CEO Steve Jobs. For the year 2013, Google was ranked higher than Apple in Forbes'[g] list of Most Innovative Companies in the World.[24]

LEVERAGING EMPLOYEES IN FOSTERING INNOVATION

Right from its startup days, Google believed in heavily leveraging on the strengths of its employees to foster the spirit of innovation at the company.

'70/20/10' INNOVATION MODEL AND 'INNOVATION TIME OFF'

In the year 2005, Google's former CEO, Eric Schmidt. introduced a business resource management model called the '70/20/10' innovation model for the employees. Under this model, Google's employees dedicated 70 percent of their working to core business tasks, 20 percent to projects related to the core business, and 10 percent to projects which were totally unrelated to their core business.[25] This model led to better utilization of the skills of its employees and helped the company come up with new products and technologies. The option to work 10 percent of their time on projects not related to their core business gave the employees a lot of freedom to work on any task they liked and come up with new and innovative ideas. The success of the '70/20/10'

---

g Forbes is a biweekly American business magazine which features articles on finance, investing, economy, and marketing.

model led to the total organization of Google under this philosophy underlying the total organization of Google for a long time.

In the year 2010, Google introduced a new HR policy dubbed 'Innovation Time Off,' where employees were given some leeway to work on their preferred tasks for some time every week. The initiative was mainly backed by Page and Brin. Innovation Time Off was inspired by a work policy at Stanford University where professors were given one full day every week to exclusively focus on their research interests. Under the policy, every Google employee was given 20 percent of their weekly working time to focus on any company related work of their choice other than their regular tasks. This unique HR policy gave Google's engineers the flexibility to work on their selected tasks and innovate new ideas. The 'Innovation Time Off' policy showed spectacular results. By 2009, half of all Google's products originated from the program.[26]

Both Google and analysts credited the new policy for several of the advances made at Google.[27] Many of the highly successful products from the company's stable like Gmail, Google Transit, Google Talk, Google Moderator, and Google News were developed by Google's engineers during the 20 percent time allowance.[28]

TGIF AND FIXITS

Google practiced a liberal communication strategy to facilitate easy communication within the organization. The company believed that discussion and feedback from its employees were an important part of doing business and of helping its employees to raise questions and solving them. It started several initiatives to encourage open communication among the employees as well as with the top management *(Refer to Exhibit VII for various channels for Google's employees to express themselves)*. The first initiative followed by Google to engage its employees was to create a two-way dialogue on important issues.[29] Every Friday, Google held a forum called 'Thank goodness it's Friday' (TGIF) where issues facing the company ranging from product decisions to internal people related policies were discussed. TGIF forums also included live questions from employees to the management. These forums resulted in a high level of employee participation, fostering a culture of transparency and an intimate atmosphere. The second strategy was to engage people in solving problems through initiatives like FixIts which utilized the complete resources of employees to solve specific problems faced by the organization.[30]

GOOGLEGEIST

Other initiatives like Googlegeist which enlisted volunteer employee teams to solve major problems improved group cohesiveness among the employees. Cafés on the campuses too were designed in such a way as to promote easy interaction among the employees. Google followed an open door policy and encouraged its employees to freely interact with their superiors. Any employee of Google could mail the top leadership of Google on any company related issue. Internal review meetings were conducted periodically where new product ideas were presented to the company's management.[31] Google kept its innovation pipeline full by tapping into the ideas of its employees and letting them 'percolate up' through the various different communication channels. Commenting on the utilization of different communication channels to let employees' ideas percolate up, Laszlo Bock, Senior Vice President of Google's People Operations said, "We try to have as many channels for expression as we can, recognizing that different people, and different ideas, will percolate up in different ways."[32]

GOOGLE MODERATOR

In the year 2008, Google introduced an innovation management tool called Google Moderator. The tool allowed anyone to pose a question and everyone else to rank the questions they would like answered in a meeting.[33] The basic idea behind the tool was that there would be lot of good questions to be asked within a limited period of time at every meeting. But it would be difficult to decide which of the questions the attendees wanted answered and discussed. Google Moderator let the best questions rise to the top and hence best utilized the limited time available during company meetings. The tool which was also made available to the public, enabled Google to best utilize the limited time available at its internal meetings and leverage on the knowledge and ideas of its employees. During the financial crisis of 2007–2008[h,] Google set up a site called 'Tip Jar' to get innovative money-saving tips during difficult times.[34] The website generated a lot of useful tips for the company to survive the crisis.

---

h   The 2007–2008 financial crisis was the worst financial crisis that the world had seen since the Great Depression of the 1930s. The crisis resulted in a large scale closure of financial institutions around the world, bailouts of banks by governments, and downturns in the stock markets.

OTHER INITIATIVES

The company made it a point to recruit the top talent and subsequently bolstered their capabilities through training and development. Potential recruits at Google were scrutinized to see if they had the right combination of technical skills, intellectual agility, and "entrepreneurial DNA". They had to often clear 20 interviews before they were selected. The employees were compensated as per the industry norms and they were also rewarded for their contributions to innovation. For instance, in 2004, the 'Founders Award' was instituted at Google wherein restricted stock options were given quarterly to teams that came up with the best ideas to increase the profitability of the company. The company had a flat organizational structure with employees working on small teams. Leaders of the teams were rotated on teams and Google engineers were allowed to work on more than one project and also allowed to switch teams. Project teams working on new projects could approach the Google Product Council comprising the top management and engineering team leaders, for formal project funding. The project teams received assistance from the Google Product Strategy Forum to develop a business model and set milestones. If the model was found viable, the company focused on how the Google's core elements might be leveraged to enable the emerging business model.[35]

GOOGLE X AND THE 'MOON SHOT MENTALITY'

Even when Google came up with new products in response to competition, it strove to offer benefits that had been unimaginable till then. For instance, when the company launched Gmail, it offered users 100 times as much storage as they could get anywhere else. In August 2011, Google acquired Motorola Mobility LLC[i] for US$ 12.5 billion in order to make its own hardware for smartphones, tablets, and other devices.[36] Google had been eyeing Motorola for a while for its vast patent portfolio and manufacturing expertise.[37] Some technology companies like Apple made their own software and hardware which gave them full control over the devices made by them. This control over both hardware and software also gave it an edge over competitors like Microsoft and Google which only made software. Google too wanted to gain an advantage in future gadgets powered by its Android and Chrome OS[j]. More and more people were using portable gadgets like smartphones and tablets to access the internet

---

i   Motorola Mobility LLC, headquartered in Libertyville, Illinois, USA is a leading telecommunications company in the world.

j   Chrome OS is a Linux-based operating system developed by Google. Unlike the other traditional PC operating systems like Windows, Chrome OS primarily works with web applications.

and smartphones were emerging as the first devices through which people in less developed countries were accessing the internet for the first time. On the eve of the acquisition of Motorola, Page said, "Many users coming online today may never use a desktop machine, and the impact of that transition will be profound."[38] Analysts said that Google sought to achieve better control over these portable devices through the acquisition of Motorola. According to Page, there was a lot of room for innovation in hardware. As for instance, how to substitute the easily breakable glass used in handsets to more durable material.

However, rather than a simple iterative approach to innovation, Page wanted Google to develop a 'moon shot mentality' where it would be inspired to create products and services that were 10 times better than the competition. Google X, a separate division which was established in early 2010 to come out with 'moon shot' projects, was Page's brainchild. The secret facility was located about a half mile from the corporate headquarters and was overseen by Brin.[39]

In 2010, Google started to invest heavily in developing technologies which were both related and unrelated to its core business. Most of these products were innovative and were totally new to the world. One of the most hyped up technologies developed by Google was 'Google Glass'. Google Glass was a wearable computer which came with its own optical head-mounted display (OHMD)[k]. This wearable computer performed many of the tasks traditionally performed by other portable gadgets like smartphones and tablets.[40] Google Glass could connect with other portable devices like smartphones and tablets to transfer data and display it on its screen, placed right before the eyes. The device also had a tiny camera to take pictures and record videos, a touchpad, and could also be controlled through voice. The main goal of developing Google Glass was to develop a new category of computing devices which could shake up the technology market. According to analysts, Google wanted to put the internet right before the eyes of customers with Google Glass. This could help boost its services and advertising revenues. Commenting on Google Glass, Page said, "Glass is a new category and quite different from existing computing devices. Our main goal is to get happy users using Glass. We want to make sure we're building experiences that make people happy."[41]

Another important technology that Google had been working on was the Google Driverless Car project. This project was aimed at developing autonomous cars which would drive on their own without the need for any physical drivers. The technology worked on software developed by Google as well as the cameras and sensors fitted on to the car. Google was testing cars which ran using this technology across the

---

k   OHMD displays use an optical mixer made of silvered mirrors. These displays have the capability to reflect projected images besides allowing the user to look through them.

world and was expected to release it for the mass market once it obtained the legal clearances. Google wanted to leverage on its existing services like Maps to make the driverless car project a success.

There were two other innovative technology projects of Google aimed at improving the accessibility to people around the world. The more ambitious of the two was Project Loon which aimed to bring internet access within the reach of people living in remote parts of the world. Despite the rapid spread of digital technologies, nearly two-thirds of the world's population did not have access to the internet.[42] Project Loon was a network of balloons which floated high in the stratosphere[l] and circled the earth in rings. These balloons could connect with special ground antennas issued by Google and provide broadband internet access which was comparable to current 3G[m] speeds.[43] Each balloon would cover an area of approximately 40 km (25 miles) and was remotely controlled from the ground. The radio and flight equipment in the balloon was powered by solar panels which did not need frequent servicing.[44] Through Project Loon, Google aimed to get more people connected to the web and thereby increase the number of consumers using its various internet services as well as clicking on Google ads. Another new service that Google was experimenting with was Google Fiber which promised to bring very high-speed internet access (100 times greater than the prevalent broadband speeds) within the reach of everyone.[45]

KEEPING THE SPIRIT OF INNOVATION ALIVE

Google constantly strove to ensure that its growing size did not come in the way of its innovation driven culture. Google kept its commitment for innovation and risk at a constant level by following several policies like having a corporate mission that could guide them, constantly looking for new ideas everywhere, working for continuous innovation rather than instant perfection, proper usage of data, etc. (Refer to Exhibit VIII for the Google's Eight Pillars of Innovation). Google tried its best to maintain the nimbleness of a startup. Commenting on the steps taken by Google to keep its spirit of innovation alive, Susan Wojcicki, Google's Senior Vice President of Advertising, said, "As we've grown to over 26,000 employees in more than 60 offices, we've worked hard to maintain the unique spirit that characterized Google way back when I joined as employee #16."[46]

---

l   The stratosphere is the second layer of the Earth's atmosphere which is located just above the troposphere and below the mesosphere.

m   3G is a telecommunication standard referring to wireless networks which can transfer data with a minimum speed of 200Kbit/s.

Google did not let even failures come in the way of its striving for innovation. Many of the ambitious projects it started ended up failing due to several reasons. Some of the biggest failures were in the areas of social networking. Google's first social network, Orkut, never really took off in key developed markets. Its other attempts to break into the booming social networking space like 'Google Buzz' and 'Google Wave' too ended up being colossal failures. Google Wave, launched in 2009, was perceived by users to be very complex and many of them could not understand it properly.[47] Google discontinued the development of Google Wave in 2010. It made it a point to learn from its past mistakes and to correct them in future. Learning from its mistakes in social networking, Google launched a new social network called 'Google +' in 2011. Google + borrowed a number of features from other successful social networks like Facebook and added some new features. It was well received in the market and started growing fast. It emerged as the second largest social network surpassing Twitter and had a user base of 500 million registered users by May 2013. There were speculations among some analysts that Google + might emerge as the top social network in the world.

LOOKING AHEAD

As of August 2013, Google was chugging ahead with its future innovation plans. The top management team including Page, Brin, and Schmidt had always believed that a lot more innovation was possible than had been achieved. Commenting on future possibilities at Google, Page said, "Today, we're still just scratching the surface. Google is working on so many innovations. I get goose bumps about it."[48] Google was even looking to enter new product categories by launching new types of gadgets. In August 2013, Google confirmed that it had acquired Android smartwatch maker WIMM Labs.[49] The acquisition led to speculation among industry observers on Google entering another lucrative wearable gadgets category.

But not all was well with the culture of innovation at Google. The company discontinued the 'Innovation Time Off' initiative in August 2013 as employees were finding it difficult to get enough time to finish their regular day's jobs. Any employee who still wanted to utilize the 20% time perk needed to first get approval from the management.[50] Some analysts even questioned the viability of some of Google's latest projects like Glass and Project Loon. Google Glass was a new to the market product whose viability in the market had not been proven. While the product could be a refreshing addition to the growing number of wearable gadgets that were available in the market, its utility for the normal man was still questionable, according to them. Disruptive technology products like the iPhone had a proven market for smartphones before they were released in the market, which was not the case with Google Glass.[51] Commenting on the viability of Google Glass, Alex Roth an analyst at Tech Radar[n], said, "Is Glass cool and entirely novel? Yes, it certainly is. Is it a device that will change the life of, or even just prove useful to, the average consumer? That's doubtful."[52] Just like any technology company, Google was also facing pressure from investors on new innovations like Project Loon whose commercial viability was questionable. Kerry Rice of Needam & Co[o] said, "There are people on Wall Street who would like Google to quit spending on things that may not actually materialize in generating significant revenue."[53] One of the main reasons for the increasing criticism was the growing share price of Google which increased the expectations of its investors. Google's share price reached an all-time high of US$ 926.47 in July 2013 *(Refer to Exhibit IX for the chart of Google's share price).*[54]

For the year 2013, Google was ranked No. 47 on Forbes' list of Most Innovative Companies in the World. Google's rank for the year 2012 was No. 24 and for the year 2011 was No. 7 *(Refer to Exhibit X for the top innovative technology companies in the world).*[55] Bruce Upbin, managing editor of Forbes, said, "It's not necessarily true that Google's innovation has slowed down. But maybe investors think that driver-less cars won't pay off like search has."[56] But some long time industry observers also felt that Google's new projects should be seen in terms of their long-term viability rather than their immediate financial viability. They opined that increased internet access resulted in more people using Google's services which could lead to increased revenues. Charles Golvin of Forrester Research[p] said, "They're not underwriting these efforts for the benefit of the Internet community. They look at the big picture that these efforts are going to generate."[57]

Like that of any other technology company, Google's future too hinged on meeting the expectations of investors and keeping its innovation engine chugging. Page also acknowledged that it was not easy to come up with moon shots. Even though it would be a real challenge to keep the company's entrepreneurial spirit alive as Google grew through innovation, he was enthusiastic about the prospect of it becoming a million employees company and was excited about the prospects of all that the company could do with many more employees. Page quipped, "We could add people and still be really innovative. That would be great for us. We're one of the bigger companies of the world, and I'd like to see us do more stuff—not just do what somebody else has done, but something new."[58]

---

n   Tech Radar was a major online publication focusing on technology and gadgets.

o   Needham & Co, headquartered in New York City, New York, US is a leading investment bank and asset management firm. It specializes in advisory services and financings of growth companies.

p   Forrester Research, headquartered in Cambridge Massachusetts, USA, is a leading technology and market research company. It advices its clients on the potential impact of technology on their businesses.

Exhibit 25.1

Revenues, Profits, and R&D Expenses for 10 Years (In US$, Millions)

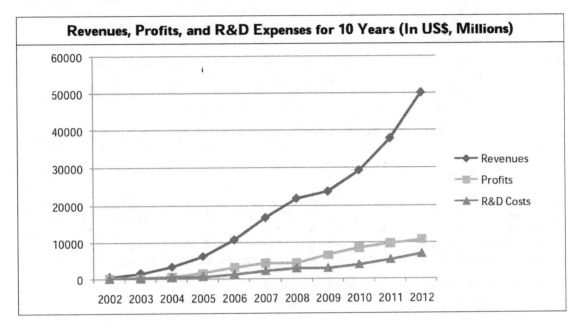

Source: http://investor.google.com/financial/tables.html.

Exhibit 25.2

Profiles of Google's Top Management

NAME	DESIGNATION	DESCRIPTION
Larry Page	CEO and Co-Founder	One of the co-founders of Google, Larry Page has a Master's degree in computer science from Stanford University. He is responsible for the day to day operations of Google as well as leading its product development and technology strategy. He was the first CEO of Google until 2001. He later worked as the president of products from 2001 to 2011.
Eric E. Schmidt	Executive Chairman	Eric E. Schmidt has a PhD in computer science from the University of California. He worked as the CEO of Google from 2001 to 2011. As the executive chairman of Google, he is currently responsible for the external matters of Google like building partnerships, government relationships, technology thought leadership, etc.
Sergey Brin	Co-Founder	Sergey Brin has a master's degree from Stanford University. He is now takes care of special projects at Google. He worked as the president of technology from 2001 to 2011, where he took care of company's day-to-day operations.

NAME	DESIGNATION	DESCRIPTION
Nikesh Arora	Chief Business Officer and Senior Vice President	Nikesh Arora has an MBA from Northeastern University. He joined Google in the year 2004 and is currently responsible for all its revenues, customer operations, marketing, and partnerships.
David C. Drummond	Senior Vice President and Chief Legal Officer	David C. Drummond has a JD from Stanford Law School. He joined Google in 2002 as vice president of corporate development and currently takes care of legal, government relations, corporate development, and new business development.
Patrick Pichette	Senior Vice President and Chief Financial Officer	Patrick Pichette has an MA in Philosophy, Politics, and Economics from Oxford University and is responsible for all the financial operations at Google.

Other members of the senior management team were Alan Eustace (Senior Vice President, Knowledge), Salar Kamangar (Senior Vice President, YouTube & Video), Sridhar Ramaswamy (Senior Vice President, Ads & Commerce), Sundar Pichai (Senior Vice President, Android, Chrome & Apps), Susan Wojcicki (Senior Vice President, Ads & Commerce), Urs Hölzle (Senior Vice President, Technical Infrastructure, and Google Fellow) and Vic Gundotra (Senior Vice President, Social)

Source: http://www.google.com/about/company/facts/management/.

Exhibit 25.3

Google's '10 Things'

1 Focus on the user and all else will follow.

2 It's best to do one thing really, really well.

3 Fast is better than slow.

4 Democracy on the web works.

5 You don't need to be at your desk to need an answer.

6 You can make money without doing evil.

7 There's always more information out there.

8 The need for information crosses all borders.

9 You can be serious without a suit.

10 Great just isn't good enough.

Source: http://www.google.co.in/about/company/philosophy/

Exhibit 25.4

Market Share of Google's Key Products

PRODUCT	MARKET SHARE (%)
Search	70.98
Email (Gmail)	8.43
Mobile OS (Android)	79.3
Google Adsense	74
Google Adwords	23
Google +	26
Google Chrome	43
Mobile hardware	1.7

* Data as of 2013.
Compiled from various sources.

Exhibit 25.5

Selected Financials of Google from 2008–2012 (In US$, Millions)

	2008	2009	2010	2011	2012
Revenues					
Google websites	14,414	15,723	19,444	26,145	31,221
Google network members' websites	6,715	7,166	8,792	10,386	12,465
Total advertising revenues	21,129	22,889	28,236	36,531	43,686
Other revenues	667	762	1,085	1,374	2,354
Total Google revenues	21,796	23,651	29,321	37,905	46,039
Total Motorola mobile revenues	-	-	-	-	4,136
Total consolidated revenues	21,796	23,651	29,321	37,905	50,175
Costs					
Costs of revenues	8,622	8,844	10,417	13,188	17,176
Cost of revenues—Motorola Mobile	-	-	-	-	3,458
Total of Google and Motorola cost of revenues	8,622	8,844	10,417	13,188	20,634

Continued

	2008	2009	2010	2011	2012
Traffic acquisition cost	5,939	6,169	7,317	8,811	10,956
Other cost of revenues	2,683	2,675	3,100	4,377	9,678
Research & development	2,793	2,843	3,762	5,162	6,793
Sales & marketing	1,946	1,984	2,799	4,589	6,143
General & administrative	1,803	1,668	1,962	2,724	3,845
Charge related to the resolution of department of justice investigation	-	-	-	500	-
Total costs & expenses	15,164	15,339	18,940	26,163	37,415
Net Income	**4,227**	**6,520**	**8,505**	**9,737**	**10,737**

Source: http://investor.google.com/financial/tables.html.

Exhibit 25.6

Google and Apple: A Comparison

	GOOGLE	APPLE
Revenues	US$ 50.18 billion	US$ 156.51 billion
Net Income	US$ 10.74 billion	US$ 41.73 billion
Investment in R&D	US$ 6.8 billion	US$ 3.4 billion
No. of Employees	44,777	72,800
Year of Founding	1998	1976
Forbes Innovation Rank	47	79
Fortune 500 Rank	55	6

* Data as of 2013.
Compiled from various sources.

Exhibit 25.7

Various Channels for Google's Employees to Express Themselves

Google Cafes	Cafes which are exclusively designed to facilitate interactions between employees and teams
Direct Emails to Company's Top Management	All employees of Google can directly Email to the top leadership of Google on anything
Google Moderator	In-house innovation management tool to share new ideas with others as well as vote on others' ideas
Google + Conversations	Conversations between Google employees on their own social network
TGIF (Thank goodness it's Friday)	Weekly meetings where employees can ask directly ask questions to company's top management
FixIts	24 hour sprints in which employees expend their 100 percent energy on solving a specific problem
Googlegeist	Survey which seeks feedback on issues and then enlist volunteer employee teams to solve the major problems
Internal Innovation Reviews	Meetings where executives present product ideas to their superiors

Source: Laura He, "Google's Secrets of Innovation: Empowering its Employees," www.forbes.com, March 29, 2013.

Exhibit 25.8

Eight Pillars of Innovation

1. Have a mission that matters
2. Think big but start small
3. Strive for continual innovation, not instant perfection
4. Look for ideas everywhere
5. Share everything
6. Spark with imagination, fuel with data
7. Be a platform
8. Never fail to fail

Source: Susan Wojcicki "The Eight Pillars of Innovation," http://www.google.com, July 2011.

Exhibit 25.9

Chart of Google's Share Price from September 5, 2008 to September 4, 2013

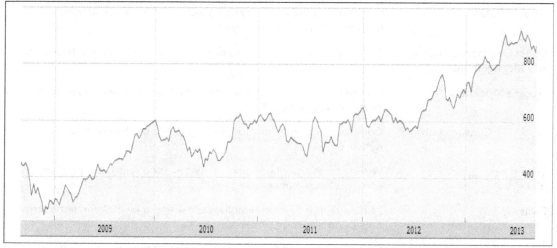

Source: https://www.google.com/finance.

Exhibit 25.10

Top Innovative Technology Companies in the World

COMPANY	COUNTRY	RANK	INNOVATION PREMIUM* (%)
VMware	United States	3	63.7
Baidu	China	6	60.6
Amazon	United States	7	60.2
Yahoo Japan	Japan	38	32.8
Tata Consultancy Services	India	40	32.6
Tera Data	United States	42	31.5
Google	United States	47	30.9
Infosys	India	53	29.1
SAP	Germany	72	22.7
Apple	United States	79	22.3

* Innovation premium is the measure which shows the premium the stock price of a company put by investors up above the value of its existing business on the basis of future innovative results.
Source: "The World's Most Innovative Companies," http://www.forbes.com.

NOTES

1 Christopher Jackson, "Is Google the Most Innovative Tech Company on the Planet," http://thenextweb.com, September 8, 2012.

2 Quentin Hardy, "Google's Innovation—And Everyone's?" http://www.forbes.com, July 17, 2011.

3 Steven Levy, "Google's Larry Page on Why Moon Shots Matter," www.wired.com, January 17, 2013.

4 *Ibid.*

5 http://www.google.co.in/about/company/

6 Michael S. Malone, "Surviving IPO Fever," www.wired.com, March 12, 2003.

7 "Google IPO Priced at $85 a Share," http://edition.cnn.com, August 19, 2004.

8 Eric Schmidt, "How I Did It: Google's CEO on the Enduring Lessons of a Quirky IPO," http://hbr.org, May 2010.

9 Caroline Thomas, "Google: The IR Behind its IPO," www.insideinvestorrelations.com, September 1, 2004.

10 Simon London, "U.S. Fund Criticizes Google's IPO Structure," www.msnbc.msn.com, May 4, 2004.

11 Geoff Duncan, "T-Mobile Launching First Android Phone?" www.digitaltrends.com, August 15, 2008.

12 Robert C. Wolcott and Michael J. Lippitz, "Google: An Ecosystem of Entrepreneurs," www.benzinga.com, September 29, 2010.

13 Evan Niu, "How Google Surpassed Apple in Design—and How Apple's Coming Back," http://www.fool.com/, June 12, 2013.

14 Nicolas Bry, "Google Versus Apple," http://www.innovationexcellence.com, June 2, 2011.

15 "Redesigning Google: How Larry Page Engineered a Beautiful Revolution," http://www.theverge.com, January 24, 2013.

16 Larry Popelka, "Google is Winning the Innovation War against Apple," http://www.businessweek.com, May 20, 2013.

17 Nicolas Bry, "Google Versus Apple," http://www.innovationexcellence.com, June 2, 2011.

18 Larry Popelka, "Google is Winning the Innovation War against Apple," http://www.businessweek.com, May 20, 2013.

19 Juliet Lapidos, "Why is Gmail Still in Beta?" http://www.slate.com, April 7, 2009.

20 Herstatt, Cornelius, and Eric Von Hippel (1992), "From Experience: Developing New Product Concepts Via the Lead User Method: A Case Study in a "Low Tech" Field", *Journal of Product Innovation Management*, 1992;9: 213–221.

21 "Finding Lead Users for Innovation," http://innovateonpurpose.blogspot.in/, November 4, 2010.

22 Bianca Bosker, "Google Glass 'Winners' Can Buy Glass Now," http://www.huffingtonpost.com, May 22, 2013.

23 Jennifer Riggins, "Through the Eyes of the First Google Glass Surgery," http://www.smartplanet.com, September 2, 2013.

24 Gregg Keizer, "Apple Plunges to No. 79 on *Forbes* Innovative Companies Ranking Google Ranks Higher at No. 47, But Microsoft Doesn't Even Make the List," www.computerworld.com, August 14, 2013.

25 Aimee Groth, "Everyone Should Use Google's Original '70-20-10' Model to Map Out Their Career," http://www.businessinsider.com, November 27, 2012.

26 Dan Schawbel, "How Big Companies Are Becoming Entrepreneurial," http://techcrunch.com, July 29, 2012.

27 "Google's Staff Now Too Busy for 20% Time off Perk, Claim Former Employees," http://www.dailymail.co.uk, August 29, 2013.

28 *Ibid.*

29 "'Involve Your Employees,' Says Google, CEB," http://www.businessweek.com, December 11, 2009.

30 *Ibid.*

31 Laura He, "Google's Secrets of Innovation: Empowering its Employees," www.forbes.com, March 29, 2013.

32 *Ibid.*

33 Michael Arrington, "Use Google Moderator to Crowdsource Group Questions," http://techcrunch.com, September 2008.

34 Leena Rao, "Google's Tip Jar Uses Crowdsourcing to Help People Save Money," http://techcrunch.com, March 5, 2009.

35 Robert C. Wolcott and Michael J. Lippitz, "Google: An Ecosystem of Entrepreneurs," www.benzinga.com, September 29, 2010.

36 Robin Wauters, "Google Buys Motorola Mobility for $12.5B, Says 'Android will Stay Open'," http:// techcrunch.com, August 15, 2011.

37 T.C. Sottek, "Google Acquires Motorola Mobility: The Full Story," http://www.theverge.com, May 19, 2012.

38 Rob Waugh, "Google Buys Motorola for $12.5 Billion—Paving the Way for Even More Google-Branded Gadgets," http://www.dailymail.co.uk, May 22, 2012.

39 Spencer Ante, "Hype and Hope: Test Driving Google's New Glasses," *Wall Street Journal*, September 11, 2012.

40 James Rivington, "Google Glass: What You Need to Know," http://www.techradar.com, August 8, 2013.

41 Sharon Gaudin, "Google CEO on Innovation: 'We're at 1% of What's Possible'," www.computer-world.com, May 15, 2013.

42 "What is Project Loon?" http://www.google.com/loon.

43 Steven Levy, "The Untold Story of Google's Quest to Bring the Internet Everywhere—By Balloon," http://www.wired.com, August 13, 2013.

44 David Tom, "Google Explains How Project Loon will Provide Stable Internet Coverage," http:// www.techspot.com, September 2, 2013.

45 "About," https://fiber.google.com/about/.

46 Susan Wojcicki, "The Eight Pillars of Innovation," http://www.google.com, July 2011.

47 Christopher Jackson, "Is Google the Most Innovative Tech Company on the Planet," http:// thenextweb.com, September 8, 2012.

48 Sharon Gaudin, "Google CEO on Innovation: 'We're at 1% of What's Possible," www.computer-world.com.

49 Natasha Lomas, "Google Confirms it Had Acquired Android Smartwatch Maker WIMM Labs," http://techcrunch.com, August 31, 2013.

50 "Google's Staff Now Too Busy for 20% Time off Perk, Claim Former Employees," http://www. dailymail.co.uk, August 29, 2013.

51 Haydn Shaughnessy, "Why Google Glass will not be Another iPhone," http://www.forbes.com, June 25, 2013.

52 James Rivington, "Google Glass: What You Need to Know," http://www.techradar.com, August 8, 2013.

53 "With Balloons and Fiber, Google Experiments in Web Access," http://www.dailymaverick.co.za, August 16, 2013.

54 Romain Dillet, "Google's Stock Price Opens at All-Time High Ahead of Q2 2013 Earnings Release Later this Week," http://techcrunch.com, July 15, 2013.

55 Gregg Keizer, "Apple Plunges to No. 79 on *Forbes* Innovative Companies Ranking Google Ranks Higher at No. 47, But Microsoft Doesn't Even Make the List," www.computerworld.com, August 14, 2013.

56 *Ibid.*

57 "With Balloons and Fiber, Google Experiments in Web Access," http://www.dailymaverick.co.za, August 16, 2013.

58 Steven Levy, "Google's Larry Page on Why Moon Shots Matter," www.wired.com, January 17, 2013.

READING 25: QUESTIONS FOR THOUGHT

- What is the "launch and iterate" process used by Google? Why do you think it has been effective for launching successful innovations?

- What has Google done to make innovation an "everyday process"? How has this helped foster innovation?

- What is the 70/20/10 innovation model that Google employs? How is this helpful in identifying new areas for innovation?

CONCLUSION

Innovators create the future. Yet the innovation process is often shrouded in mystery and is sometimes under resourced or even completely overlooked in some organizations. As we have seen across the readings, companies that do not properly focus on innovation may find their business models disrupted. While companies that embrace innovation, particularly breakthrough innovation, can reap the rewards of access to new markets and new customers. Several of the companies profiled in this book have leveraged their innovation efforts to become among the largest companies in the world.

If you are studying innovation and have completed reading this book, you now have a better understanding of why innovation is critical to all organizations and how innovation can be achieved. And if you are lucky enough to work in the fascinating field of innovation, I hope I have provided you with some insights to improve your innovation efforts and better enable you to implement and spread innovation techniques throughout your organization.

There are a few key takeaways from this book that I am listing below as a reference to help your innovation efforts:

- All companies need to focus on innovation—even profitable market leaders.

- Foster a culture of innovation that creates the environment in which innovation can take place.

- Pursue innovations at both ends of the spectrum: incremental innovations and breakthrough innovations.

- Start innovation efforts with the customer—understand their needs, problems, and what they are trying to accomplish.

- Utilize various creative techniques and engage large and diverse groups of employees to generate ideas to solve for customer problems.

- Evaluate ideas using an array of objective exercises to ensure the optimal selection of ideas to design and develop.

- Leverage systematic experimentation using prototypes to design new products and services

Throughout this book we have seen examples of companies that applied many of the above points successfully. Amazon places the customer first and builds innovations leveraging core customer insights. Google is continuously experimenting with new product and service ideas. And Philips leveraged creative techniques to make a revolutionary improvement to the DVD player.

You can immediately apply many of the principles in this book in any organization you are a part of. Even if you are in an entry level position you can benefit from the innovation tools and mindset put forth in this book. In every role in an organization people serve customers. Sometimes those customers are external, as we traditionally think of the customer. But, more often, people in an organization serve an internal customer—that is, someone who uses the output of your work. If you serve an internal customer, you can readily leverage the lessons of this book to make positive changes to the output and the experience that you deliver.

Now, go forth and innovate!